Afrofuturism and World Order

NEW SUNS:

RACE, GENDER, AND SEXUALITY

IN THE SPECULATIVE

Susana M. Morris and Kinitra D. Brooks, Series Editors

Afrofuturism and World Order

Reynaldo Anderson

THE OHIO STATE UNIVERSITY PRESS
COLUMBUS

Copyright © 2025 by The Ohio State University.
All rights reserved.

Library of Congress Cataloging-in-Publication Data
Names: Anderson, Reynaldo, 1964–, author.
Title: Afrofuturism and world order / Reynaldo Anderson.
Other titles: New suns: race, gender, and sexuality in the speculative.
Description: Columbus : The Ohio State University Press, 2025. | Series: New suns: race, gender, and sexuality in the speculative | Includes bibliographical references and index. | Summary: "Locates Afrofuturism within an African geography of reason, situating the past, present, and future of people of African descent at the intersection of speculative philosophy, science fiction, futurology, artificial intelligence, climate change, and geopolitics, illuminating how Afrofuturism participates in an increasingly multipolar world"—Provided by publisher.
Identifiers: LCCN 2025016259 | ISBN 9780814215944 (hardback) | ISBN 9780814284308 (ebook)
Subjects: LCSH: Afrofuturism—History and criticism. | Speculative fiction—Black authors—History and criticism. | Black people—Intellectual life—21st century.
Classification: LCC PS153.B53 A53 2025 | DDC 809.3/9352996—dc23/eng/20250528
LC record available at https://lccn.loc.gov/2025016259

Other identifiers: ISBN 9780814259559 (paperback)

Cover design by Laurence J. Nozik
Text composition by Stuart Rodriguez
Type set in Palatino

CONTENTS

Introduction	The Second Race for Theory	1
Chapter 1	The New Atlantis, the Anglo World Order, and the Genesis of Afro-Modernity	24
Chapter 2	The Rising Tide of Color and Creating a New Race	44
Chapter 3	The Rise of the Deep State and the Technostate	75
Chapter 4	The Dark Enlightenment and the Collapse of the Anglo Liberal World Order	102
Chapter 5	The Nommo of the Black Speculative Turn	121
Chapter 6	AI Nationalism and the New World Order	145
Epilogue	Dark MAGA, BRICS+, and the Biofunk Era: A Brave New World Order	163
Acknowledgments		175
References		177
Index		203

INTRODUCTION

The Second Race for Theory

Afrofuturism is the intellectual progeny of African thought that can be traced back to a philosophy of Nile Valley and Nubian civilization in the forms of St Tpy (The First Time) to Whm Mswt (The Beginning), indicating the need to retrieve something that will aid in the future (Nehusi, 2023). One idea long associated with ancient Kemet is the observation that Constantinople was not the only or even the major route for the transportation of Nile Valley knowledge to Europe. Before 1453, primarily through the Greeks (James, 1954; Bernal, 1987/1991; Browder, 1991), and through the Moors in their occupation of the Iberian Peninsula (Lane-Poole, 1990; Jackson, 1970; Van Sertima, 1993), Kemetic philosophy was transmitted and subsumed into European cultural reality, effectively shaping much of the philosophical and esoteric thought therein. Finally, at the end of the Byzantine Empire, the remaining legacy of Nile Valley civilization was also transferred to Western Europe, after the sack of the city of Constantinople by the Ottoman Turks in 1453, where it helped educate and illumine Europeans out of what they referred to as the Dark Ages (Louv, 2018). The knowledge from Nile Valley civilization was distorted over the centuries into a model and hierarchy reflecting the bias of Neoplatonism as well as doctrines derived from Hebrew scriptures, Roman Catholic and Protestant theology, select Eurocentric angelology, and the Kabbalah (Louv, 2018). Its chief proponent or adept in the Anglo-speaking world was John Dee. Dee, a scientific advisor, mathematician, and alchemist, was an advisor to Elizabeth I who invented the phrase *British Empire* and developed the metaphysical blueprint of both the British and American empires and the secret societies that influenced Europe and America (Louv, 2018). While Portugal, Spain, France, and other nations and cultures are mentioned in this book, the networked Anglo world order established by Great Britain and its successor, the United States, is the most powerful by far (Ferguson, 2008, 2019).

On the other hand, Afrofuturism is a product of the African response to the Anglo world's and by extension European and Arab usurpation of the Nile Valley Nubian civilization and distortion of African history and agency. African knowledge is a tributary to the Black speculative tradition, coined as Afrofuturism late in the 20th century. Afrofuturism first emerged as a concept in the 1990s during the post–Cold War period and the beginning of a phase of neoliberal globalization as a conversation between a small community of intellectuals in New York City that later led to discussions among creatives and thinkers on internet platforms. Contemporary Afrofuturism is a philosophy that emerged from the culture of the African diaspora and the continent and empowers people of African descent to situate themselves in time and space with agency.

The Afrofuturism of the 21st century is a strategic formulation reflecting Black speculative thought as a critical project with the mission of laying the groundwork for a humanity that is not bound up with the ideals of white Enlightenment universalism, critical theory, science, or technology (Anderson & Jones, 2016; Rabaka, 2010; Rollefson, 2008, p. 91). According to Anderson & Jones (2016), contemporary expressions of Afrofuturism emerging in the areas of metaphysics, speculative philosophy, religion, visual studies, performance, art, and philosophy of science or technology that are described as "2.0," in response to the emergence of social media and other technological advances since the middle of the last decade (p. ix). Additionally, Anderson and Jones define Afrofuturism 2.0 as "the early twenty-first century technogenesis of Black identity reflecting counter histories, hacking and or appropriating the influence of network software, database logic, cultural analytics, deep remixability, neurosciences, enhancement and augmentation, gender fluidity, posthuman possibility, the speculative sphere, with transdisciplinary applications and has grown into an important diasporic technocultural 'Pan-African movement'" (p. x).

Afrofuturism occupies a liminal space between science and spirituality and is not based on a racial phenotype but on a geography of reason that locates Africa as the origin of the human species and is indebted to not only Nile Valley civilization but to different regions in Africa and its diaspora. It envisions a future shaped by African and African diaspora experiences and practices and is a product of a complex historical process. Contemporary Afrofuturism emerges from a confluence of technological and historical forces that trace back to Nile Valley civilization and the defeat of African empires of the 15th and 16th centuries, like the demise of the Keita dynasty—a period marked by the onset of Arab and Muslim conquest, European expansion, and the European transatlantic, trans-Saharan, Indian Ocean / Arab slave trade.

This era saw the dismantling of powerful African states and the forcible displacement of millions, laying the groundwork for centuries of racial oppression and cultural disruption. Simultaneously, by the early 17th century, the publication of Francis Bacon's *The New Atlantis* (1900), a racially biased utopian narrative that projected European ideals of progress and scientific mastery onto an imagined society, speculatively illustrated this new worldview. *The New Atlantis*, with elements appropriated from archival knowledge of African Nile Valley civilization, was a work that was emblematic of the transition undergone by Europeans from what they referred to as their renaissance to a burgeoning modern era heralding a new Euro-centered worldview that emphasized empirical knowledge and technological advancement, underwritten and financed by the destruction or enslavement of non-European cultures and knowledge systems.

The modern era also led to the intertwined phenomena of racial capitalism and Enlightenment racism. Racial capitalism refers to the development of a global form of capitalism that intricately linked economic exploitation with racial hierarchies, a system that commodified African bodies and labor. Enlightenment racism, meanwhile, emerged from the intellectual currents of the Enlightenment, which, despite advocating for universal human rights and rationality, also formulated pseudoscientific racial theories that justified European domination and African subjugation. Consequently, the world order dominated by European peoples emerged during this period in the Peace of Westphalia in 1648, theoretically based on a balance of power among nation-states, and reformed in 1815 at the Congress of Vienna, the Treaty of Versailles at the end of World War I, and Bretton Woods at the end of World War II. However, early in the 21st century, since the 2008 financial crisis, the world order that was religiously, philosophically, and politically organized around Western racial and ethnic praxis is unraveling due to a rising challenge from the non-Western world (Diesen, 2024).

World order is "the international distribution of power and legitimacy that marks how states and nonstate actors should conduct themselves for order to prevail over chaos" (Diesen, 2024, p. 2). However, following the collapse of the American-led financial system in 2008, new power centers from Eurasia are emerging that are challenging Western hegemony, laying the foundation for a multipolar system that is in opposition to the Western-dominated, rule-based system in favor of a negotiated system that bears resemblance to the Westphalian system of the past but is more pluralistic and inclusive (Diesen, 2024). Correspondingly, the geo-economics of the world were restructured to this logic using bureaucratic violence to pursue relative advantage and impose a new geoculture or system of ideas in concert with the economic and political order (Wallerstein, 1991).

New geopolitical, geo-economic, and geocultural conditions influenced the formation of a new type of intellectual in the African diaspora, one engaged in a critique of European theory and practice. In pursuit of this practice, the contemporary progressive Black or African scholar (in the eyes of the Eurocentric academy) commits heresy, creating a new critical discourse or doxa when questioning the doxa of Western intellectual formations which utilize "systems of classifications that reproduce their logic . . . imposing their principles of social reality" (Bogues, 2015, pp. 12–13). Additionally, "Black radical intellectual production engages in a double operation . . . an engagement with Western theory and then a critique of this theory . . . breaking the epistemic limits established by the Western intellectual tradition." Furthermore, "For the black radical intellectual, 'heresy' means becoming human, not white, or imitative of the colonial, but overturning white/European normativity" (Bogues, 2015, p. 13).

Therefore, it became necessary to evaluate received knowledge formations as axiomatic. Furthermore, questions arise regarding approaching an epistemological break with Eurocentric ideas of knowledge production. A plausible analysis lies in the historical underdevelopment of critiquing racism and white supremacy in institutional frameworks or structures, continental philosophy, and the limited understanding of the theory and praxis of African or Black activists and intellectuals. For example, in contrast to what Jean-Jacques Rousseau articulated as a social contract, which holds that societies should be structured and regulated by a "defensible moral code," the racial contract "is characterized as an unjust exploitative society, ruled by an oppressive government and regulated by an immoral code" (Mills, 1997, p. 5), rather than a morally defensible code.

This racial contract rests on three existential claims: "White supremacy both local and global exists and has existed for many years; white supremacy should be thought of as itself a political system, and finally, white supremacy can be illuminatingly thought of as based on a contract between whites"

(Mills, 1997, p. 7). This racial contract has white elite signatories, with all whites as beneficiaries of what W. E. B. Du Bois described as the psychological wages of whiteness (Du Bois, 1920; Mills, 1997, Roediger, 2022). Mills (1997) explains that "this situation has led to a crisis in Western society where . . . the Racial Contract prescribes for its signatories an inverted epistemology, an epistemology of ignorance, a particular pattern of localized and global cognitive dysfunctions . . . producing the same ironic outcome that whites will be unable to understand the world they have made" (p. 18).

Afrofuturism, Afrocentricity, and the Metamodern Moment

Modernism took shape toward the end of the 19th century and came into full view in the early 20th century, during the Industrial Revolution and the societal changes brought about by rapid urbanization and technological advancements (Yousef, 2017). Modernist art sought to break away from traditional forms, challenge conventional norms, and emphasize the individual artist's subjective experience, experimentation, and innovation. Notable modernist figures include Henry James, Jean Toomer, Joseph Conrad, A. E. Housman, T. S. Eliot, and Virginia Woolf (Yousef, 2017). In the mid-20th century, after World War II, postmodernism emerged as a reaction to the perceived rationality of modernism and the flux of modern life. By the 1960s, it rejected the notion of universal truth and instead embraced skepticism and irony. Postmodernist art often incorporated pastiche, intertextuality, magical realism, and temporal distortion and can be found in the works of artists like Andy Warhol and Jean-Michel Basquiat and writers like Jorge Luis Borges and Salman Rushdie, who embraced postmodern sensibilities (Yousef, 2017).

Metamodernism, a relatively recent artistic movement appearing in the late 20th century and early 21st century, is characterized by structured feeling and its oscillation between modernist and postmodernist sensibilities, or how its aesthetics can be linked back to political goals of early modernism (Brunton, 2018). Modernism was primarily epistemologically focused on its aims and objectives, whereas postmodernism was a skeptical response to the modernist project, primarily ontological in orientation (Yousef, 2017). By contrast, metamodernism acknowledges the skepticism of postmodernism while seeking to relocate to a sense of wholeness and reinterrogate older forms of modernism (Yousef, 2017). Artists like Wes Anderson and Lana Del Rey, poet Evie Shockley, and writers like David Foster Wallace and Zadie Smith have been associated with metamodernism. Metamodernism acknowledges the merits of both modernism and postmodernism, recognizing the need for innovation while engaging with and critiquing the past. However, it needs to be improved in the politics of form and failure (Brunton, 2018). For example, the new aesthetic regime of metamodernism largely ignores the question of whose time and space is privileged by its definition within the preservation of modernist practices vis-à-vis contemporary realities and aesthetic sensibilities (Brunton, 2018). This brings us to how the contemporary Afrofuturist project is an intentionally aesthetic and political formation engaged in the metamodern moment from a geography of reason and hermeneutics that privileges the sensibilities of the African diaspora and Africa (Janz, 2017).

Afrofuturism and metamodernism are cultural movements that have recently gained significant attention and recognition. Afrofuturism, rooted in the experiences of the African diaspora and Africa, envisions alternative futures that challenge dominant narratives and celebrate African culture and creation. On the other hand, metamodernism embraces the paradoxes of contemporary existence and seeks to reconcile diverse perspectives between modernism and postmodernism (Yousef, 2017). Contemporary Afrofuturism emerged as a response to the historical dislocation caused by the destruction of African civilization, enslavement, scientific racism, colonialism, imperialism, and continued marginalization of African peoples within the modern world system. It encompasses various expressions, including literature, philosophy, science, music, visual arts, and film. Afrofuturist works often explore mythology, technology, and spirituality themes that reflect Africa and the African diaspora's history and future. By envisioning alternative futures and reimagining narratives, Afrofuturism challenges existing power structures and offers a platform for Black voices to shape and reclaim their own stories (Anderson & Jones, 2016).

However, metamodernism, focused on embracing paradoxes and navigating the complexities of contemporary existence, shares some common ground with Afrofuturism. Both movements acknowledge the multiplicity of identities and challenge binary oppositions. Metamodernism's oscillation between sincerity and irony resonates with Afrofuturism's ability to blend ancient traditions with cutting-edge technologies, merging past and future and celebrating the complexities of African identity. Moreover, both movements reject simplistic categorizations, explore cultural evolution nuances, and intersect on several thematic levels. Both movements challenge dominant narratives and power structures, seeking to dismantle oppressive systems and envision more inclusive and equitable futures.

Both frameworks embrace inspiration from diverse sources and traditions. Afrofuturism's exploration of spirituality, mythology, and cosmology finds echoes in metamodernism's engagement with metanarratives, as both movements seek to understand and reshape our collective understanding of truth and existence. However, Afrofuturism's willingness to engage with the politics of Black life in an anti-Black world is where traditional metamodernism's utility is insufficient. In this historical context, Afrocentricity is utilized as a corrective to the predominant Euro-centered worldview and order and acts as a corrective regarding data, culture, orientation, and agency of people of African descent. Afrocentricity liberates African peoples from a specific geographic bias that has paraded itself as universal. It begins to offer their vision of the future and what that order should look like about other human beings (Asante, 2007). Moreover, Afrocentricity is not the inverse of Eurocentrism. It does not make universal or totalizing claims as Eurocentric scholarship does, nor does it claim that no progressive European scholarship is worthy of engagement (Keto, 1993). From an Afrocentric world-order approach, based on negotiation, a pluriverse or multipolar environment operates in Africa's interest as opposed to the European Western, rule-based world order that is slowly unraveling in the wake of the Eurasian land war that began in Ukraine in (Diesen, 2022; Keto, 1993).

The process of epistemic decolonization and restructuring of international relations in the 21st century, therefore, can begin along the following principles: Africanist philosophies are applied to determine the analytic perspectives of this theory as identified by Modupe (2003) and are embedded within the following frameworks: (a) Grounding, scholarly and creative practice centered on African/African diaspora life, culture, history, and geography; (b) Orientation, having a healthy psychological and intellectual disposition to African phenomena; and (c) Perspective, an indication of self-awareness in thinking and influencing the environment in a way that signifies the interests of African peoples (Rapanyane, 2021). In this vein, Afrocentricity offers Afrofuturist studies an intellectual *djed*—the ancient Kemetic notion of foundation or stabilizing force—and stasis to advance African agency into the future (Anderson & Carr, 2023).

Consequently, contemporary Afrofuturism stands at the intersection of these historical and contemporary currents. It reimagines and reclaims African identities and futures suppressed or distorted by these centuries-old dynamics. Afrofuturism challenges the legacies of colonialism, imperialism, and oppression by fusing elements of speculative literature or science fiction, the arts, technology, social science, and African cultural heritage, offering alternative narratives that celebrate Black visionary potential. This movement critiques historical injustices and empowers Black communities to envision and construct new possibilities for the future, free from the constraints of past oppressions.

Previously, scholars like W. E. B. Du Bois were interested in establishing a method for retrieving accurate information concerning people of African descent, so they started the Encyclopedia Africana project to address this archival issue of theory and practice of liberation during the Industrial Revolution, a period of transformation. The politics of knowledge, culture, and information continued into the 20th century with the Harlem Renaissance and movements like the Garvey movement, negritude, and decades later, various movements around the diaspora and Africa. In a US context, toward the end of the Cold War, a new cohort of theorists began to critique the social reality of African peoples between 1987 and 1993. During this period, many creative intellectuals started to expound on the materializing phenomenon of Afrofuturism—among the first to do so were Mark Dery, Kodwo Eshun, and Alondra Nelson. At the end of the 20th century, early Afrofuturism characterized the intersection between Black people in the US and diaspora, sci-fi, musical composition, technological innovation, and artwork. Contemporary Afrofuturism is Pan-African, transnational, and translocal, embodying the intentional positioning of African influence within historical and spatial contexts. Its scope includes metaphysics, aesthetics, social science, theoretical and applied science, and programmatic areas (Anderson, 2016). After the COVID-19 pandemic, there was a massive shift in economic production as digital platforms became the main arena. There were also several other significant shifts happening in tandem at this time. These were society-shifting phenomenon like the acceleration of technology, the materialization of the metaverse, and the rapid increase of climate change. These conditions present the challenge of theorizing, forecasting, and identifying how these potential threats might affect people of African descent specifically.

When drawing on the African intergenerational archive, it is possible to determine the significant works that intellectuals contributed during the post–civil rights, post–Black Power era regarding intellectual output just before Web 1.0, which began to take shape in the early 1990s. Among these are works such as *The Afrocentric Idea* (Asante, 1987), *The Signifying Monkey: A Theory of African American Literary Criticism* (Gates, 1988), *The Black Atlantic: Modernity and Double Consciousness* (Gilroy, 1993), and others by African and diasporan intellectuals at that time. Though one shortcoming of *The Black Atlantic* is that it omits Afro-Latinos, many continue referencing Gilroy's work. This period also marked the onset of what would come to be known as the *culture wars,* a term first publicly introduced by paleoconservative US politician Pat Buchanan (Anderson, 2022b). At the 1992 Republican National Convention, he explained: "My fellow Americans, this campaign is about philosophy. . . . It is a cultural war, as critical to the kind of nation we shall be as was the Cold War, for this war is for the soul of America" (Anderson, 2022b).

A few works explored the Africological rejoinder to this period and examined Black futures. Mark Dery coined the term *Afrofuturism* in his 1993 interviews with Samuel R. Delany, Tricia Rose, and Greg Tate, a writer for the *Village Voice,* commenting on the growing power of Silicon Valley in the post–Cold War period and African American cultural production (van Veen, 2014). Prominent scholars known as the Temple Circle in the 1990s, from the African American Studies Department (currently the Africology and African American Studies Department) at Temple University, commenting on African futurity, were also staking out a post–Cold War perspective on Africana thought. In his 1993 book *The Africa-Centered Perspective of History and Social Sciences in the Twenty-First Century,* C. Tsehloane Keto (1993) asserted, "As a futurologist, she or he can speculate, engage beyond the next century . . . to create in sharp contrast a time map on which to trace the events of the past, create history through action in the present, and plot the path of possible future action" (pp. 120, 122). That same year, Molefi Asante published *Malcolm X as Cultural Hero and Other Afrocentric Essays* (1993), in which he grapples with Africological space and time. Additionally, one of the first scholars to use Afrocentricity to critique the World Wide Web was Anna Everett in her essay "The Revolution Will Be Digitized: Afrocentricity and the Digital Public Sphere" (2002), in which she established an Africological perspective on the Web 1.0 era.

More recently, there are several books published on the topic of Afrofuturism, covering issues ranging from the esoteric or occult to slavery, religion, the arts, music, ethnic identity, and science fiction, such as Ytasha Womack's *Afrofuturism: The World of Black Sci-Fi and Fantasy Culture* (2013). Womack's treatment of the topic is a scholarly link in several areas in her attempt to make Afrofuturism digestible for a popular audience and to connect Afrofuturism to the concept of post-Blackness. However, this project is the first to argue three points in a book-length form. First, Afrofuturism is emerging in dimensions about class, race, sexuality, gender, migration, and geopolitical tension and is one of the primary tributary, cultural, and intellectual forces in contemporary African diaspora culture in the early 21st century. Second, the book is the first scholarly rendering of the topic across several disciplines considering the new developments of social media, significant contributions by continental African intellectuals and artists, the speculative turn (Binetti, 2021), and the emergence of other philosophical perspectives such as Afropolitanism, Afropessimism, metamodernism, and transhumanism or posthumanism. Third, the book calls into question the orientation of other scholarly frameworks used in books on the topic. For example, the book *Black Utopia: The History of an Idea from Black Nationalism to Afrofuturism* (2019), by Alex Zamalin, does advance key historical actors attributed to the study of Black Nationalism in the American tradition, yet he does not locate Afrofuturism within an African geography of reason, as he relies primarily on alternative theoretical legacies to critique African and African American phenomena and does not draw on the work of contemporary Afrofuturist scholars to build his argument more substantially. Also, substantial volumes of scholarship are found in the books *Afrofuturism and Black Sound Studies* (2017), by Erik Steinskog, and *Sun Ra's Chicago: Afrofuturism and the City* (2020), by William Sites. They are vital in content and progressive in the arguments and ideological perspectives. Still, the philosophical reliance on European hermeneutics or American liberal orthodoxy around race relations framing the emergence of Afrofuturism does not advance the discipline of African / African American studies from a theoretical perspective.

Afrofuturism Rising: The Literary Prehistory of a Movement (2019), by Isiah Lavender, is a generous contribution to the Afrofuturist literary canon. However, the author's claim that slavery is the beginning of Afrofuturism dislocates enslaved African agency from the knowledge traditions enslaved peoples brought with them from Africa that would influence the societies they created for themselves and lived in. A tenet of African / African American studies is that Black or African diaspora history does not begin with slavery. Regarding religion, comics, and music, the books *The Dreamer and the Dream: Afrofuturism and Black Religious Thought*, by Roger Sneed (2021), the edited volume *Toward Afrodiasporic and Afrofuturist Philosophies of Religion*, by Jon Ivan Gill (2022), and *The Future of Black: Afrofuturism, Black Comics, and Superhero Poetry*, a volume edited by Len Lawson, Cynthia Manick, and Gary Jackson come close to engaging in similar aspects of the conceptual framework that *Afrofuturism and World Order* is focused on, yet they do not look at the interlocking structures that Afrofuturism engaged, in relation to the forces of the *State* and *geopolitics*. Furthermore, *The Future of Black* and *Boogie Down Predictions: Hip-Hop, Time, and Afrofuturism*, edited by Roy Christopher (2022), offer frameworks for niches within Afrofuturism; however, the cultural anthropology they both draw on does not situate their work within the Black speculative tradition from which Afrofuturism emerges. For example, while comics, novels, poetry, music, and movies are legitimate sources of inspiration for the study of Afrofuturism, there are gaps in understanding the connection of the Black speculative tradition or Afrofuturism to scientific racism, technology, politics, and how it overlaps with other systems of thought, like Africana esotericism within the diaspora or Africa. Finally, the recent appearance of the book *The Future of Black Studies*, by Abdul Alkalimat (2022), which attempts to promote Black studies as Afrofuturism, does not break new ground. For example, the text's opening chapter does reference *Afrofuturism 2.0: The Rise of Astro-Blackness* (Anderson & Jones, 2016); however, the transition into historical materialism as an analytic framework is different from where the field is now for a couple of reasons. First, contemporary Afrofuturism engages quantum theory and new materialism that embraces Indigenous epistemologies and cosmologies (Leonard, 2020). Second, the book's reliance on the geography of reason or sensemaking derivative of European historiography as well as the anthropological error of Marx and Engels when they formulated historical materialism limits the volume's utility. As other scholars have aptly asserted, "One of the most critical failures of the historical theory composed by Marx and Engels was its misappropriation of cultural and intellectual development" (Dove, 1995; Robinson, 2020, p. 19). Still, much work has been done on Afrofuturism in the last decade, which is qualitatively and quantitatively different from the results he cites to build his case. Finally, the books *Afrofuturisms: Ecology, Humanity, and Francophone Cultural Expressions* (2023), by Issac Joslin, and *Challenging the Black Atlantic: The New World Novels of Zapata Olivella and Gonçalves* (2020), by John Maddox, make substantive contributions to the field of Afrofuturism studies; they are focused on the influence of francophone and Latin American characteristics of Black diasporan and African speculative thought, yet I consider their contribution parallel to what this volume attempts.

The First Race for Theory

Coined by sociologist Elise Boulding (1996), the term *200 year present* is particularly striking because, at this moment, there are people who were born 100 years ago, and at this very moment, a new child is being born whose life will span the next 100 years. Moreover, nations and societies generally typically have about a 200-year lifespan before undergoing massive change. Two hundred years ago in the United States, around 1820, enslaved Africans were revolting. I speculate that scholars in digital humanities will go and collect the data from archives about ten years from now, when there may begin to be yearly Black meetings of scholarship. Since 1830 there has not been a year where Black people in the US had no religious or political forum to discuss what was happening in the country.

Roughly three phases have occurred in the last 100-plus years of transnational struggle, during which Black intellectuals have done archival work (i.e., reassembling institutional knowledge). The first phase, which revolved around the concept of the *Encyclopedia Africana*, began around 1901 when W. E. B. Du Bois conversed with Edward Blyden, an intellectual forerunner who influenced generations of African thinkers and many of Du Bois's thoughts. During the period that Rayford Logan called the nadir or the Age of Imperialism, spanning from around 1880 to 1921, other cultures were developing encyclopedias to archive and reassemble knowledge and make sense of what was happening.

Forty years after that period was Black Power, an anticolonial period when modern Black studies emerged, primarily driven by activists or scholars who came of age between 1955 and 1975. Then, the term *Africology* appeared in the late 20th century toward the end of the Cold War, when postmodern scholars and thinkers like Michel Foucault, Jacques Derrida, and similar thinkers began to have a significant influence. Eventually, this created a particular intellectual conflict regarding terminology and theory. In her article "The Race for Theory," Black feminist scholar Barabara Christian (1987) argued that theoretical writing was becoming largely incomprehensible for laypeople when it came to literary criticism. In the postmodern era, from roughly the late 1970s to 1993, thinkers like Derrida and Jean-François Lyotard had effectively sunk the notion of grand narratives. From around 1977 to the late 1980s, Molefi Asante's theorization of Afrocentricity, the Black feminist practice of bell hooks, Michele Wallace's manifesto on Black feminism, and other published works set the trend for a generation. Public intellectuals like Cornel West, Henry Louis Gates, bell hooks, and others also began to rise in influence during this time, highlighting the end of a particular type of knowledge production that had formerly been developed from 1945 to about 1988.

The Second Race for Theory

According to Moore's law, knowledge doubles about every 18 months to two years because of the impact of transistors in the emerging technology industry. Gordon Moore made this observation in 1965, commenting on the growth of the microelectronics industry, when he noted a doubling of necessary elements on a produced chip once every 12 months (Mack, 2011). In contemporary times, the COVID-19 pandemic pushed society toward what some might call Moore's law+ in recognition that so much of knowledge production has shifted to online platforms. This quickened and displaced our sense of time and beingness for about two years. In response to the digital surge, I and other scholars lean toward the artificial intelligence (AI) explanation, which critiques Moore's law regarding its current rate of acceleration and possible decline by the late 2020s and changes in computational science (Shalf, 2020). Change is more rapid now than it was under even the 1960s model of Moore's law due to society's shift from Web 2.0. toward Web 3.0, roughly between 2016 and 2018 (Ma, 2023). Correspondingly, during this technological shift, artmaking has been revolutionized with the advent of nonfungible tokens combined with distributed ledger technology, specifically blockchain. Currently, we are experiencing what might be termed a second race for philosophy in the Black speculative field in which roughly three or four ideas compete with Afrofuturism 2.0. Critical theory scholar Kara Keeling (2019) and communications scholar Amber Johnson (2019) explore queer temporalities in Black speculative cultural production and racial capitalism. Poet and author Sofia Samatar (2017) and political theorists and historians Achille Mbembe and Sarah Balakrishnan (2016) use the term *Afropolitan* as a transnational lens, as opposed to Pan-African, to discuss African expatriates and their global lived experiences. Finally, Pamela Phatsimo Sunstrum (2013) considers the differences between Afrofuturism, articulated by Mark Dery as an African American phenomenon, and African futurism to locate a specific continental African sensibility using Indigenous African mythos.

Afropessimism, attributed mainly to Frank Wilderson (2008), asserts that Black people do not function as political agents due to the possibility of social death. Afropessimism is a theoretical framework that examines the persistent and ongoing oppression of people of African descent, particularly the history of colonialism and slavery. It argues that historically affected African people's social, political, and economic conditions are characterized by a fundamental sense of hopelessness and despair, resulting in pervasive cultural pessimism. Afropessimism was first articulated in the late 20th century by scholars such as Frank Wilderson, Orlando Patterson, and Saidiya Hartman, and it has since been developed and expanded on by several thinkers in various disciplines. It challenges traditional approaches to understanding race and racism, which often emphasize progress, reform, and the possibility of eventual equality. According to Afropessimism, the experiences of slavery and colonialism have created a unique form of social death for people of African descent, in which they are excluded from the realm of human recognition and subject to ongoing violence and exploitation (Wilderson, 2020).

By contrast, Afrofuturism 2.0 rejects the ontological nihilistic attributes of Afropessimism as articulated by theorists like Frank Wilderson and Calvin Warren, who essentially argue, based on the continental European tradition, that there is an "utter absence of ontology for Black people" and lack of subjectivity (Coleman, 2023, p. 51). Furthermore, Afrofuturism 2.0, or contemporary Afrofuturism, has at least five dimensions that include and engage metaphysics that "includes and engages ontology or the meaning of existence, relations between the epistemological and ontological or truth-functional aspects of knowledge, cosmogony or origin of the universe, cosmology or structure of the universe" that draw on African diaspora or African metaphysical praxis (Anderson & Jones, 2016, p. x). Moreover, Afrofuturism's approach to history and temporality offers a unique way to grapple with Afropessimism. Rather than viewing history as a linear progression from past to present, Afrofuturism sees history as a nonlinear process, where the past, present, and future are interconnected while also envisioning a future where this legacy can be transcended. In this context, Afrofuturism can be used as a hermeneutic tool to reinterpret the traumatic history of slavery. Colonialism and its ongoing impacts create space for envisioning a future that promotes the potential for liberation, empowerment, and transformation. Therefore, through its emphasis on Afrocentric cosmologies and spiritualities, Afrofuturism allows for the reclamation of cultural narratives and practices that were erased or distorted by the forces of slavery and colonialism.

The work of Anna Everett is one of the first to connect Afrocentricity to Afrofuturism directly through her examination of digital media and technology. For example, Everett (2002) argues that digital technologies have provided African diasporic communities the tools to engage in cultural production that affirms their unique experiences and histories. This perspective resonates with Afrocentric ideals, emphasizing the importance of African agency and voice in shaping narratives about the African experience. Furthermore, Everett sees these digital technologies as tools for envisioning and creating alternative futures, a core component of Afrofuturism. She highlights how African diasporic communities use digital media to imagine and articulate visions of the future grounded in African and African diasporic perspectives, histories, and experiences (pp. 126–127). This ties into the Afrofuturist idea of using science fiction and speculative narratives to interrogate the present and envision future possibilities for the African diaspora.

Moreover, Everett's work uniquely connects Afrocentricity and Afrofuturism by recognizing that both movements are concerned with reclaiming and centering African narratives. Everett's analysis of digital media and technologies demonstrates how these tools enable African diasporic communities to engage in Afrocentric cultural production while envisioning Afrofuturistic possibilities. Her work thus provides a compelling insight into the interconnectedness of Afrocentricity and Afrofuturism. As a cultural and intellectual movement, Afrocentricity emphasizes the importance of viewing African history and culture from an African perspective. Conversely, Afrofuturism, as defined by Charles E. Jones and me in *Afrofuturism 2.0: The Rise of Astro-Blackness* (2016), represents a rising speculative movement of literary and cultural aesthetics combining art, science fiction, speculative fiction, magical realism, and Afrocentric perspectives with non-Western cosmologies. At their intersection, these two concepts offer a robust framework for reimagining the past, present, and future of the African diaspora.

Afrocentricity, a term coined by scholar Molefi Kete Asante in the 1980s, is a paradigm that repositions Africa as the center of one's worldview. Instead of viewing African history and culture through the lens of European or Western perspectives, Afrocentricity urges us to view Africa through an African lens. Afrocentricity is not the inverse of Eurocentrism and does not make the same totalizing claims. It asserts that, despite the diversity across African peoples, an African cultural matrix is standard to all African people, with different geographic and local sociocultural particularities constituting this lens. This perspective applies to historical interpretations and extends to social, political, and economic analyses. I coined the term *Afrofuturism 2.0* in a brief conference dialogue with Alondra Nelson in 2013 and, in collaboration with Charles E. Jones, conceptualized and developed an anthology on the topic, updating Afrofuturism for the 21st century and its connection to Africana studies. While the original concept of Afrofuturism, coined by Mark Dery in 1994, focuses on the African American future, including technology and speculative fiction, Afrofuturism 2.0 expands these boundaries. My formulation of Afrofuturism 2.0 recognizes the entire diaspora and its connection to Africa as a source of a geography of reason. It also underscores the intersection of technology, race, gender, and class in these futuristic African realities.

The intersection of Afrocentricity and Afrofuturism 2.0 provides a unique perspective on the African diaspora's past, present, and future. We can understand and appreciate Africa's rich history and culture through Afrocentricity, unfiltered by Western or Eurocentric lenses. This understanding forms a solid foundation on which Afrofuturism 2.0 can build. Afrofuturism 2.0, with its speculative framework and design elements, allows for reimagining Africa's future. These frameworks frequently incorporate African history and cultural elements, making Afrocentricity a crucial component in their creation. The interplay between Afrocentricity and Afrofuturism 2.0 helps to decolonize the mind, providing an avenue for the African diaspora and Africa to envision a future free from the constraints of a Eurocentric worldview.

One critical aspect of Afrofuturism 2.0 is its emphasis on Pan-Africanism, acknowledging the complexity of identity in the African diaspora. This intersection is where Afrocentricity's focus on an African-centered perspective and Afrofuturism 2.0's consideration of future possibilities converge. Together, they create a more holistic view of the African diaspora and Africa in the emerging world order. Thus, developing an Afrocentric perspective has been a long and progressive journey, with key figures and movements contributing to its formation and evolution. From the foundational work of W. E. B. Du Bois, the Garvey movement, through the transformative Black studies movement, to the groundbreaking research of Cheikh Anta Diop, Molefi Kete Asante, Wade Nobles, C. T. Keto, Maulana Karenga, and Anna Everett, the Afrocentric perspective has emerged as a powerful tool for reframing the understanding of African history and culture. By centering Africa in historical, cultural, and social analyses, the Afrocentric perspective provides an alternative to the dominant Eurocentric view, enabling a more comprehensive and nuanced understanding of the African experience.

The Revenge of Geography and the Age of Acceleration

Following the Cold War at the end of the 20th century, the world order established at the end of World War II began to unravel, and the history of geography, geopolitics, and technology began to assert itself as the reality of climate change began to make its presence felt. The rapid pace of globalization and accelerating change triggered a wave of theories and perspectives on the world's future. Two theories, outlined in Robert Kaplan's (2013) *The Revenge of Geography* and Thomas Friedman's (2017) *Thank You for Being Late: An Optimist's Guide to Thriving in the Age of Accelerations,* offer distinct views on the forces shaping our global future. While Kaplan emphasizes the enduring influence of geography on human affairs, Friedman focuses on the accelerating forces of technology, globalization, and climate change.

Robert Kaplan posits that geography shapes the destiny of nations despite the rapid pace of technological and social changes. He suggests that while globalization, technology, and human agency play a significant role in shaping events, they are still subject to geography's fundamental constraints and opportunities. According to Kaplan, the physical characteristics of a place, including its climate, topography, and location, significantly influence its inhabitants' political, social, and economic behaviors and act as a limiting factor to the possibilities of human actions and interventions. For example, he suggests that Russia's vast Siberian plains and severe climate have historically made it difficult to invade, thus shaping its geopolitical strategy.

On the other hand, Thomas Friedman emphasizes the impact of three accelerating forces: technology, globalization, and climate change. According to Friedman, these three "accelerations" rapidly reshape our world, with profound implications for individuals, societies, and nations. Friedman argues that technology, particularly the exponential growth in computing power, is reshaping every aspect of our lives, from how we work to how we communicate. Globalization, influenced by advances in technology and the liberalization of markets, is integrating economies and societies like never before. Finally, the acceleration of climate change, driven by human activity, poses new challenges to our survival and prosperity.

While, briefly, the two theories may seem to be in opposition, there is a level of complementarity between them. Based on geography's enduring influence, Kaplan's theory provides a framework for critiquing the realpolitik that shapes human activity. It reminds us that despite our advanced technology and interconnectedness, we are still fundamentally bound by physical realities. On the other hand, Friedman's theory highlights the transformative power of accelerating forces, suggesting that our world is increasingly defined by rapid change and complexity. His perspective does not negate the importance of geography but rather illustrates how these accelerations interact with and often amplify the effects of geographical realities.

Climate change, one of Friedman's three accelerations, is deeply influenced by geography. A country's geographical location can determine its vulnerability to rising sea levels, extreme weather events, and other climate-related phenomena. At the same time, technology and globalization, the other two accelerations, often shape how countries respond to these geographical realities, whether through migration, infrastructure development, or international cooperation. Finally, it is broadly acknowledged that the emergence of a multipolar world after the Ukraine–Russia conflict has ended the world order established after World War II (Diesen, 2024).

Afrofuturism in a Multipolar World

Pan-Africanism and Afrofuturism represent two radical perspectives on the future of Africa and the global African diaspora. While Pan-Africanism is rooted in a historical and political narrative, advocating for the unity and self-governance of African nations, Afrofuturism is a cultural and philosophical movement envisioning an advanced technological and social future for Africans and people of African descent. These two perspectives, although distinct, share a common vision of an empowered and autonomous Africa and its diaspora. However, they face significant geopolitical challenges, particularly around the issue of energy security. This raises the question of what the implications are for the revenge of geography and the three principles of acceleration for Afrofuturism 2.0 and Pan-Africanism. For example, the current conflict between the NATO countries, select nations of the Economic Community of West African States (ECOWAS), and the Pan-African revolt by counties in the Sahel and central African nations illustrates an emerging new world order fracturing along several dimensions, including energy and development.

Some of the challenges that Afrofuturism and Pan-Africanism must grapple with to realize the ideals on which they are founded are, first, the geopolitical instability of many African nations, which produces political instability, conflicts, and governance issues that often hinder the execution of cohesive energy policies and infrastructure projects for African nations; and second, climate change and environmental destruction resulting from the exploitation of fossils and which disproportionately affects African nations. For Afrofuturism to realize the technologically advanced Africa that it envisions, it must also set out to accomplish this reality within the framework of environmental sustainability. Third, significant sway over energy resources and technologies, which many developed countries and multinational corporations hold, shapes the global power dynamics and presents a significant challenge. The control of these entities over energy resources and technologies can hinder Africa's ability to achieve energy independence, which, in turn, reinforces neocolonial structures.

For Pan-Africanism and Afrofuturism to address these challenges, a multipronged, cooperative approach is necessary. This includes investment in renewable energy infrastructure, strengthening regional political and economic cooperation, and fostering Pan-African technological innovation. Furthermore, these movements must address the power asymmetries in global energy politics, pushing for fairer trade agreements and tech transfers and advocating for the interests of African nations on the global stage. Thus, energy security is a significant challenge to realizing Pan-African and Afrofuturistic ideals. These challenges are multifaceted, encompassing resource availability, geopolitical stability, environmental sustainability, and global power dynamics. However, Pan-Africanism and Afrofuturism provide a framework for creative, strategic cooperation rooted in an African worldview that will empower African nations to address these difficulties and pave the way for a future that embodies the principles of Pan-Africanism and Afrofuturism.

The evolving nature of globalization and the increasing complexities of a multipolar world necessitate the application of unique insights to understand the ongoing dynamics. Thomas Friedman's three principles of acceleration provide such a perspective. These principles—the market and Moore's law—relate to economic globalization, climate change, and technological advancements. Pan-Africanism, which encourages solidarity and collaboration between African nations, can be examined through these lenses to highlight its challenges in a multipolar world. Friedman's first principle, the market, encapsulates the rapid changes in the global economy, highlighting the acceleration of financial flows, goods, services, and people across borders. Pan-Africanism, rooted in the desire for collective self-reliance, economic cooperation, and integration among African nations, is greatly influenced by these economic dynamics. In a multipolar world, where economic power is dispersed among various international players, African nations face the challenge of maintaining their sovereignty while engaging in international trade and investment. The market acceleration has opened opportunities for African economies to participate in global trade. However, it has also exposed them to increased competition and the risk of economic exploitation. To navigate this, Pan-Africanism must adapt to promote economic policies that capitalize on aspects of globalization while safeguarding the interests of African nations. This might include negotiating more equitable trade agreements, fostering regional economic integration through bodies like the African Union, or investing in sectors that can compete globally while providing local benefits.

Friedman's second principle is climate change, which refers to the accelerating pace of climate change and biodiversity and species loss. With its diverse ecosystems, Africa is particularly vulnerable to these environmental changes. Lack of precipitation, floods, climate migration, and other extreme weather events threaten the agriculture sector on which much of the continent's population depends for livelihood. Through a Pan-African lens, these environmental challenges necessitate collective action. A unified approach to sustainable development and climate resilience can harness the power of shared resources, knowledge, and technology, potentially mitigating the impact of environmental change. However, in a multipolar world, environmental diplomacy becomes a complex endeavor. Balancing the urgency of climate action with the need for economic development, particularly in the face of demands from more affluent nations, is a significant challenge. Pan-Africanism, therefore, must involve advocating for fair and equitable global environmental policies that consider Africa's unique circumstances.

Friedman's third principle, Moore's law, pertains to the exponential growth of computing power, which is representative of the broader acceleration in technological innovation. Technology presents vast opportunities for African nations, especially in the realms of education, healthcare, and economic productivity. However, the technological divide between Africa and more technologically advanced regions presents a significant challenge. While technology has advanced rapidly in Western countries, many African nations still lack access to basic technological infrastructure like reliable internet connectivity and electricity, all while being exploited for the materials that make these and other technological advancements possible in the West. The West relies on resource extraction in African countries to fuel the demand for minerals and rare-earth elements in Western technologies, like smartphones, smart televisions, and laptops. This extraction often has negative social and environmental impacts, including displacement of local communities and ecological damage.

Thus, while the West ravages African countries and people for technological enrichment, many African nations lack technological infrastructure, hindering economic development, education, and healthcare. Moreover, an essential aspect of national security and economic growth is energy security, but many African nations still need help to secure reliable, sustainable, and affordable energy sources. This energy insecurity is a significant roadblock to realizing Pan-African and Afrofuturistic ideals. Since most African nations do not control their own energy production, there is a dependency on foreign nations and corporations, undermining the self-sufficiency that Pan-Africanism and Afrofuturism envision.

Bridging this gap should be a fundamental aspect of an Afrofuturistic Pan-African approach to technological acceleration. This gap is primarily due to Western companies often holding patents and intellectual property rights over advanced technologies, which limits the ability of African countries to develop and produce their technology solutions. Faced with the accelerating technological boon, the encroaching metaverse, the rise of AI, and increasing global disorder and divergence in a multipolar world, Afrofuturism is faced with the task of adapting to these conditions. Part of that endeavor must include establishing ethics concerning a pluriversal world (Anderson, 2022c). This might involve investing in digital infrastructure, fostering tech entrepreneurship, and implementing policies encouraging digital literacy and inclusion. In a multipolar world, the geopolitics of technology also come into play. Issues of cybersecurity, data sovereignty, and the influence of tech giants are all factors in the emerging great power competition between the United States and China, despite the African Union's recent admission to the G-20 and the defiance of African states like Burkina Faso, Mali, and Niger to the neo-imperial tendencies of France.

Chapter 1, "The New Atlantis, the Anglo World Order, and the Genesis of Afro-Modernity," discusses the emergence of Black speculative thought and its links to select African continent and diaspora regions. For example, it demonstrates how Black/African speculative theory and praxis reflected a geography of reason that survived the Middle Passage and destructive attacks on West African civilization and faced Enlightenment racism and the rise of scientific racism. Furthermore, the chapter looks at the engagement with science and speculative thought within this tradition by figures and phenomenon such as conjure feminism, Hoodoo, Vodun, Benjamin Banneker, Paschal Beverly Randolph, and Martin Delany and how they would engage the emergence of scientific racism and white supremacy.

Chapter 2, "The Rising Tide of Color and Creating a New Race," focuses on modern Black and African life emerging in modernism and the esoteric ideas that influenced; for example, how the emerging international relations order and politics of the Jazz Age and the ideas of the mystic G. I. Gurdjieff and A. R. Orage impacted Americans. Important figures like W. E. B. Du Bois, Zora Neal Hurston, Jean Toomer, and others were vital in developing what would later be known as the Harlem Renaissance. Furthermore, figures in the Nazi movement during Germany's Weimar period developed an occult worldview that was rising to challenge the Anglo-led world order.

Chapter 3, "The Rise of the Deep State and the Technostate," explores the intersection of astroculture, the Cold War, and the space race in the 20th century that catalyzed a unique cultural awakening, birthing a genre often referenced in the Black speculative / Afrofuturist tradition. This period blends speculative fiction, science fiction, and fantasy with African diasporic cultural and historical themes. Central figures in this movement include Sun Ra, Samuel Delany, and Octavia Butler, each contributing to reimagining Black identity and future possibilities through their creative works. Sun Ra's avant-garde jazz and cosmic philosophies challenged conventional narratives and offered a vision of Black liberation through extraterrestrial mythos (Szwed, 1997). Samuel Delany's science fiction explored complex social issues, including race, sexuality, and power dynamics, thereby pushing the boundaries of the genre (Tucker, 2004). Octavia Butler's narratives provided profound explorations of race, gender, and human evolution, positioning her as a pivotal figure in speculative fiction (Canavan, 2016).

Chapter 4, "The Dark Enlightenment and the Collapse of the Liberal World Order," explores the intricate intersections between Nick Land's "Dark Enlightenment," the collapse of progressive ideology, the disintegration of the Washington Consensus or what was also known as the Bretton Woods Agreement, and the ascendance of my theory of Afrofuturism 2.0. The analysis begins with Nick Land's "Dark Enlightenment" concept, which critiques modern liberal democracies and posits a return to hierarchical and anti-egalitarian principles (Land, 2023). This ideological shift is contextualized within the broader collapse of progressive ideology, marked by increasing disillusionment with globalism, multiculturalism, and the welfare state

(Murray, 2017). Amid these shifts, the chapter highlights the rise of Afrofuturism 2.0, as I have theorized. Afrofuturism 2.0 extends beyond its original cultural and artistic dimensions to address issues of technology, science fiction, and speculative thought about the African diaspora and Africa in the 21st century (Anderson & Jones, 2016). This theoretical framework provides a counternarrative to the dystopian visions of the Dark Enlightenment by envisioning futures where Black cultural and technological contributions reshape the global landscape. By juxtaposing these seemingly disparate intellectual movements, the chapter demonstrates how they reflect broader societal transformations and ideological realignments in contemporary global politics. It argues that understanding these intersections is crucial for comprehending the complex dynamics of the current geopolitical and cultural landscape.

Chapter 5, "The Nommo of the Black Speculative Turn," delves into the Black Speculative Arts movement (BSAM), exploring its aesthetic politics. The BSAM, an umbrella term for creative works that engage with Black speculative fiction, Afrofuturism, and other genres, is a critical space for reimagining Black futures and histories (Anderson & Fluker, 2019). Through a multidisciplinary approach, this chapter examines how BSAM artists and allies use speculative aesthetics to challenge dominant narratives and propose alternative realities reflecting Black existence's complexities.

The aesthetic politics of BSAM are rooted in a desire to surpass and transcend the restrictions imposed by historical and contemporary forms of racial oppression. By employing speculative fiction, visual arts, and performance, BSAM practitioners create works that envision liberated Black futures, thereby offering resistance against systemic inequities (Thomas, 2019). These artistic practices are not merely escapist fantasies; they are deeply political acts that assert the presence and agency of Black people in shaping their destinies. BSAM provides a platform for articulating an aesthetic politics that acknowledges the multiplicity of Black experiences and identities, thus fostering a more inclusive understanding of humanity. These examples demonstrate how BSAM artists navigate the intersections of race, gender, and technology to produce innovative and transformative visions of the future. In conclusion, the Black Speculative Arts movement offers a rich terrain for exploring the intersections of aesthetic politics and social ontology. By imagining alternative futures and challenging existing power structures, BSAM enriches the cultural landscape and contributes to broader conversations about justice, identity, and human potential.

Chapter 6, "AI Nationalism and the New World Order," explores the dynamic interplay between Afrofuturism 2.0, the emerging multipolar world order, AI nationalism, and the pressing issue of climate change. Afrofuturism 2.0, characterized by its engagement with digital technology, speculative fiction, and African diasporic narratives, provides a unique lens to examine how marginalized communities envision and navigate future scenarios (Eshun, 2003; Anderson & Jones, 2016). Afrofuturism 2.0 challenges dominant narratives and offers alternative visions of technological advancement and societal evolution by integrating elements of African culture, history, and futuristic aspirations.

The multipolar world order, marked by the decentralization of global power away from a unipolar dominance toward a more distributed geopolitical landscape, significantly impacts global governance and international relations (Acharya, 2018). This shift necessitates rethinking how nations, particularly Global South nations, engage with technology and climate policies. A re-evaluation of global strategies to address climate change, emphasizing the need for inclusive and equitable approaches, is spurred by regional powers gaining more prominence and the heightened importance of transnational networks (Hurrell, 2006). AI nationalism, the phenomenon where nations prioritize developing and controlling artificial intelligence technologies to assert their sovereignty and global influence, further complicates this landscape (McCauley, 2020). The strategic importance of AI in national security, economic competitiveness, and societal governance underscores the urgency for robust policy frameworks that balance innovation with ethical considerations. Nations increasingly leverage AI to tackle climate challenges, from optimizing energy use to advancing climate modeling and disaster response systems (Vinuesa et al., 2020). Climate change, an existential threat with disproportionate impacts on vulnerable populations, intersects with these themes by highlighting the necessity for resilient and adaptive strategies. Chapter 6 argues that Afrofuturism 2.0 offers critical insights into how communities can harness technology and cultural heritage to build sustainable futures in the face of climatic disruptions. By examining case studies and theoretical frameworks, the chapter illustrates how the principles of Afrofuturism 2.0 can inform global responses to climate change, fostering innovation that is both inclusive and contextually relevant (Yaszek, 2006; Nelson, 2019).

CHAPTER 1

The New Atlantis, the Anglo World Order, and the Genesis of Afro-Modernity

Human variation resulting from the rise and fall of empires, which add different geographies to their polities as they expand their borers and reach, has been a prevalent reality throughout history (Smedley & Smedley, 2005). The ancient world's empires were diverse in composition and features, and often these populations would eventually be assimilated into the larger imperial populations (Smedley & Smedley, 2005). However, with the emergence of the transatlantic slave trade from the 16th century onward, the concept of race emerged as an idea among the English-speaking people, and by the end of the 17th century, it was a primary focus of the relations between European, African, and Indigenous people of the Western Hemisphere. Asians were later added within the classification system occupying a space between Europeans and Africans. By the 18th century, scientists like Linnaeus and Blumenbach introduced human classification systems for the entire human race (Smedley & Smedley, 2005). During this same period, roughly 1687–1789, a group of elite European thinkers consisting of Descartes, Kant, Rousseau, Voltaire, Diderot, Condorcet, Paine, Benjamin Franklin, and others established a systematic body of thought that would generate a series of scientific and political developments that would destroy millennia-old cultures and civilizations to sustain an undefined but conceived of as universal modern world (Monteiro-Ferreira, 2014, p. 41).

The roots of modernity lay in the reconquest of southern Europe from North African peoples and Arabs, finalized by 1492, solidifying Iberian kingdoms on the peninsula (Monteiro-Ferreira, 2014). Furthermore, a profit motive combining the influence of the Roman Catholic church and the kingdoms of Portugal and Spain combined the religious, commercial, and military rationale underwritten by the slave trade and the existence of gold and silver mines in the Western Hemisphere, financing the expansion of latifundium—the ancient Roman term for plantation estates. Therefore, from the 16th into the 19th century, the Atlantic occupied an international strategic position, "a triangular platform through which raw materials, mineral resources . . . and enslaved free labor circulated creating a global racist and capitalist world order" (Monteiro-Ferreira, 2014, p. 49).

It is during this historical period of European exploitation and expansion that Afro-modernity was born. Afro-modernity illustrates a unique understanding of the modernity and subjectivity of African peoples (Hanchard, 1999). It represents incorporating and synthesizing selective discourses and technologies from Western modernity to develop a relatively alternative modernity unique to the sociocultural political practice of African peoples distinct from their European counterparts. Afro-modernity is a response to the Middle Passage and technosocial conditions of the societies where African peoples found themselves in the Western Hemisphere and the Eurosphere of influence. It is characterized by three things: a supranational formation of people based on the experiences of the Middle Passage and trans-Saharan slave trade; the development of alternative international cultural and political networks across national boundaries and temporal time; and an explicit critique of the process of the Enlightenment, modernity, citizenship, and sovereignty (Hanchard, 1999).

At the same time, detractors of Enlightenment social, cultural, and political dogma began their work. We know who the philosophers and prose writers were: men such as Montesquieu, Bayle, Voltaire, Rousseau, and Locke. Since genuine intellectual plurality was not a goal of all Enlightenment thinkers, a search for this other side will provide a glimpse of the pragmatic importance of precedence without claim to absolutist legitimacy (Serjeantson, 2024). For example, it was Thomas Jefferson, who, influenced by the ideas of the Enlightenment, rationalized the treatment and natural inferiority of the enslaved Africans on his plantation in his book *Notes on the State of Virginia*, establishing the philosophical roots for American-style scientific racism at the beginning of the 19th century (Smedley & Smedley, 2005).

The idea of the New World took on very diverse characteristics in 18th- and 19th-century thought. For some, the concept of a perfectible New World instilled hope and confidence. The New World was not a romantic ideal of academic interest only. First, the idea of an ideal New World, and second, the very notion of America as images of social, cultural, and political reform, or as mirrors of prospective strife and chaos, are unique to the 18th-century period, at least in the degree of their adoption and impact. Now, by the New World, I do not mean the American colonies but rather an idealized society that was considered the ideal society envisioned by artists, writers, philosophers, and eventually political leaders who agreed with or at least had sympathy with Enlightenment principles. Such thought experiments were by no means invented during the Enlightenment. They were, after all, a time-honored theme in utopian literature, but the concept of the New World developed during the Enlightenment deserves special attention (Zavala, 2022). The European Enlightenment was a highly influential philosophical, literary, and sociopolitical movement that dominated European discourse during the 18th century through the late 1700s. Although the Enlightenment was extraordinarily broad in scope, Enlightenment thinkers share a few essential commonalities, such as liberal religious toleration; rejection of tyranny as a legitimate form of government; appreciation of proportion, harmony, and beauty in art, architecture, and design; and the critique of dogma and deference to established authority, whether it be political, social, or intellectual (Levitin, 2022).

Francis Bacon's *The New Atlantis*: Utopian Vision and Scientific Progress

Among his other political theory works Francis Bacon wrote several significant utopian works. While most of Bacon's philosophical work emphasized the importance of empirical investigation as freeing reason to develop rational methods from dogmatic beliefs, Bacon only mentions mental inventions that clarify things because of considering the error—all actual scientific progress results from drawing inferences from the observation of nature. Moreover, here is where I want to dwell. The longer scientific reason held sway, the more concerned the scientists became with their inability to improve humanity. So desperate were some that they turned to questionable chemicals and texts, distorted remnants of the hermetic tradition, hoping to prolong life (Yuan, 2022; Remmling, 2022).

On the eve of the European Enlightenment, there was a renaissance of ancient knowledge, mainly focused on Rosicrucianism and Egyptology. Bacon wrote one of the first and most notable books in this Europe-wide search to recover ancient wisdom. While condemning ancient knowledge and extolling only the virtues of modern science, Bacon presents a utopian vision of a pagan, ancient civilization in his book *The New Atlantis*. In so doing, he reveals some fascinating tensions in the development of the early Enlightenment. He demonstrates the importance of a specific type of knowing commonly associated with Rosicrucianism in the rise of the European Enlightenment (Dolgoy & Hale, 2020).

Bacon's work *The New Atlantis* was begun in 1623 as part of his third proposed part of the *Instauratio* but was never completed. Following Bacon's death, it was published posthumously in 1627. It is the story of a roving, determined group of characters known variously as Strangers, Venturers, Sons of Science, and the Family of Solomon the King who sail in search of places and come upon the mysterious island nation of Bensalem. The island has a theocratic government composed of a college of general priests led by a single head priest, known as the Ruler. Established by the inapprehensible inspiration of the Divine Spirit, it is governed by true religion and God's secret wisdom. Here, the Testament of Job, The Minority of God in Supremacy and his government, and The Strong Mind of Solomon the King, together with the New Proposta, are translated and shown to the amazed visitors who realize that the founders of Bensalem, working under the guidance of Divine Providence, had also received advanced science and what they believed to be pagan philosophy (Ghorban Sabbagh, 2020).

Bacon's Influence on Enlightenment Thought

At any rate, if not the New Atlantis as a conceptual pattern, in most other doctrines, it was the initiator of a tendency in Enlightenment thought, which was to become more insistent in the movement's second half-century, the actual realization of freedom and equality among men. Bacon was the first European to claim the necessity of the sciences for man's happiness. Such a government would not only have to work little to maintain its rule but would have largely unpaid personnel who could spend most of their time contemplating the divinity and receive an enduring education in another state known as the Solomonic House. The design approach imitated the stability of a favored government. The clarity of its concept would saturate English Enlightenment thought (Bacon, 2020).

Because of the secrecy surrounding the sizeable educational plan of Francis Bacon, it is difficult to determine at this late date to what extent it was an inciting influence on thinkers in the two centuries following his death. *The New Atlantis* was much read and praised and occasionally ridiculed. However, we do not know whether anyone has considered putting any of the ideas it contains to any practical test. An experiment in state education could hardly have been conducted in secret, unless the only purpose its sponsors intended to serve was to adumbrate the steps to be taken by an enlightened few in that direction. Bacon, being a philosopher, one who was engaged with the politics of his time, did not have to rely as much on mystification as some of the natural philosophers, and he rarely proposed doing anything remotely resembling an engagement with mysticism.

Rosicrucianism: Mysticism, Alchemy, and Enlightenment Ideals

Rosicrucianism was a 16th-century intellectual and social movement considered the most important stimulant to the 17th-century scientific revolution and the European Enlightenment. Their most easily understood, though not typically emphasized, side is the association with alchemy. This is because the Rosicrucians considered alchemical knowledge the key to those changes required for achieving their utopian goals. Also leading to a misunderstanding of their intentions is the dissemination of popular misconceptions by various types of initiates under the supposed Knightly Order of the Rose Cross (Atkinson, 2023).

The label Rosicrucian designates those who believe that a spiritual-philosophical "Knightly Order of the Rose Cross" exists and that it is a secret society that is directly descended from certain late Hermetic and Kabbalistic writings (inherited from Egyptian civilization) supposedly produced by the synthesis of the society's teachings and initiates appropriately qualified aspirants to whom its members studiously refrain from informing about their rank or mere membership (Atkinson, 2023). However, they often provide hints in their own published works. Moreover, those who, having learned about the order from published works of established or putative members or the historian's pronouncements about them, imitate the propagandistic practices of the reputed members of the order by writing or believing popular accounts that convey whatever they understand to be the theme or spirit, ordinarily identified with the supposed order or its teaching (Atkinson, 2023).

Rosicrucianism

Inside the tomb, the mythical personage Rosenkreuz had left behind a series of cryptic writings, which prophesied the return of the members of his society at the dawn of the new millennium and described some of the wondrous "secret knowledge" that they had gathered during their 16th-century travels through the Middle East. Once established, the society was said to hope to complete Rosicrucianism's true purpose of founding a new, secret school of wisdom that would guide humanity toward a more fortunate future (Waite, 2020). Rosicrucianism first appeared in a series of pamphlets, or advertisements, published through European printers from around 1606 through 1616. Each of these pamphlets claimed to establish a foundation for the Order of the Rosy Cross, an organization that none had ever seen nor met. However, its reputation as a group whose members were engaged in the study and practice of occult arts was already widely known at the time of publication (de Vries, 2022). The first of the pamphlets, an anonymous treatise called "Fama Fraternitatis" (The Brothers' Report), introduced the society to the public and announced its purpose of providing a new solution to the problems currently plaguing Christian Europe. Claiming to have originated in 15th-century Germany, the Fama described how the body of the founder of the society—scholar Christian Rosenkreuz—had been discovered in a vault beneath a medieval chapel, where, following his death, it had been preserved in a lifelike state through alchemical techniques of introversion and encasement within a container of transparent glass (Waite, 2020).

Rosicrucianism's Impact on Scientific and Philosophical Discourse

The scientific academies of the 17th and 18th centuries were, by no means, neutral institutions. Rather, they were shaped by specific Western philosophical and esoteric ideologies that were part of a broader invisible hand which comprised epistemological control, economic structures, and religious institutions. Rosicrucianism was one such ideology that heavily shaped the scientific academies during the esoteric movement of the early 17th century, but which would come to be seen as problematic in mainstream scientific and academic circles with the epistemological shifts brought about during the onset of the Enlightenment Era. Francis Bacon tried to connect intelligence and political order to achieve his utopia. However, science and politics were together in opposite camps when Machiavelli first claimed the need to support imposing the order from above, and Blaise Pascal finished by stating the necessity of special knowledge to support the order from below (Zeitlin, 2021). Ultimately, the French Revolution was also a revolution of scientific education. These aspects demonstrate the longevity of the connection between science and control and the abrupt changes in the spirituality of the relations of force (Zeitlin, 2021).

At the start of the Scientific Revolution, Rosicrucianism came on the stage as a mixture of religious and philosophical beliefs. It proposed a utopian society based on science, where the members had an image of workmates, and the "invisible colleges" had the image of secret societies that strive to control the world using their unique knowledge. Historians emphasize the contrast between the secrecy of the invisible colleges and the public character of the members of scientific academies like the Royal Society or the French Académie des Sciences. With this, they outline the connection between the early forms of modern scientific societies and the secret societies in the Age of Enlightenment (Willard, 2022).

Egyptology: Ancient Wisdom and Enlightenment Curiosity

To unravel the essence of this power of influence in the Enlightenment, we need to analyze and understand the nature, matches, and differences between ancient knowledge and Enlightenment knowledge. How the Egyptian way of building an individual or the making of the enlightened was depicted, given shape, and claimed to be constituted not only during the Renaissance and the Enlightenment but also afterward, until our present day. Moreover, the rise of Egyptology corresponds to a specific pattern of thought demonstrating how the use of ancient Egyptian heritage's political and administrative suggestions, guidelines, aphorisms, and symbols extend from Francis Bacon and *The New Atlantis* to the Enlightenment project (Yaffe, 2020).

Western Europe's curiosity toward ancient Egypt was triggered by the Ottoman Empire's defeat of the Mamluk dynasty in 1517 at the battle of Ridaniya. Correspondingly, European powers saw the opportunity to establish engagement for political, military, and trade reasons. The Mamluks, Sunni Muslims, were the descendants of enslaved white Turkish, Circassian, Greek, and Christian peoples. This military caste dominated Egyptian life for several centuries until their defeat. Egypt would remain under the control of the Ottoman Empire until 1798, when Napoleon I of France, a Rosicrucian adept, invaded Egypt. According to scholars within the discipline of Enlightenment studies, some claims regarding ancient Egypt and its production/fabrication in Europe during the Enlightenment were valid. There was, of course, a wide range of instant wisdom sample books fabricated for the use of diplomats, travelers, generals, writers, and other elites with cliché Egyptian wisdom and symbols of sages, that the enlightened culturally elevated of Europe wanted to appear in Egyptian dress at least in their books (Conermann, 2021; Wilkinson, 2020).

Exploration and Rediscovery of Ancient Egyptian Civilization

The spice route of moving enslaved people, spices, precious gemstones, silks, textiles, porcelain, Indian elephants, and seacraft (virtually without and perhaps entirely without a direct connection between the Catholic transoceanic travels and present or anticipated Muslim opposition) was a near-perfect compromise—right up until the renewed application by Turkey and (subsequently) France and Sweden that access to the straits of Malacca had been granted by the Portuguese to the Spanish Crown with the approval of the 1529 Treaty of Zaragoza (Wilkinson, 2020). Nonetheless, this identification of the cultural breadth of Rome and its forerunners resulted in the evolution of those African civilizations into the substance of personal or imperial aspiration. This was essentially an Egypt of fantasy, designed to honor the Goths and the Vandals who claimed high status from their destruction of the long-busted classical empire Greater Egypt, with Goths and Vandals as its rival Egypt, and was acquired only vestigially and through a haze of anachronism (Wilkinson, 2020).

In many royals' courts, particularly in the Iberian Peninsula, iconography illustrates the belief that these people saw themselves as the heirs of Egyptian civilization. For example, in 1826 the Brazilian monarchy transported many Egyptian artifacts to Rio de Janeiro to start a "civilizing mission" to Europeanize the country during the reign of King Joao VI (Chaves, 2018). This Egypt of the imagination might have appeared to promise even more than the allusion to the authentic non-Oriental cultural, moral, and intellectual substance of the Greek past—indeed, Coptic and Christian identification might have meant spiritual salvation—but it is likely that, in any event, research into the civilization of the Pharaohs would have proved to be less profitable than the purchase and strategic employment of modern Egypt itself (Wilkinson, 2020).

European exploration of the primarily ancient world's buried and derelict wealth was at the heart of these events. Europeans knew something, at least, about the invasions of Greek and Roman soldiers and colonists into Egypt. However, even stone statues were buried so deep that they seemed to be from a hopelessly remote past. Alternatively, this was how Christian cosmology held a European imagination that was not so disconnected from

Egypt after all: not literal evidence, but, in any case, a divinely imposed period of distance from the revelation that the incarnation would bring (Wilkinson, 2020). As an intellectual and emotional concept, ancient Egypt now found itself increasingly and literally in an imperial context. Political and military control of Egypt gave added clout; its hieroglyphic language and the fact that it translated the unqualifiable divinities of ancient Egypt into a scriptural language of written signs was particularly intriguing and religiously helpful. New European perceptions of the nature of the past and the potential of history monetized the hunting, acquisition, interpretation, and, occasionally, the restitution of what Europeans might take to be their property (Anderson, 2022b).

Egyptology's Influence on European Thought and Culture

The center of the actual study of ancient Egypt remained in Egypt until the dominant paradigm of the post-Renaissance European scholarship rendered it obsolete. For the 15th- and 16th-century humanists, Egypt remained more than just a repository of wisdom and knowledge of the ancients. The favorite precedent and justifications for their exercise of critical original thinking reside in the memory of Egyptian wisdom. They called themselves philosophers, direct descendants of the ancient Egyptian priesthood bearing the Holy Grail of Thoth and revealing those hidden truths that would prevent human beings from falling into corrupt and vile conduct. Their mission was one of unmitigated cultural rescue: resurrecting the seed of knowledge sown by those ancient sages and thereby rejuvenating the Old World, which was found to be degenerate considering the brilliance of lost Egypt (Yaffe, 2020). By doing so, they hoped to supply the early modern reformists with the tools necessary to combat and mitigate the moral decay of their contemporaries. However, by trying to prove that the roots of wisdom run deep in ancient Egyptian soil, these thinkers took on an even more daunting task. They hoped to restore the culture that had let knowledge flourish in the first place, recreating the society that had generated those insights of the past imagined as the present and future. Their main task, as they saw it, was to articulate ways in which knowledge could be rendered socially efficacious, ways in which wisdom could be transformed into action that would have tangible beneficial consequences in the geopolitical concerns of their times. The land of the Nile pointed back to the past and the future.

The idea of revealing secrets from the past was by no means new to the Europeans of the 16th and 17th centuries. For over one and a half millennia, ever since the contact of the Western world with the remnants of that great civilization was re-established by Greek and Roman soldiers, Greek and Roman emperors, Catholic priests, and mercenaries had traveled the territories of ancient Egypt seeking to find knowledge and wealth, and through them, the power such knowledge and wealth could buy. Meanwhile, Europeans debated about the history and philosophy of the ancient Egyptians, revering them as the foundation stone of the classical culture from which they believed themselves to have sprung. Besides the viewpoint of the traditional biblical narrative, another key to the evolution of European interest in ancient Egypt was the vast number of Egyptian words incorporated into a variety of languages they spoke and the mysterious characters they saw in the hieroglyphic inscriptions on the most important surviving relics of ancient Egyptian civilization, their very own monuments (Yaffe, 2020).

The Convergence

Interest in Bacon's *The New Atlantis*, Rosicrucianism, and early Egyptology was more than curiosity. By the intellectual and political incline of the 1640s, diagrams in Descartes's (d. 1650) *Principes de Philosophie* (1644/2009), the philosophers' hunger was for a New World. Seventeenth-century interest in the creation of a perfectly just society is well-known. However, the roots of the enlightened arguments can be found by questioning why (and by whom) the earliest philosophical landscaping tool—a new literary device, the utopian-educational novel—was liberated from the grasp of humanism. The solution holds the unity of the two fundamental aspects of the content of this thesis. Both are derivatives of a mystical paradigm involuntarily brought upon the scene by the narrative structure of a philosophical theme developed by Bacon in *The New Atlantis*. In 1791 Lemprière asserted that Bacon had formed the plan of a Universal Society and left to his followers to reduce into practice the grand design (Lemprière & Lord, 1825). Why would a prominent historian admire a figure like Sir Francis Bacon in the middle of the Enlightenment, considering what Lemprière would like the world to believe? The answer, a paradox not limited to France and England, is that the temper of the sophisticated thinkers of the day led them to yearn for a new age.

Background of the Enlightenment and Scientific Racism

European Enlightenment introduced new systematic approaches to explaining the workings of the world. The middle of the 19th century was a time of unstable change when science was still poorly funded, and experimental data was mainly reported to serve the demands of both intellectual and commercial progress. Increases in transatlantic commerce and global expeditions inspired Darwin's theory of natural selection, and it was also a time of radical experimentation with the fiction of time, space, and humanity (Yao, 2021). Rasheedah Phillips (2024) argues this period in question reaches its zenith in the late 19th century, whereby the time, space, and agency of Africans and their diaspora were geopolitically dislocated and chronometrically reorganized by European powers during the International Meridian Conference of 1884 to reinforce colonial and global capitalist power structures.

The 19th century was an extremely speculative age in multiple senses because it was an experimental scientific epoch characterized by new scientific discoveries, trading, and migration. It was a time of empire and the expansion of global trade routes and relocations. The world in Western consciousness at the time was more frequently thought of as something to be acted upon, something that could be transformed. At the same time, Western views of difference focused on understanding biological differences came to the fore, inheriting Enlightenment ideas. The thought of the cruel and violent expropriation and transformation of so much of the planet and the concomitant exclusion of so much humanity from the fiction of human potential is at the center of Western science fiction. Differences from the Western ideal as manifested in whites were attributed to the inheritance of presumably degenerating traits that Black bodies carried due to the bestiality of their African origins (Gaukroger, 2020).

The European Enlightenment was a period of exciting and rapid transnational intellectual change. During this time, various entangled and alternative traditions came together in new ways. The Enlightenment, more than anything else, saw substantial sociopolitical change in this period, which brought about the rights and liberties of specific kinds of people. The problem of this kind of "other" in Enlightenment thought, especially in forms that could be considered unusual or outside of the norm, was worked out across a diversity of different registers, one of the most powerful of which involved the question of race (Lok, 2023).

African Diaspora Speculative Counterdiscourse

Black speculative thought, amorphous and slippery as it is, has become the topic of more attention within mainstream culture circuits such as Afrofuturism over the last decade. For example, in the 19th century, the

African diaspora was involved in critiquing the impact of the influence of Egyptology and the Enlightenment. It sowed the seeds for their counter-Enlightenment project. People like Frederick Douglass, post-emancipation, and Edward Blyden traveled to Egypt for insight. The African church in America focused more on America than on Egypt, in contrast to the white counterparts who saw America as the New Israel. As such, confronting the alleged motivations and origins of these systemic foundations, such as anti-Blackness, comes with an interest in speculation. In Cuba a free African man, Jose Antonio Aponte (1760–1812), was executed for developing a speculative book influenced by the Haitian Revolution, illustrating a Black utopian society, where the founding emperors like the Haitian Dessalines and the enslaved African Cuban population executed all the island's white males and used the surviving white females for other services (Braham, 2022). In Brazil, Joaquim Felicio dos Santos (1822–1895) wrote *Pages from the History of Brazil Written in the Year 2000* (1868–1872) characterizing the backwardness of Brazilian society, the abolition of slavery, and describing a Brazil led by African and Indigenous peoples that technologically dominates the United States by the year 2000 (Braham, 2022). Also, in the 19th century, African Americans like David Dorr (1858), by contrast, describing the attempt by white Americans to create an Egypt of the West in the New World in 1858, wrote his book *A Colored Man Round the World*, calling Americans the Medes and Persians of the 19th century and reflecting how Egyptian civilization had fallen to invasion (Trafton, 2004, p. 20). This example of Black cultural life "occupies space between European American imperialism and African American oppression, between White ambivalence and Black Identification, between interconnecting images of pharaohs, slaves, homeland and exodus" (Trafton, 2004, p. 21). Therefore, the roots of the Black speculative tradition as a speculative counter-rhetoric to the "Enlightenment" of the 19th century wielded powerful tools that would challenge European-centered science fiction in the future.

The African Diaspora Speculative Tradition's Response to Scientific Racism

Afrofuturism has been proposed as a speculative counter-rhetoric to the Enlightenment, particularly as articulated anew in 19th-century scientific racism. Following this period, Blacks began appearing more frequently in Western literature, often used as fodder for narratives of scientific racism or as marginal ethnic types used as apes of white popular characters proliferating in Oriental fiction. Considering these disempowering characterizations, Black speculations into the future, futures as conceptual constructs, and theories of science and technology that Black characters, or an overly Blackened modernity, can and should serve to challenge the terms used to create those agents. Afrofuturism is a citation of the creation of every kind in resistance to the denials of both time and identity that scientific racism represents (Toliver, 2021; Scott, 2021).

In African interpretations of science and technology, Black identities generally tangibly appear in and around scientific discussion as the argumentatively empty origin of something tacitly agreed upon in scientific discourse. As they present ways that Black and African people might have produced knowledge, 19th-century science fiction written by or dealing directly with Blacks and Africans has a wealth of responses that incorporate speculative narratives and esoteric practices. These works, of course, serve to belay or subvert the narratives of scientific racism codified in and around 19th-century Western science fiction in several ways. They offer alternative stories taking Black and African agency, looking to alternative worlds of creation where scientific racism would not exist or where they could contest the science fiction that deals with them directly in new marginal types that create new subjectivities and show new realities.

Vodun in the Haitian Revolution

Vodun was the means for achieving the secular-first ethical ends propounded by the colonial Enlightenment as the only means for achieving economic prosperity. Vodun resembles the Dogon religious practices of Mali and their symbol of the Pole Star, like the entities of Legba and Gede (Levenda, 2008). To Saint Domingue's Haitian Revolution, Vodun provided the moral and leadership parameters resembling those in place after the Western political "descent of Moses" to Mt. Sinai (except many in Saint Domingue had rarely known the Western notion of freedom). At the beginning of the Haitian onset, when Haiti became the only place where enlightened aspirations were affirmed for all, interest in the colonially forgotten Vodun customs and language (marked forgotten on Enlightenment's maps of the world) renewed. Vodun began attracting attention from outsiders wanting to know how it could transform enslaved African-originated populations—the stateless, crashing, destitute, brutish, lawless, and short lives of the enslaved served as a critique of John Locke's and Thomas Hobbes's notions of political agency (Levenda, 2008).

Celestial Ascent

African belief systems survived the experience of the Middle Passage. They thrived throughout the Americas, and if there was any mixing, it was with other African systems of thought, even if there was a surface borrowing attributed to Catholicism and Protestantism (Du Bois, 2011; Levenda, 2008). Vodun originated in West Africa, specifically among the Fon and Ewe peoples and their various subgroups. The rituals that take place in the Haitian peristyle or temple are represented by the four cardinal directions with a pole in the center called the poteau mitan, analogous to the axis mundi, that reaches down into the Vilokan, to contact the loa, or Haitian deities that ascend the pillar to participate in the ritual (Levenda, 2008). Importantly, Vodun is not a static ideology but continues to play a significant role in contemporary African and Haitian societies. The Fon and Ewe, who had a shared origin and met in present-day Togo, have developed a solid connection to Vodun over the past millennium and a half, creating a conventional faith as a foundational element of their cultures. Over time, Vodun has become the central religion for specific groups in Congo and its neighboring region of Muchiote, which were once the heart of Afan, the central religion of the homogeneous groups. The early stages of Vodun also demonstrate a connection between Orisha and N'Kisi, gods of water and iron, respectively, known in Dahomey and Congo. In the Caribbean, these deities became syncretized with the pantheist beliefs of the Valley, which Caribs and Arawaks shared (Thornton, 2023).

In the African Vodun cosmology, religious beliefs influenced all elements of life and the universe. Enslaved people acknowledged numerous deities, each with their distinct role and area of influence. Beliefs in the spiritual and animistic aspects of existence affected how nature, animals, and plants were viewed, forming a dominant faith and belief system among Bedford villagers and Jamaican plantation communities. As a result, religion not only reflected their faith and beliefs but also guided their community customs and practices, as well as imposed constraints on their thoughts, emotional distress, and physical enslavement (Thornton, 2023).

Conjure Feminism and Hoodoo

Conjure feminism, hoodoo, and other Afrodiasporic esoteric traditions are powerful intellectual and womanist tractions that inform Black women's world-making and politics (Brooks et al., 2021). Conjure feminism and hoodoo are complex and multifaceted because they are rooted in the lives and experiences of generations of Black women, living at the intersection of race, gender, and sometimes class. For the members of the Black community whom these traditions serve, they risked their lives, morals, and reputations to uphold their spiritual practice to better their existence in a society that was created to cull the Black population. These faiths, practices, and traditions are more than just spiritual; they can function as identity movements in the social identity theory tradition and seek social justice, equality, and visibility (Mulkey, 2024).

Conjure or rootwork has been characterized as two steps to the left of African traditional religion and one step to the right of Christendom. Conjure empowers the individual (or a member of their ancestral legacy) to affect change with tools and methods that obstructed surveillance on enslaved African people's cultural practices. There have been many hoodoos, those who practice hoodoo, and some of those happen to be conjure women or root doctors. Hoodoo is a distinctively African spiritual heritage that holds other spiritual traditions at the forefront. Conjure feminism does draw spiritual practices from Black practices that originated in Africa, are motherland specific, slave memory encrypted, and southern African American conjure/hoodoo practices (Failla, 2022).

Healing, empowerment, and self-defense are the primary purposes of conjure feminism. These principles are evangelized throughout the conjure feminist living tradition and are accomplished through the practice of hoodoo, a folk magical system that is widely and openly practiced throughout the Black American South. Unlike many traditions of contemporary Wicca, or even Hermetic and Kabbalistic magical systems, adherence to conjure or hoodoo as a system of personal development and spiritual practice does not in any way conflict with one's adherence to the principles of another religious or atheistic tradition. Conjure and hoodoo are systems of utility, embodied sets of practices designed to provide practical results and support human beings in their struggles to move effectively through the world (Fox, 2023; Page & Woodland, 2023).

Benjamin Banneker's Astro-Liberation Theology

Benjamin Banneker (1731–1806) was heavily influenced by his family's non-denominational faith, which emphasized religious unity, and his father's knowledge of colonial instructional material about scripture. He incorporated his family's values and understanding of numerology to create his unique perspective on mathematics, astrology, and theology. Banneker's interpretation of biblical repetition and use of numerology to make his formulas and interpretations showcase his deep understanding of astro-theology. He believed in the significance of specific numbers, such as four and five, and their role in religious and astronomical contexts. Banneker's insights were complex and reflected his analytical approach to interpreting astro-theological concepts. Banneker assisted the astronomer and surveyor Andrew Ellicott (1754–1820) in surveying the federal territory that would become the District of Columbia. Banneker's work connecting the cosmos and science to liberty is now considered apparent in his almanacs for 1792 through 1797; the philosophy of astronomy concerning the condition of the enslaved Africans was theological, revolutionary, and abolitionist (Walker, 2014).

This unique interpretation created a way to attempt to break down the inherent constituents of the system. In this case, astrophysics goes beyond science and adopts and politicizes cosmology, philosophy, and theology. To move around the limits imposed by racist science and philosophy, the dynamics of African spirituality, like Vodun, can be used as a literary resource. This connection between Hellenism, Blackness, and Indigenous cultures can be found in the study of astro-theology proposed by Banneker in 1793. The writer, astrologist, mathematician, and man of letters linked Africa with the symbols of the ancient world by producing educational and emancipating counterdiscourses that deserve to be studied (Herschthal, 2021). Furthermore, Banneker's spirited literary response to Thomas Jefferson's *Notes from Virginia*, acknowledging the importance of examining Banneker from a perspective beyond his ties to African American heritage, is essential. The Enlightenment's resistance to racism is also shown through fictional characters who faced slavery and class disparities in the capitalist system while also representing the fight for freedom. Some African American authors have used speculative fiction to imagine a different reality and depict potential antiracist societies that go beyond scientific traditions that have marginalized Black experiences.

Pascha Beverly Randolph

Paschal Beverly Randolph (1825–1875) can be considered one of the principle founders of the African American esoteric tradition and influenced other occultists like Helen Blavatsky and Aleister Crowley, and his influence and spiritual innovation is noted by the African American novelist Pauline Hopkins (1859–1930) in her seminal text *Of One Blood*, noting that the esoteric tradition is a product of African roots (Finley, 2015). Furthermore, Randolph's book *Ravalette* (1863) is one of the earliest African American speculative writings to appear with its combination of Rosicrucianism, a man's journey to wed a preadamite woman, and a dueling vampire distinguishing it from the staid Victorian culture of the period in question. Randolph emerged from a matrix of his sympathetic involvement with the abolitionist movement, early involvement with the Spiritualist movement, and reputation as an occultist coinciding with his civil war activities. However, it was Randolph's book *Dealings with the Dead: The Human Soul, Its Migration and Its Transmigrations* (1862) that demonstrates a sophisticated esoteric philosophy, denoting different types of spiritual phenomena, sex magic, and angelic presences that became the seed of the occult revival in the late 19th century in America.

Furthermore, Randolph's work would have a lasting impression on the work of occultist Helen Blavatsky and novelist Pauline Hopkins. For example, Blavatsky borrows Randolph's work in her publication *Isis Unveiled* in 1877, launching her career as an international occult adept. Also, it is not a coincidence that when Randolph moved in 1867 to the Beacon Hill community of Boston, Massachusetts, where he lived until 1872, the same neighborhood as a young Pauline Hopkins, his exploits and reputation as a Rosicrucian resemble the character of Reuel Briggs in her 1903 novel *Of One Blood* (Finley, 2015). Despite his rise to fame as an orator, he was undone by his brand of racial politics, demonstrating that he was also infected with the taint of scientific racism when he made remarks distinguishing himself in intelligence due to his fairer complexion (Finley, 2015). A publisher of free love literature, a critic of Christianity, a promoter of sexual literature, and a purveyor of drugs and magic, Randolph was considered a pariah by the African American upper class that was under siege by the politics of post–Civil War Reconstruction politics and cultural norms and died at his own hands by suicide in 1875, although Helen Blavatsky claimed to have killed him by occult assassination (Deveney, 1996; Finley, 2015).

Martin Delany and Egyptology

Martin R. Delany (1812–1885) is commonly understood as the Father of Black Nationalism and a believer in African self-determination. Delany practiced medicine, served as an officer in the Union army during the American Civil War, and traveled to Yorubaland, Africa, in search of a possible new homeland for Africans in the Western Hemisphere to emigrate to. Delany is also the author of one of the first speculative narratives to promote an alternative speculative history in his book *Blake: Or the Huts of America*, which describes a slave revolution and the attempt to establish a free Black Republic. However, what is less known is the fact that Martin Robinson Delany was one of the first Americans to attempt to visually articulate, reset, and decode Egyptian hieroglyphs in a book entitled *Principia of Ethnology: The Origins of Races and Color, with an Archaeological Compendium of Ethiopian and Egyptian Civilization, from Years of Careful Examination and Enquiry* (1880). Delany attempted to refute the scientific racism of his time and drew upon his background in freemasonry, esotericism, and understanding of symbolic language and references to Renaissance art and architecture (Beatty, 2005).

Delany's work was engaging the work of the French scholar Jean-François Champollion, who discovered the Rosetta stone in the wake of Napoleon's invasion of Egypt and discovered after a millennium how to interpret the Egyptian language (Beatty, 2005). Champollion was partially motivated by the influence of freemasonry and its esoteric praxis, and his discovery allowed scholars to study the different stages of Egyptian civilization. Delany used the hieroglyphs to critique his Christian outlook and interrogate his historical perspective. His work ultimately accomplished two things. First, in refuting the Eurocentric scholarship done on hieroglyphs, he challenges the white supremacy and nexus they had established for themselves and descendants of Kemetic civilization, and second, he provides a geography of reason and historical stasis, or *djed*, for the study of Egypt that would be completed by Senegalese scholar Cheikh Anta Diop 100 years later.

Intersections with Black Speculative Thought

This interpretation of Vodun in the Haitian Revolution, Randolph's esotericism, Benjamin Banneker's astro-theology, and Martin Delany's *Blake or The Huts of America* and *Principia of Ethnology* offers a new perspective on liberation movements in the region and Black speculative fiction. By examining the symbolic and secret gardens of Vodun at Bois-Caïman, Banneker's astro-theology, and Delany as a Black speculative realist, this study contrasts the Enlightenment's intellectual racism. I argue that Vodun in the Haitian Revolution represents a liberating practice rooted in African metaphysical practices. These practices reimagine and support realistic truths beyond the Enlightenment's intellectual racism. This integrative Afro-speculative critique promotes Vodun's emphasis on liberation and demonstrates how Black speculative thought can serve as a tool for radical organizing (Eddins, 2022).

In the forest, with radical agency, which shook the core of Western colonial Enlightenment's theological imperialist plans, it was the symbolic and material beginning action and rehearsal for the subsequent Haitian Revolution—which Vodun leaders and healers at Bois-Caïman initiated. Vodun figures not only created the free space, communal, gender-calibrated architectural models, political and intellectual theories, professional, secular, and medical infrastructures of the transformative art spaces that enabled the revolutionary acts at Bois-Caïman and beyond and yesterday, today, or any tomorrow, but Vodun was diverse in organizing the center of their community.

Revolutionary esoteric Black speculative discourse should be the logical opposite of prosaic racist pseudoscientific projects. These specially conceived counterdiscourses take their unique place with another element as the speculatively imagined counterpart of the Eurocentric scientific racism discourse. Delany's character Blake's quest establishes a key metaphysical element that suggests Black esoteric possibility. These actions parallel Bacon's *New Atlantis* recounting of how knowledge of the activities of individuals enabled inquiries to discover whether teachings inspired applications. Therefore, knowledge of what was attributed to personages in the Bible, such as the building of Solomon's temple, was valued as a guide to possible foreseen future activities.

Conclusion

I have sought to excavate the suppressed and underappreciated contributions of crucial radical African diasporic thinkers/revolutionaries and situate their theories within and as advanced Black speculative thought stemming from different geographies of the Black Atlantic. The Enlightenment is, of course, a significant intellectual moment. It is the birth of the European modern and unleashes human potential with industrial production, science, and governance breakthroughs. However, the European Enlightenment project was stubbornly shadowed by racism and sexism. It is the toxic stain that taints the advancements of that era with slavery, colonization, and repression. Moreover, given the racial terror being performed across the globe at present, it should not be surprising that Africans and their diaspora were able to produce coherent alternative cosmologies and astro-theological syntheses of the modern world just as they toppled many of the regimes driving it.

Moreover, with Banneker, Randolph, Delany, and Vodun, we see a sustained African intellectual counterdiscourse to scientific racism and Western Enlightenment across time. These Afrodiasporic theories are as ancient as they are modern. These thinkers of old organized paradigms confront and sustain Western knowledge, governance, and religious theories on behalf of enslaved bodies and spirits; the impact of their efforts cannot be overstated. Indeed, just as whites dominated and exploited their bodies, native institutions, and sacred sexual practices, they sought to discredit and hide the efforts of Blacks from the annals of history. Commercial hegemony was not enough; Europeans sought to dominate the world of thought itself. So, through Vodun, Banneker's astro-theology, and Delany's proto-Africology and speculative writing, the groundwork was laid for resistance. Moreover, by the 1890s, the emergence of the Japanese Empire following the Meiji restoration representing their transition into modernity and the defeat of the Italian forces by the Ethiopian general Ras Makonnen in 1896 signaled that despite the rise of international white supremacy, the struggle for freedom against Western hegemony characterized as imperialism was just beginning.

CHAPTER 2

The Rising Tide of Color and Creating a New Race

The end of the 19th century saw the emergence of what we know as science fiction around a group of science fiction writers in London. This was during a period of crisis in the British Empire, which was worried by the threat of Eurasia and the rise of the Dark World. As a result, Great Britain was rethinking its geopolitical standing and imperial policy. By the early 20th century, the challenge to white Anglo domination, following what writer Lothrop Stoddard called the white civil war or World War I, had begun in earnest, and in the American literary artistic sphere it was expressed in the emergence of what philosopher Alain Locke called the New Negro or Harlem Renaissance. The preoccupation of white elites with race was directly tied to their desire to maintain global white hegemony, to which many viewed the Harlem Renaissance as a direct threat (Vitalis, 2015). This was consistent in the scholarship represented by men like Ralph Bunch and Alain Locke in the early 20th century, characterizing what is now termed "international relations" as "racial development," reflecting the era's dominant Eurocentric ideologies that justified imperialism and hierarchical global governance through pseudoscientific racial theories (Lauren, 1996; Vitalis).

Halford Mackinder, a British member of parliament, authored *The Geographical Pivot of History* in 1904 that argued that the powers of Germany, Russia, China, and Japan would strive for the control of the Eurasian landmass, and that whoever controlled that territory controlled the world. This would be a direct challenge to the Anglo world order. Moreover, following World War I, the writer Oswald Spengler wrote *The Decline of the West*, which argued that because of World War I, the West would never recover its civilizational vitality. Lothrop Stoddard went further in his own book *The Rising Tide of Color* to argue that due to what he called the international white civil war, immigration and miscegenation would destroy the West, and that the hegemony of the West depended on the domination of Africa and Latin America. In this chapter, we explore the intersection of the esoteric or occult with science fiction, race, and geopolitics. This intersection has been historically prevalent and has consistently raised the same concerns. These domains focused on phenomena that explored contemporary technological, sociopolitical, and cultural complexity and became a significant aspect of European high culture during that time—this singularity was recognized even then (Higgins, 2021; Vint, 2021).

The Rising Tide of Color and Decline of the West

Lothrop Stoddard's 1920 pamphlet *The Rising Tide of Color Against White World-Supremacy*, Oswald Spengler's 1918–1922 two-volume work *Decline of the West*, and the development of geopolitics were critical works in the intellectual geographies of Europe and America in the decades just before and after World War I. In a matter of years, a racial pyramid had inverted: the solid, unassailable supremacy of the white race in a solar civilization had been questioned and turned on its head as the nonwhite races began to assert their autonomy against an empire dedicated to their inferiority. Against the idea of progress that bloomed in the 19th century, apocalyptic visions of civilizational decline flourished in Europe and America decades after the fin-de-siècle. Behind this was an ancient struggle for global vitality rooted in geography, biology, and an irrevocably historical past.

Lothrop Stoddard's book *The Rising Tide of Color*, published in 1920, is notable for its early exploration of race and the associated themes of race and civilization, race and geopolitics, and the "colored" races of the world. Stoddard was a politician, author, and political-thriller writer. He received his bachelor's degree from Harvard, visited Europe with his family, and traveled to the Middle East with a Yale expedition in his early career. Returning to the East, he turned to politics, working as a secretary for the Progressive Party campaign of 1912 in Massachusetts before expanding his interests to writing. Stoddard published works on topics such as immigrants, the rising birthrate of Blacks, and miscegenation. He contended that race was the key to the history and greatness of civilization (Welton, 2021).

The theme of race and civilization examines the relationship between the two, emphasizing the importance of white race dominance. Stoddard argues that rising birth rates and pressures from the colored races threaten the existence of the white race, resulting in a daily interaction which, coupled with the white race woman (the rise of women in the West), presents a double danger. For Stoddard, the increasing birth of the colored (non-Hispanic) races in North America, Europe, and Asia is paramount, calling for measures to prevent this from occurring across the world. Within the first chapter of *The Rising Tide of Color*, he introduces three key concepts: the white race, the colored races, and the great races. The use of the terms *great races* or *colored races* suggests ethnology over racism, presenting large cohesive units united under specific color characteristics and underlying social, economic, and political development concerning similar historical traditions. According to Stoddard, civilization is a race product, capable of only a few races (white, yellow, and brown). He categorizes world races as great races based on the knowledge and understanding of anthropology and ethnology at the time. He attempts to explain the world and its history through this distinction as a historian (Krenn, 2022; Stern, 2022; Welton, 2021).

Race and Civilization

According to Stoddard and Spengler, race had always been one of the most influential factors in the development of civilization, including the unfolding of destiny, the rise and decline, and the cultivation and maintenance of a nation-state. Lothrop Stoddard's *The Rising Tide of Color* during the late 1910s, Oswald Spengler's *The Decline of the West* during the early 1920s, and several geopolitical concepts had similar understandings of civilization seen through the lens of race, particularly modern civilization as a product of the Nordic race. Civitas Gradialis characterized all forms of civilization as gradual, implying that later civilizations, darker races, are relegated to a lower category of civitas than early civilizations, the white race. Hence, the commonsensical notion of the rise and decline of nations assumed a racial component; Stoddard even posited a bold theory to use race as a predictor for the rise and decline of race and civilization (Aragon, 2021; Baldwin, 2022; Bell et al., 2022).

Spengler's concept of a great cycle, spanning a thousand years, was composed of eight subsuming civilizations, of which the Occidental (the West) race and modern civilization was one, believed to experience an inevitable decline. Before this, flourishing and rising periods would occur that were all evinced by urbanization, grandeur in politics and economy, monumental architecture, literature and painting, and more, all indicative of European races and Northern American nations. To explain the decline of the West, other races' ascendance was postulated. Although astonishing and outlandish theories in modern sensibility, the captivating idea of racial destiny was common and believed to be veracity in this era. Such theories coalesced and circulated like a snowball, expanding in spheres of influence and application until the world collapsed in the ashes of World War II (Al Bidh, 2023; Kimmage, 2020). This became "the first true world" war between the protagonists of the great cycle that vertically divided civilization across racial lines: the black, brown, yellow, and white races, and emerging nation-states like Japan, China, and India fighting for supremacy and an entire region on the chessboard. The dominant role of geography, especially the racial component, was recognized and utilized in warfare.

Mackinder's Heartland Theory

Mackinder's "heartland" is a geopolitical designation of Russia and surrounding countries, like China, as the lands that comprise the land power in Mackinder's framework. Moscow, Mackinder argued, was one of the key centers of influence in Eurasia, since it bordered the center of power in Eastern Europe. Such expansionism would take place at the expense of the transitional nations of Eastern Europe, and a defeat would endanger India; therefore pan-Germanism and pan-Slavism would endanger British and Anglo-Saxon political hegemony (Rosenboim, 2015). Mackinder perceives Russia ultimately—as more than French and German expansionism—as semibarbaric and from an alien race that harbors ambitions for Russia to hold hegemony.

The focus of Mackinder's geopolitical thought is first defined along the question "Why has Britain ceased to be the world's first power?" This question is predicated on motives that Britain ceased its imperial expansion in terms of Asia and Africa in the late 19th century, primarily not from the Boer War in South Africa or the success of the American experiment or the success of its imperial conquest after the Berlin Conference of 1885. The British Empire, by far, was the largest the world had ever seen. The need for colonies to oversee themselves in the face of alarming railway competition—both within the empire and from rival powers—is pervasively denoted from 1880 by several figures. Perceived political unification and systemization was necessitated by the increased rail traffic volumes. Stringent regulation had to be undertaken to tackle, head-on, the immense size of transport, which, they argued, could not be grappled with efficiently unless through centralization and control (Flint, 2022).

Nationalism and Ethnicity

Throughout the second half of the 19th century, an unprecedented wave of mass migration substantially altered the ethnic composition of several metropolitan and provincial cities within the newly established New World nations of the Americas and Australia. Though a variety of different immigrant groups arrived in differing historical and demographic circumstances, one consequence of this mass migration was a rapid growth in the demographic weight of new, non-Anglo-Saxon ethnic groups (at least in Anglo-Saxon-dominated societies such as the United States, Canada, and Australia). This trend was most evident in American cities such as Chicago, which more than doubled in size between 1880 and 1890, adding three-quarters of a million new inhabitants and more than 100,000 new immigrants in only a single decade (Manning & Trimmer, 2020; Spickard et al., 2022).

The rise of fascism had not yet fully manifested itself on the global stage during World War I when the theoretical advancements of Germany and France were combined to pursue innovative uses of technology for modern warfare. The writer H. G. Wells exemplifies the contradiction inherent in the British scientific and social philosophy of the time. It is within this historical context that three revolutionary intellectual pursuits would grow. Practical industrial and applied science, science fiction, and the search for a unified field theory of physics, which was conducted on the fringes of scientific orthodoxy, were all impacted by imperialism's social and military expansion. Each of these pursuits would have a significant impact on war and form a connection during the conduct of the coming Great War.

Inspired by the American and French revolutions and driven by the rise of the Industrial Revolution, the Western world established a clear hierarchy among global powers and the resurgence of imperialism. Motivated by the belief in manifest destiny, Britain extended its control over a large portion of the world's land and people, seeking to promote its abstract ideals and advanced technologies developed through revolutionary advancements in science, technology, and engineering. Both oppressive motives and noble intentions drove these actions. The rise of global ideological influence is closely tied to both economic inequality and social development. Ultimately, this influence led to a significant transformation in the tactics and strategies of war across all aspects of its conduct and nature (Ikenberry, 2020).

Racism and Social Darwinism in the Victorian Era

Race played an enormous role in shaping attitudes, policies, and general culture during the Victorian era and was the most important factor in shaping British imperial policy during that time. Following the emergence, acceptance, and elevation of Darwinism, ideas rose within society concerning hierarchy. Some races were better than others, with civilization corresponding to position within that hierarchy. Given that the English were at the top of both civilized and social rankings, questions were raised concerning the apparent inferiority of those further down the social ladder. This inferiority was both cultural and biological, for rank was believed to be something inherited, denoting social Darwinism in manner that accosted the very foundation of Victorian society (Gallagher, 2013). Arthur de Gobineau provided the notion of eugenics in 1853, to examine the downfall of empires. He proposed that the Aryan race was superior, that other races were degenerative, and that intermingling only served to destroy that which was good. This perspective became more popular with the Anglo-Saxons in Britain, who viewed themselves as the purer breed of Aryans (the Celts having been displaced) and actively sought to defend their position—justifying colonialism, for, by virtue of race, they were better than Africans and Indians (Ong, 2019).

Imperialism and Colonialism

The late 19th century began the age of imperialism, where people from industrialized countries migrated to rural, agricultural nations to colonize and exploit resources in the name of their respective governments. While colonization was officially justified as a means of improving the lives of the colonized through education and modern sanitation, some argue that economic interests were the true motivations rather than any humanitarian concern for the primitive or outdated nature of the occupied territories. Around 80% of the world's land was colonized or "imperialized" by approximately 20% of the global population (Manjapra, 2020).

The age of imperialism period typically refers to the time from around 1870 to the First World War. During this era, capitalists pushed to invest in less developed regions that had not yet been included in the expanding global capitalist market. This resulted in economic and political conflicts between the Indigenous societies and the colonial powers, mainly industrial capitalist societies. According to Scott (2021), these conflicts have significantly impacted the third world's history since at least 1870. Over the course of this century, approximately 80% of the world's land came under the control of about 20% of the population, consisting of the industrialized, primarily Christian, capitalist countries of the Global North (Leigh, 2020). With its overwhelming power, this geopolitical truth emerged as the unequivocal weapon against the terror of emptiness that plagued the all-encompassing imperial consciousness. It also fought vehemently against the affliction of imperial hubris, which sowed doubt in the empire's quest for unwavering sovereignty. In its essence, this profound truth embodies the relentless quest of humanity for the embodiment and efficacy of divine universal rule, but tragically, it ultimately unravels as a poignant narrative of political deception and betrayal (FitzGerald, 2020; Wood, 2020). The two main principles represent the central aspect of the specific type of science fiction being discussed: imagining apocalyptic events and scenes of racial tension in a distant future text. This is achieved using the narrative technique of prophetic foresight and the creative portrayal of religious beliefs and ideas about the end of the world. As a result, it carefully examines, reproduces, and questions the physical and nonphysical aspects of life in literature, as well as in sacred texts, while striving to uncover deeper spiritual truths through the mysterious world of (supernatural) science (Nunn, 2023; Morgan, 2020).

The supernatural, as opposed to the fantastical, is not typically viewed as having a significant connection to imperialism. It is widely understood that an empire, which is built and maintained through the oppressive exercise of power by one nation over another, arises due to specific historical circumstances rather than to belief in ghosts, curses, or prophecies. However, it is essential to recognize that there is a need for a narrative to establish dominance over any given vision of the future. The influence of imperialism on science fiction writing during this time is significant. The themes of empire, science, science fiction, religion, race, and the occult are central to this chapter. While the focus here is on the overlap of these themes in a specific time and place—primarily Britain during the late 19th and early 20th centuries—a broader perspective is taken; this is because the historical and theoretical significance of this subject extends beyond such temporal or geographical constraints. Furthermore, the British Empire could not have arisen without a specific set of connections between science, the narrative of science fiction, racial and religious taboos, and fantasy (Parrinder, 2021).

Science fiction serves as the opposite or alternative to established science, providing a vast realm of imagination and creativity. It takes a daring approach by not disregarding taboo topics when exploring the significant influence of specific religious beliefs on the survival and demise of any imperialist. As the genre is more profoundly engaged, it delves into the uncharted territories of Helena Blavatsky's ideas about the origins of different races, speculating narratives that demonstrate the dominance or downfall of various ethnic groups in the future. Science fiction embraces the boundless possibilities of the human mind, propelling us into a world where the limits of imagination are stretched beyond comprehension. By pushing the boundaries, it continually challenges our perspectives on society, culture, and the very essence of humanity itself. Within the incredibly expansive science fiction universe, every thought and idea are magnified, every hypothesis expanded upon, and every assumption questioned. It captivates and astounds us with its ability to transport us to distant galaxies, parallel dimensions, and future timelines that defy our current understanding. With its endless potential, science fiction ignites a spark within us, inspiring a hunger for exploration, discovery, and the infinite possibilities that lie within the realm of the unknown (Parrinder, 2021).

Impact on Global Politics and Societies

Upon initial examination, these narratives of imperial dominance might appear to simply uphold Britain's reputation. However, it is crucial to bear in mind that the Victorian period saw a vast range of Anglocentric literary production. The emphasis on such narratives of British strength may be a sign of underlying national uncertainties, shown through the promotion of specific cultural beliefs. As Jackson (2020) argued, the novel was the most effective tool in its ability to ideologically influence populations of readers and the middle class. When considering the profound impact of imperialism on global politics and societies during the late 19th and early 20th centuries, it becomes crucial to investigate the extensive realm of science fiction literature that significantly influenced shaping these dynamics. The prevalence of captivating fantasy and science fiction narratives that intricately explore and emphasize British imperialism and its global dominance indisputably serves as compelling evidence of Britain's unparalleled control over foreign territories and societies. Works of fiction, such as the H. Rider Haggard's *King Solomon's Mines,* published in 1885, and *The Ghost Kings,* released in 1908, effectively depict and exalt the strength and impact of the British imperial system. Intertwining elements of adventure, suspense, and imagination, these literary motifs unequivocally suggest that the mere consideration of the breakdown or upheaval of Britain's imperial influence remains incredibly improbable and inconceivable. The visionary power of science fiction literature unveils the profound depths of a seemingly unbreakable empire, which left an enduring impression on the historical portrayal of the era (Bird, 2021).

Late 19th- and Early 20th-Century Science Fiction

Throughout the ages, science fiction writers have consistently employed the genre to shift paradigms and guide humanity's consciousness. Heinrich Heine and James Merrill were two such poets who claimed to receive messages of advanced human knowledge from otherworldly entities in the form of science fiction stories. They believed these entities were spirits from the afterlife and sought theosophical knowledge (Denisoff, 2021). Heine wrote these messages with the entities, and symbolists and decadent writers used theosophical and occult knowledge to influence the present and culture through abstract and symbolic use of science fiction and future-tense narratives. This fusion of mystical and scientific concepts reflected the cultural fascination with the unknown and the possibilities of the future. Science fiction is a style that was made for symbolism writers. It is full of fantastical imagery and advanced technology, and it peers ahead into the future. Decadent and symbolist writers were heavily fixated on time: time as it progresses, the passage of time, and history. That time had to go somewhere generally meant that it went it two directions: the future was being charted, and the past was fixated upon.

Futuristic imagery contained within science fiction held an allure for writers who sought out both symbolic significance and theosophical ideas. Jules Verne and H. G. Wells were two of the foremost and most impactful science fiction creatives. Symbolist writers who made use of science fiction cloaked symbolism in signifiers having to do with advanced technology, flying machines, technology from Atlantis, strange and artificial beings or monsters, alien races, and planet environments. The far future would now be hidden lore or metaphysical meaning of this strange and wonderful imagined world (Denisoff, 2021). While science fiction originated in the late 19th and early 20th century, the term *science fiction* was first used in 1851 by William Wilson in *A Little Earnest Book upon a Great Old Subject*. Edward Bulwer-Lytton's novel *The Coming Race* depicted a technologically advanced society called the Vril-ya. This society was run on Vril, a latent energy derived from higher-dimensional geometry, and the Vril-ya were closely aligned with theosophy, a mystical belief system. The psychic powers of the Vril-ya were accessed through meditation, ritual, and a connection with the earth's energies. Understanding this early history is crucial to comprehending the genre's association with imperialism and Romantic-era occult politics (Kiran, 2021).

H. G. Wells

The acclaimed English author Herbert George Wells was born on September 21, 1866. Wells rose to prominence as an author of science fiction in the late 19th and early 20th century. Wells invented the silent war between worlds, as well as the one-off ruthless vengeful attacks either by invaders escaping a doomed planet, or pursuing, or escaping a dying race. Wells's early works inspired imitators like Edgar Rice Burroughs and influenced later authors John W. Campbell and Arthur C. Clarke—all authors of "Boys Own Adventure" stories (Vinson, 2011). Science fiction grew out of the scientific and technological advancements and the genesis of modernity of the 19th century. Works of "impossible" voyages and "lost" races, as early science fiction might be called, appeared. Such literature was speculative within the then-context of emerging sciences of anthropology and the social sciences more generally, which would come in the decades following to fundamentally reconceptualize and dismantle theories surrounding modern progress. Wells's scientific romances emerged in the context of literary tradition, considering which they can perhaps be better understood. His scientific romances belong to the emergence of the genre of science fiction (Riesenberg, 2014). The term emerged decades following Wells's seminal works in the field to categorize a new mode of literature that could not quite be placed in the then-existing frames of fiction or nonfiction. However, in the aftermath of the unraveling of modernity and its genocidal and catastrophic consequences, an inquiry into science fiction may return to originally specified anthropocentric epistemic and ethical issues, thus reconsidering Wellsian science fiction in the aftermath of the recent "ancient" unfolding of what some contemporary scholars refer to as the Anthropocene era (Ong, 2019).

Wells's utilization of the themes and elements prevalent in the science fiction genre to amplify his commentary on imperialism in *The War of the Worlds* (1898) is a monumental task (Ong, 2019). However, Wells's treatment of the theme would evolve over time regarding both genre and subject matter. For example, H. G. Wells, as a Victorian novelist and proto-futurist, wrote some of the earliest works in science fiction, often criticizing social developments. Wells's critical approach to imperialism and racism, particularly in two of his essays, "The Future in Space" and "The Discovery of the Future," and two of his novels, *The Time Machine* and *The War of the Worlds*, examines his condemnation of the practices of imperialism, the prejudices of empire, and the implications of social hierarchies. Wells wrote his critical works and novels in the latter half of the 1890s, a time of colonial expansion and the British Empire's greatest geographical coverage.

Esoteric Philosophy in the Late 19th and Early 20th Century

In the wake of the emergence of science fiction, scientific naturalism failed to fully encompass the profoundness of human experience and the deep connection individuals have with the world and struggled to captivate society's attention. However, against this lack of regard, a multitude of occultist groups emerged in conjunction with the theosophy movement, with many incorporating theosophical methodologies into their own practices. The "invisible college" concept played a pivotal role within these societies, linking their endeavors to an ancestral line inherited from age-old and unbroken spiritual customs. These cherished traditions offered a means to authenticate their convictions within an ever-increasingly materialistic world. As these groups flourished, their influence expanded, gradually weaving its way into the intricate tapestry of society, fanning the flames of curiosity and enticing the imagination of those yearning for a bridge between the seen and the unseen realms (Hanegraaff, 2020).

Their blend of esoteric knowledge and ancient rituals evoked a sense of wonder, beckoning individuals to explore the mysteries that lay beyond the confines of mundane existence. By channeling what they believed to be the collective wisdom of the ages, they sought to unravel the enigmas that perplexed humanity, offering alternative paths of understanding and illuminating the duality of the human experience (Hanegraaff, 2020). As the mystical currents mingled with the currents of progress, society witnessed a delicate dance between the intentional quest for knowledge and the personal exploration of the unknown. The allure of these occultist groups persisted, drawing in those who dared to venture beyond the confines of conventional thinking, lured by the prospect of glimpsing hidden realms where the beauty of the inexplicable interweaved with the threads of mortal existence. Through the lens of the invisible college, these seekers of truth tapped into a reservoir of ancient wisdom, finding solace and inspiration amid a rapidly changing world (Hanegraaff, 2020). Their beliefs, ever resilient in the face of skepticism, served as a testament to the enduring human need for connection, purpose, and a transcendental awareness that goes beyond the bounds of direct observation.

Helena Blavatsky, founder of the Theosophical Society, revealed interesting knowledge through her literary works. Two of her publications, *Isis Unveiled*, first published in 1877, and *The Secret Doctrine*, first published in two volumes in 1888, became sources of influence—despite the apparent unacknowledged work of Paschal Beverly Randolph in the text—illuminating the minds of countless practitioners in the vast West and the Indian subcontinent. This influential society, which came into existence in 1875, was dedicated to disseminating and promulgating Blavatsky's concepts. The very term *theosophy* was meticulously coined, artfully crafted from the harmonious fusion of two Greek words resonating with timeless vibrancy, namely Theos, signifying the eternal and divine essence of God, and Sophia, symbolizing profound and sacred wisdom (Hanegraaff, 2020).

The core tenets of Blavatsky's theology were masterfully woven together by the fundamental conviction that the ultimate truth, all-encompassing and omnipresent, resides within the very fabric of every religion. However, this impact is all too often concealed beneath layers of mundane fallacies, and unfounded superstitions. Blavatsky asserted that through the extraordinary lens of a diligently trained interpreter, the veil of ignorance and misinterpretation could be lifted, thereby honing their ability to discern the essence within each belief system (Hanegraaff, 2020). Blavatsky transcended the bounds of conventional wisdom by proclaiming her unwavering belief in the manifestation of spiritual archetypes throughout human history. These emanations of energy would influence the world with their celestial presence, to guide and uplift humanity's collective consciousness (Hanegraaff, 2020).

The Intersection of Science Fiction, Imperialism, and Esoteric Philosophy

A highly significant and profound relationship not only exists but thrives between the development of science fiction and the remarkably pervasive and deeply imperialist and racist ideologies that were so deeply prevalent and inescapably omnipresent in not just the Victorian era but also within the contemporary, cultivated, and perpetually advancing modern world.

The implications and ramifications of this phenomenally revelatory and paradigm-shifting connection are important, to the extent that it may be posited, with conviction and plausibility, that historical periodization of popular literature and sociopolitical concerns may be subjected to a comprehensive re-evaluation. That is, if we are to attain even a glimpse of understanding and grasp the multifaceted minutiae and complexities of this dimension of the human experience.

The writings left behind by H. G. Wells stand as a testament to the intricate and troubling nature of the relationship. A prime illustration of this consequential and thought-provoking connection can be found in Wells's powerful and evocative work, resounding through the depths of time and echoing in contemporary halls of intellectual inquiry and discourse, where he believed and opined that the single-minded mission and cherished purpose of the British Association lay in the resolute and unwavering endeavor to suppress and eradicate the reprehensibly distorted and dehumanizing portrayal of human beings as nothing more than insentient creatures addicted to the consumption of mind-altering substances, as postulated by certain individuals of the physiologically inclined persuasion (Canavan, 2021; Young, 2020).

The rise of science fiction as a coherent literary body resulted in several significant themes and motifs, primarily reflecting technological and cultural developments. Notable among these are the following: man's relationship to the unforeseeable consequence of his own actions; the themes of evolution and degeneration, culminating in the proposal of intelligent life not resident within material form; the interpenetration of dimensions of space, and the exploration of the consequences of feeling that one is not the sole vehicle of conscious will within the cosmos; the study of pathologies and alternate wills, as embodied either in grotesquely modified humans or manifesting themselves through unknown technology or a desire to engage with totally nonhuman design; the theme of entropy which points to the question of the consequences of an inevitable technological age; and finally, the consequences of extraordinary mental power (Bina et al., 2020).

The Relevance of Julius Evola, Aleister Crowley, and Filippo Tommaso Marinetti

Julius Evola (1898–1974), an Italian philosopher and esotericist notable for his extreme right-wing views and antimodernism, was primarily concerned with the nature of tradition and its decline, particularly with the fall of the

Roman Empire. Despite his aristocratic background, Evola disavowed contemporary social classes, advocating for a caste system based on spiritual endowments. He contended that traditional societies were hierarchical, ordered according to individuals' transcendent realities and earthly capacities. As he saw it, the decline of these societies epitomized a crisis of the masculine principle dominated by materialism. Although Evola believed there was a premodern age where civilizations of a superior archetypal nature existed, he also contended that tradition was cyclical, allowing for degenerations and recuperations. Evola joined the Italian army during World War I, where he was injured in battle. Following the war, he embarked on a series of ventures in art, philosophy, technology, and psychoanalysis, contributing to magazines such as *L'Italiano, Renaissance,* and *Krur* (Tutors, 2020; Teitelbaum, 2021). His philosophy was deeply rooted in a division of the world into the spiritual (supernatural), mundane (natural), and quantified (artificial) realms. His critique of the modern world was not a mere pragmatic lamentation of the degradation of the spiritual order but the uncovering of an underlying 2,500-year-old esoteric war between the martial, contemplative tradition and the materialist, quantitative tradition. The greatest weapon of the latter is the manipulator, the demiurge addressed in Evola's theurgy. It is yet another expression of the Gnostic mythos. Evola's critique does not stop at a diatribe against industry and machines but is directed at the deepest spiritual foundations of the current civilization (Marino, 2024; Pedretti, 2021).

Aleister Crowley (1875–1947), born in Royal Leamington Spa to a royal family, was an English occultist, ceremonial magician, poet, and novelist. He became a prominent figure in the early 20th-century occultist movement. Educated at Cambridge University, Crowley traveled widely in the East, experiencing various spiritualities and rituals, including an initiation into the esoteric Hermetic Order of the Golden Dawn. In 1904 he claimed to have received communication from the Egyptian deity Horus, leading him to document an esoteric philosophy called Thelema. Notably, this philosophy espoused concepts of divinity, the nature of the human spirit, and conducive forms of praxis. Crowley experimented with a variety of evocations, invocations, and similar magical rites due to the supposed creative powers of the Gnostic/Athenian art form. Such a process became integrated into his writings about his initiation into the same art form after evocations of Horus and the signature of the Beast, concepts considered brand-new in terms of praxis at the time (Bogdan, 2024; Hedenborg White, 2021).

Crowley, having founded the religion of Thelema, produced a body of work, including *Liber AL vel Legis* (The Book of the Law), and trained a cult of initiates in right and left types of magic. Crowley's notion of the Great Work resonated deeply with members of the artistic avant-garde, especially those with a leftist bent, and led to the creation of various popular, liberatory, syncretic, and synesthetic magics. Crowley's work also inspired Dadaists to change the lunar calendar. The absurdist ritual (un-Chien Andalou) filtered Crowley's ideas into later surrealist work and the cult of events like the "Fifty-Year-Long Performance" enacted at the opening of the novel *The Hour of the Star* by Clarice Lispector (Beauchesne, 2021; West, 2021).

Filippo Tommaso Marinetti (1876–1944) was an Italian poet and novelist known for founding the futurism art movement. Marinetti, born in Alexandria, Egypt, to an Italian family, spent the early years of his life in Italy before moving to Paris at age nine. He was educated at the University of Pavia, where he studied law and supplemented his income by working as an art critic for Italian magazines. Marinetti's poetry often invoked themes of movement, speed, war, youth, and the machine. He is best known for the *Manifesto di Futurismo* (*Manifesto of Futurism*), published in 1909, which became the foundation of the futurism movement. With this manifesto, Marinetti sought to overcome symbolism and metaphysical abstraction in favor of a new language modeled on the dynamics of the modern world.

Marinetti posited that the metaphor contributed to the growth of a new sensibility, which, overcoming the spiritualism of the past, would bring a fresh mode involving a sense of immediacy and multitude. He was adamant in affirming that metaphors should also be factual and mechanical in terms of imagination, thus exclusionary to dreams, shadows, blazes, and semblances. In the wake of the First World War and revolutions that engulfed many countries, futurism was initially credited with being revolutionary; however, the movement was outsmarted by the avant-garde and postwar parks of surrealism and Dadaism (Mirabella, 2023; Coronelli, 2022). Although he may lack the clinical detachment of the seer, the themes of accelerationism and militant renewal are present throughout his manifesto. Marinetti's works can be read as anticipating the influential left-of-the-left-wing currents of 19th- through 21st-century carnivalism, positivism, crypto-anarchism, and transhumanism (Coronelli, 2022; Falcone, 2023).

Esoteric Praxis in the Works of Evola, Crowley, and Marinetti

The intersection of Western futurism and the occult has been explored through the works of prominent figures such as Julius Evola, Aleister Crowley, and Filippo Tommaso Marinetti. While Marinetti may not have practiced the occult the same way as Evola and Crowley, his manifestos contain elements that can be interpreted as occult. An analysis of the themes of these three figures will illuminate the connections between occult praxis and the futurist avant-garde. The works of Evola, Crowley, and Marinetti lend themselves to an analysis of mutual influences both within the aesthetic and philosophical realm as well as the personal. Marinetti is a crucial figure in this analysis because of his role as an ideologue of the late 19th-century futurist avant-garde and his intimate involvement with occultism. Crowley operated on the overlapping plane of practical occultism and literary avant-garde, sometimes soliciting commissions from Marinetti's movement. Both contributed to new formulations of magical cosmology, which Evola synthesized into a profoundly original gnosis that transcended artistic and practical imperatives (Blum, 2023). To situate the broader historical context, occultism is defined as a path to knowledge and experience of the sacred through practices such as magic, divination, alchemy, and investigation of the inner or spiritual nature of reality on both macrocosmic and microcosmic levels, including planets, stars, gods, demiurge, angels, demons, and souls. Esotericism can be communally nourished through suitable institutions, doctrines, and practices. Subaltern utopian strains of ideated aestheticism have too readily paradoxically promoted the simulacrum of the sacred by their commodification or failure to recapitulate inner experience (Kapcar, 2022).

The Esoteric Axis

The occult influenced the ideological foundations of the Nazi regime quite heavily. From philosophers like Friedrich Wilhelm Nietzsche to social Darwinists like Ernst Haeckel and H. S. Chamberlain to founders of Ariosophy or Aryan occult knowledge like Guido von List, Jorg Lanz von Liebenfels, and Rudolf von Sebottendorff, Germans before World War II espoused many notions either related to or directly taken from the then-flood of occult literature (Staudenmaier, 2020). For example, in the 1890s, an Austrian optician named Guido von List announced that a spiritual vision had opened his eyes to the revelation that he was the latest descendant of a long line of grand master occultists and messiahs. This lineage could be traced back 12,000 years and extended to every notable figure of European descent. He further claimed that the Aryan race was the genetic legacy of a superior and much older "Thule" population of survivors from Atlantis (FitzGerald, 2020).

The end of the First World War focused this interest more. The occult came into the public more, for instance, when the Thule Society assassinated a successful German politician financed by Walter Rathenau (Gellately,

2020). Many occult interests, as well as vast sums of money from many German industrialists, went to carry out this occult development, admittedly announced before the deed. Hitler, while in prison, had a long-awaited cult recognition from detractors Roehm and Goering through astrologer Wilhelm Wolf, and Germany's National Socialist papers loudly proclaimed the co-identification of Germans and spiritual, cultural elite at least of the Nazi kind in at least the elites' belief in the occult. Nazis on the high-priest level actively pursued their interest in the occult, and we can get an insight, not into spy games or political manipulations per se, but into the makings of policies by looking at what is considered esoterica, indeed considering it in esoterica's function (Gellately, 2020).

In this chapter, we have followed a hypothesis regarding the direct impact of occult or esoteric beliefs on the development of geopolitics. Occultism differs from philosophy and religion in that it supports esoteric doctrines impenetrable to the uninitiated. During the pre–Third Reich period, the German leaders of new secret societies did both: they revised texts of older or more recent mystics, and they produced new racist and anti-Semitic versions of the same basic message. The German leaders of new secret societies constructed or adopted a vision of absolute power, leading to the eradication of Judaism, capitalism, and Marxism and the consecration of mercilessness. Concurrently, they internalized this vision. Nazi ideology and practice hence covertly aimed at realizing a transmutational vision in terms of magical and irrational beliefs (FitzGerald, 2020).

The SS developed from several new secret society lodges and hence embraced occult content. It represented the transcendental and the absolute realms. Heinrich Himmler's convictions were bound up with the doctrines of the SS, which Karl Maria Willigut, the official Brigadeführer of the SS, really wrote. Willigut transmitted to the SS elements of the Thule legends and discourses. Willigut was in close contact with the Thule-Gesellschaft, a Volkisch secret society. The Thule-Gesellschaft was presided over by Rudolf Freiherr von Sebottendorff, born Adam Alfred Rudolf Glauer. Thule was attractive to people with occult leanings, for example, Tibetan Buddhists. As Deitrich Eckart did, the typical Volkisch practitioner believed in the reality of the unseen world. Eckart believed in astrology, numerology, sympathy, and contagious magic. He used the Ouija board, automatic writing, and the seance. Eckart was absorbed with the Jews and Jesuits, who he believed embodied evil, as both hatched conspiracies against the pure Aryan faith and Aryan folk (Gardell, 2023; Siepe, 2022).

The discussion of *Nazi occultism* requires a historical understanding of the concept and its usage. In the first place, individuals and movements branded with this name in popular culture were often polyphonic constructs consisting of actual people and semi- or entirely fictional persons who sometimes were pieces of enemy propaganda. In the second place, the concept is anachronistic. One of the most striking characteristics of the myth of a Nazi occult war is that it was constructed after the Second World War, was primarily influenced by the Cold War, and thus inserted ideological elements into it. Nevertheless, such an approach, as holistic as possible, may be helpful if the problematic nature of the source material and constructed myths are investigated (François & Uskalis, 2023).

However, the organized occult milieu became quite heterogeneous, encompassing a wide array of conflicting currents by the end of the Weimar Republic. Initially, the Thule Society was the source and promoter of many aspects of NS and SS occultism, a mystical group founded by aristocrats Rudolf von Sebottendorff and Walter Nauhaus. In 1917, when the Thule Society became publicly anti-Semitic, the higher social classes became interested in it, and it began to maintain and expand the political, economic, and social power of the group centered on the society (FitzGerald, 2020). There has been a great deal written about Nazi occultism, but very few studies focus on Imperial Japan, the Third Reich's ally and the third member of the Axis, during the 1930s and earlier in this regard. Many European racists, fascists, and Nazis believed the Japanese were Aryan-like—sharing certain perceived qualities with Aryans—but still viewed them as predatory Orientals.

The promotion and suppression of what is perceived as Occulture and occultism is often related to the power balance between East and West, Global North and South, or rising empires versus declining ones. In 1939 there were more than a million active occultists and spiritualists in Japan. Some researchers, artists, politicians, and military officials rely on the special forces of the esoteric to protect their souls and wished not to eliminate the Japanese national crisis. However, there is no solid definition of occult. The occult incorporates philosophical, paranormal, and psychological data from subcultures, countercultures, and cultures. The term refers to secret and cryptic sectarianism, religious mysteries, and other secretive and secretive doctrines. In Japan, by 1932 the Japanese researchers' Pan-Asiatic metaphysical society, Kokkai Tōa Shinri Kenkyūjo, was researching the occult, Pan-Asianism, the Aryan race, Homo superior, and the germ-cell disc paradigm as part of the Japanese tradition connection (Mullins, 2021; Skya, 2023).

The fact that occultism, in general, and spiritualism, in particular, relate to religious beliefs and that religious beliefs commonly can be traced back to cultural peculiarities has been clear, and it is applicable in every society at every time in history. Especially in the far east of Asia, religion, magic, and spiritualism were embedded within people's consciousness. This applies to Japan, a country of mystery and miracles, a land of religion, and an empire. Therefore, magic and mystery, psychic phenomena, or spiritualism represent this phenomenon. How can one express Japanese beliefs in these matters prior to the Pacific War? To explain the above, it is easiest to illustrate it by narrating some practical examples. Of course, one characteristic of the Japanese population was a keen interest in supernaturalism, where one could find people wandering about Japan and other parts of eastern Asia in search of a perspective that it is commonly believed to be found in nature (Rogers & Rogers, 2020).

The Black Dragon Society, or Kokuryūkai, played an important role in shaping Japan's imperialist ambitions and promoted Pan-Asianism in the early 20th century. The Black Dragon Society successfully promoted Pan-Asianism and Asian solidarity against Western colonialism, disguising their motives to advance Japanese expansionism. Founded in 1901 by Uchida Ryohei, the Black Dragon Society emerged as a secret ultranationalist group dedicated to expelling Russian influence from East Asia, particularly Manchuria and Korea. Its name derived from the Amur River ("Black Dragon River" in Chinese), symbolizing its focus on continental ambitions (Jansen, 1975). Initially composed of ex-samurai and right-wing activists, the society combined bushido ethics with fervent nationalism, advocating for Japanese hegemony in Asia. The Black Dragon society engaged in espionage, political lobbying, subversive activities, supporting Japan's annexation of Korea (1910) and later infiltrating Manchuria, laying the groundwork for the 1931 Manchurian Incident (Young, 1998). The Black Dragon Society also forged relationships with the African diaspora community in the United Sates leading up to World War II (Gallicchio, 2003).

Pan-Asianism emerged in the late 19th century as a response to Western imperialism, positing that Asian nations should unite culturally and politically to resist colonization. Figures like Japanese art scholar Okakura Tenshin and Chinese revolutionary Sun Yat-sen endorsed versions of this ideology. Okakura famously declared "Asia is one" (Okakura, 1903), emphasizing shared heritage. However, Japanese Pan-Asianism increasingly framed Japan as the "leader" of Asia, even when this vision clashed with the aspirations of other Asian nations (Hotta, 2007). While Japanese Pan-Asianists portrayed invasions of Korea and China as "liberation," these actions mirrored the imperialism they condemned. The Greater East Asia Co-Prosperity Sphere (1940–1945) epitomized this paradox, promoting regional unity under Japanese control while exploiting resources and labor.

Uchida Ryohei framed Japan's interventions as altruistic missions to "rescue" Asia from Western powers, a narrative echoed in the society's publications (Wilson, 2019). For example, the society supported the anti-Qing Dynasty revolutionaries in China and aimed to cultivate a pro-Japanese regime, not genuine independence. By portraying Manchuria as a bastion against Russian and Western encroachment, they justified Japan's military presence, culminating in the puppet state of Manchukuo (1932). However, local populations often resisted, viewing Japanese rule as another form of colonialism (Duara, 2004).

Post-1945, the Allied occupation disbanded the society, and Pan-Asianism became tainted by its association with militarism. However, Pan-Asianist ideas resurfaced in softer forms, such as postwar economic collaborations and regional forums like ASEAN. Modern scholars caution against conflating these cooperative efforts with the imperialist Pan-Asianism of the past (Saaler & Koschmann, 2007). The Black Dragon Society and Pan-Asianism illustrate the tension between idealism and realpolitik. While Pan-Asianism offered a vision of unity, its co-option by Japanese ultranationalists like the Kokuryūkai reveals how anticolonial rhetoric can mask imperial ambitions.

Geopolitics of the Supernatural

As discussed earlier, some of the Western or European occultists, such as René Guénon and Julius Evola, and theologians like Father Niklaus Prinz von Liechtenstein, thought there could be alliances between European Nazis and some Asian or Japanese "occultists," "spiritualists," or "traditionalists." They and the Nazi regime, as well as the Imperial Japanese Army and the Japanese ethnologists, thought they could notice why majoritarian Europeans or Americans could not understand that the intertwining of these or related strains of "occultism" with the geopolitics and international relations may tend to produce the grossest of genocides (Pedretti, 2021; Morrow, 2022). Western historians of the Nazi and Japanese occult tend to put the issue aside as a topic that should be treated separately from actual international political events and their analyses of these events. As a result, the role and significance of the Nazi and Japanese occult in world history have not been fully revealed and explained in Western studies. This is shown in their evaluations of the problem as censorious and detached from the study. However, evaluations always show that the issue is so essential and important that it must be studied internationally.

Thus, Western occultism had a robust impact before World War II in Europe, gaining attention through the aftermath of World War I, sociopolitical destabilization, and an emerging youth culture of novelty. The popularity of Western occultism solidified around the images of Nazi and Japanese totalitarian Oriental despotism. Personalities such as Heydrich, Himmler, and Evola represented three distinct "centers" of European occultism. The Nazis, with their concept of the Nietzschean titan rooted in heroic-will arrogance—proliferated throughout the cities of Germany—and the Evola-inspired so-called priest-warrior misfits of the Schutzstaffel (SS), including unit 91, embraced the Nordic ideology when it was appropriated. However, the Nazis and the SS were fanatical and selective in their Western occult approach of alliances and invocations as propaganda, military strategy, and cult, and they did not dream of decriminalizing or ever studying Jewish Kabbalah within their territory. In Japan, on the other hand, the military put so little pressure on scholars of the Western occult, instead employing Japanese occultists against the "gaijin"—or white European and Chinese "ghosts"—in the spiritual unconscious warfare of World War II (Truscello, 2020).

Black Speculative Modernity and Creating a New Race

The opportunities for Africans in America after slavery saw a significant increase, particularly during the short-lived period of Reconstruction in the United States following the Civil War. It was during this time that many emancipated African Americans, known as freedmen, bought land, ran for public office, and contributed to the writing of new laws. However, the backlash against this new era, which was quick, intense, and unrelenting, along with the open sabotage of Reconstruction, effectively undermined the brief but promising political progress of the newly empowered group, leaving them once again in a state of limited power like their time as enslaved people. This period of repression would be historically remembered as the Jim Crow era (Gates, 2020). However, by the beginning of the 20th century, the work of W. E. B. Du Bois was beginning to interrogate the status of people of African descent around the world and the social contract they endured as citizens and colonial subjects.

Souls and the Racial Contract

During this period, the geopolitics of world order was studied under the topic of race development until this concept came to be known by a new name in 1919, international relations (Vitalis, 2018). Building upon this concept of race development, Du Bois (1903) made his case with respect to race and international relations in the era of Jim Crow and imperialism, noting: "The problem of the twentieth century is the problem of the color-line, the relation of the darker races of men in Asia and Africa, in America and the islands of the sea" (p. 18). Furthermore, Du Bois suggested, due to their unique experience, African Americans had developed a metaphysical perspective or *veil* that bestowed a certain insight upon them on life in the West.

Du Bois was a contributor to the journal *Race Development and International Relations*, and his talent would overlap the areas of geopolitics and speculative thought. The intersections between Du Bois's *The Souls of Black Folk* (1903), his essay "The Souls of White Folk" (1910), and Charles Mills's theory of "the racial contract" is relevant to race relations and world order. Most scholarship on Du Bois's thought has worked to recognize a single criticism, departure, or seed of Mills's theory in one of the *Souls* essays, without recognizing these two texts as closely related, or more complicated and comprehensive multifaceted approaches to whiteness and white humanity. The racial contract seeks to draw attention to the alternative historical backdrop of race and the social contract against which Du Bois's ideas can be evaluated, undertaking an analysis of Mills's theory with Du Bois's *Souls* essays for new perspectives in contemporary sociopolitical discourse (Morris et al., 2021; Mills, 2022).

Du Bois's influence on race theory can hardly be overstated. While his notion of double consciousness in *The Souls of Black Folk* is often heralded as the clearest departure from the lessons of contemporary critical theory and racialized discourse itself, its effects on our broader philosophical understanding of race remain largely understudied. Written at the height of the Progressive Era, *The Souls of Black Folk* demonstrates the extensive racism, social contract racism, and racial theory characterizing the "whether and how" of understanding Du Bois and social contract theory. His analysis of Plessy v. Ferguson, the experience of freedmen's opposition, and white American hypocrisy demonstrate both the breadth of critical thought in the *Souls* essay and the persistent anxiety concerning white privilege due to its dependency on the racial hierarchy of the American settler-state (Morris et al., 2021; Mills, 2022).

A pivotal idea in this essay is the confrontation of Du Bois's *The Souls of Black Folk*, representing the Black soul and living as a person can under a racial contract, and his *The Souls of White Folk*, now living under the racial contract, each reflecting the soul of the systems they represent. It further highlights the associated readings of double spirits and the African colonization and fleshes out the full array of dual selves arising from the racial contract. Yet *The Souls of White Folk* parallels the racial contract interrogating the levels of moral action and of political action, claiming that the contradiction requires political action as a corrective. An internal critique of white virtue, therefore, is presented, constituting the third soul, which quintessentially expresses the racial contract (Hughey, 2021; Du Bois, 2023).

Sutton Griggs: *Imperium and Imperio* and the Coming of the New Negro

Sutton E. Griggs's novel *Imperium in Imperio* (1899) offers an alternative historical narrative and explores various philosophical issues, drawing from W. E. B. Du Bois's writings and speculative philosophy. Griggs presents a vision of a future where African Americans are united under a single government, known as the "Empire within the Empire," to benefit an oppressed class of African American citizens. Although he is heavily influenced by the Victorian-era sensibility of the British empire in his formulation, Griggs emphasizes the attitude of a leader of secret societies that flourished in the late 19th century, arguing that it would bring about a new life of higher spiritual attitudes and ultimately lead to the development of a "true higher civilization" through a new religious spirit for the new Black Republic (Hill, 2023; Hooper, 2024; Wright, 2021). In his groundbreaking and thought-provoking novel, Griggs skillfully unveils an expansive and captivating alternative historical narrative.

Through the intricate tapestry of Black speculative philosophy, Griggs constructs a compelling vision for the future of African Americans, envisioning a harmonious and unified existence under the auspices of a single government. Within the pages of *Imperium in Imperio*, Griggs artfully employs the tools of speculative philosophy, deftly intertwining concepts that address the profound intersections of race, politics, and the complex nature of citizenship (Tamplin, 2020). His ingenious exploration centers around the fundamental principle of "unity in diversity," embracing the nuances and diversity within African America while unifying the community under the shared purpose of collective progress. Engrossed in the timeless narrative, readers embark on a political journey stretching beyond both spatial and temporal limits. Griggs seamlessly intertwines the illuminating ideas of Du Bois and myriad other philosophical luminaries, enhancing the texture and complexity of his vision. Through this revolutionary work, Griggs beckons readers to contemplate the weighty questions of identity, power, and the elusive pursuit of justice. At the heart of *Imperium in Imperio* lies a powerful call for societal transformation and the recognition of every individual's inherent humanity and worth. With extraordinary eloquence and intellectual acumen, Griggs challenges conventional notions and sparks a resounding call to action during the Jim Crow era and imperialist age. By illuminating the potential inherent within African Americans, he inspires a collective striving for emancipation, empowerment, and a brighter future where unity intersects with civilizational complexity (Tamplin, 2020).

Following World War I, during the period referred to as the Harlem Renaissance, a group of African diasporic writers and intellectuals who lived in the Manhattan neighborhood participated in an esoteric project described as a blend of Theosophists and Rosicrucian-Hermetic discourses that were in vogue in the early 20th century promoted by mystic George Ivanovich Gurdjieff (Woodson, 2015). Writers like Wallace Thurman, Jean Toomer, Zora Neale Hurston and others were influences by the work of Gurdjieff and A. R. Orage. Toomer would become the chief literary occultist of the Harlem Renaissance as he attempted to use esoteric work to grapple with the concept of racial identity and believed himself to be the forerunner of the new human and exemplified this approach in his poem "The Blue Meridien" (Woodson, 2015).

African diasporic writers engaged in an incredibly profound endeavor, utilizing their written pieces as a profound platform for delving into the intrinsic essence of the human soul, its intricate connection with the divine, and its irrefutable position within the vast expanse of the world. In times gone by, these philosophical and theological dialogues were confined solely within the realms of academia, but now the magnificent narratives crafted by these extraordinary intellectuals have transcended these boundaries, bestowing upon a significantly larger audience the invaluable opportunity to access, comprehend, and revel in the sheer brilliance of their contemplations. Consequently, this paradigm shift ushered in a truly transformative epoch, the *New Negro*, a term coined by Alain Locke, and greatly empowered the African diasporic community through the authors' speculative ponderings, which resoundingly championed racial equality and liberation. Furthermore, it emerges as an unwavering force, effectively challenging and rebutting the suppressive influences that permeated the Gilded Age and the era following the tumultuous period of Reconstruction (Berg, 2020).

Black speculative writing has historically served as a critical method for authors and activists to create different portrayals in response to the racial oppression and political control of African diasporic peoples stretching as far back as the pre–Civil War era to the contemporary moment. However, due to the strong influence of Darwin, Spencer, and Huxley on American society in the late 1800s, such speculative writing in the form of allegory, dystopia/utopia, or futurist fiction is now being acknowledged, embraced, or recognized as a fundamental component of African American literary studies or the African American protest tradition. Academic research on African American speculative or science fiction tends to increase in the early 20th century, with the works of W. E. B. Du Bois, Pauline Hopkins, and Sutton Griggs (Jones, 2021; Warren & Coles, 2020).

The Intersection of Esotericism and the Harlem Renaissance

A new literary movement developed in the United States after World War I. Dubbed the New Negro movement, its proponents advocated for a new aesthetic, embracing Black culture openly and pursuing the loftiest standards of artistic excellence. That pursuit incorporated folk culture and naivety, which prompted a cross-generational conflict in literary aesthetics that is part of the larger narrative of the Harlem Renaissance and its afterlife (Owens, 2013). Esotericism may lend itself to various types of appropriation, but at the core of it, there seems to be some esoteric content that should account for the influences on Toomer and Hurston (Vass, 2017). The breadth and depth of the exoteric reading traditions revealed an engagement with hymns, most palpably freeing the human psyche from the interiorization of the maternal sphere of the corporeal body. Addressing the redemptive journey of the exoteric consciousness, esoteric reading traditions narrated a fall from a pristine state of nonduality into separation.

Important perspectives published in the early decades of the 20th century within the works of Jean Toomer and Zora Neale Hurston reveal a constellation of esoteric beliefs related to mysticism and the occult, albeit through different concepts and meditations. Similarly, the ideas and concerns central to Toomer and Hurston regarding Afrodiasporic folk culture and peoples bear corresponding esoteric similarities. While significant to both writers' works, the examination of this intersection briefly looks at an understanding of the practices and beliefs of esotericism and how they resonate in the philosophical, scholarly, and artistic currents of the period in question. Thus, broadly conceived by mysticism, the occult, and esotericism, the religious milieu of the 1920s and 1930s reveals the importance of Afrodiasporic esotericism in the works of Toomer and Hurston.

Jean Toomer and Esoteric Influences

Jean Toomer was an active writer during the Harlem Renaissance and embodied the quest to understand the place of non-Western spiritual traditions in America and the world of the early 20th century. Born in 1894 to a biracial family that included both freeborn and enslaved African Americans, Toomer's upbringing in Washington, DC, and later in Pennsylvania and Georgia exposed him to a range of spiritual beliefs. However, his writings also reflected a rejection of traditional Protestantism, an exploration of

Gnosticism, and a search for authenticity through folktales and spirituals. His literary career, marked by the publication of *Cane* in 1923, showcased his deep engagement with both African American culture and Western religious philosophies, giving rise to a hybrid spirituality of universalism that served as both a refuge from and a critique of modernity (Olsen, 1987).

Toomer's poetry was influenced by critical tenets of esotericism, including the search for the divine within nature, the reclamation of the body, the awareness of ancient universal wisdom distorted by modernity, and criticism of mainstream religion. His writings revealed the desire for America to transcend the divisive history and ignorance that defined the colonial relationship with Africa. Despite the potential dangers of esotericism, as with the traditional schools within Western Rosicrucianism or the Theosophical movement, Toomer's esoteric writings were predominantly explorations of alternative paths (Owens, 2013). Ultimately, *Cane* served as an entry point into this hidden Toomer, and close readings of select prose and verse illuminated how he engaged with esotericism as a cultural dialogue.

Esoteric Themes in Toomer's and Zora Neale Hurston's Works

A comparative analysis of Jean Toomer's and Zora Neale Hurston's writings examines the thematic presence of esotericism. Commonalities and divergences in this presence are explored. This section aims to identify and examine common, diverse, and nuanced thematic expressions of esotericism in the works of the two writers to ascertain how such an examination furthers scholarly knowledge of the intersection of esotericism with the Harlem Renaissance. In *Cane*, the overarching principle of a universal mind is turned to the direct idea of the mind of individuals. The notion of individuals possessed of either high or low minds, but within the dialectic of the two, are all individuals who connect to the universal mind. Hurston relied on theosophical notions of the universal mind, the principle of which was biblically contextualized but also referenced in the voice of the folk who resonated with a much older tradition.

In contrast to Toomer's abstraction of the universal mind, Hurston's grounding in folk tongue yielded a high form of mystical language in re-scenes, like that of the singing where it was taken or elevated to God. This work of Toomer and Hurston is a complimentary oscillation between what was considered high versus low culture, representing the emergence of modern African American speculative philosophy in this period. In another vein that speaks directly to Toomer, Hurston's grounding in folk tongue also yielded a form of mystical language—the regional dialect that Tea Cake and other characters used in *Their Eyes Were Watching God,* which Toomer could not understand. But in honoring high and low forms of language, Hurston straddled and transgressed the line of "voluble" and "multiloquious" (Owens, 2013). The Black speculative philosophies of Toomer and Hurston are consistent with the reemergence of the Rosicrucian tradition and a continuation of ideas that trace back to Bacon and his desire to forecast the new age.

Building on the groundbreaking work of Jon Woodson, this analysis sheds light on an often-neglected intersection of esotericism and the Harlem Renaissance through careful textual analysis of the works of Toomer and Hurston, who explore spirituality and cultural unity through innovative stylistic choices. In *Cane,* Toomer imagines an African American sacred consciousness, relying on abstract poetic imagery and stylistic fragmentation, which develops narrative coherence through religious performative repetition. However, while Toomer's abstraction contemplates unattainable totality, Hurston's *Their Eyes Were Watching God* consciously negotiates form to explore the sacred nature of art without settling into abstraction. Hurston's text acknowledges the hierarchy and tension between "high art" and vernacular expressiveness through an internal and external narrative frame, novelistic digression, and intricate dialect.

The broader significance of this intersection is twofold. First, it speaks to an emerging transatlantic and translocal consciousness through which esoteric traditions and Black experience are articulated as universal. While there are limits to this universalism in the works of both authors, the richness of their respective imaginations allows for the exploration of spirituality on both individual and cultural levels. Second, this project opens up more possibilities to explore how the authors and thinkers across locales and contexts negotiated similar questions of space, form, genre, race, and faith as modernity arose. In this way, a historic moment and a field of study emerged within the literature to examine the individuality and collective unity, esotericism and African-ness, Harlem, and the wider world.

W. E. B. Du Bois: The Comet

Du Bois's short story also comes closer to realizing the full extent of the speculative philosophical method. Du Bois's recently discovered unpublished essay "The Princess Steel" reveals an interest in the Black speculative tradition early in the 20th century (Du Bois et al., 2015). Du Bois developed this story with a character that invented a Mega-scope that could see across space and time that would amplify his ideas to study the boundary of space-time creatively, "into an optimal means for perceiving material history" (Du Bois et al., 2015, p. 820). Du Bois pushes the boundaries of bourgeois unity as effectively as any leftist intellectual. However, by making class instead of property the site of unity, he moves the confrontation out into an intersectional space that is much more relevant to the lived experience of his readers. W. E. B. Du Bois's groundbreaking speculative essay "The Comet" takes Sutton Griggs's thought-provoking analysis of the postbellum Black middle class and their complex relationship with America to unprecedented depth and insight.

Throughout "The Comet," Du Bois compels readers to critically re-evaluate the inherent power and significance of existential meaning. By skillfully appropriating the timeless narrative of the outsider, Du Bois elevates this exploration to an unparalleled degree, urging the reader to confront the profound implications that were present in American society. One must inevitably ponder: what does it truly signify when the central plot unfolds through the experiences of an individual who embodies the deepest-seated fears of society, encompassing both the nightmarish stereotypes associated with Blackness and the inherent terror that permeates the very core of American white supremacy? Moreover, within this context, it subtly alludes to the underlying reasons why the long-awaited revolution continues to elude us, providing a glimmer of understanding regarding the social mechanisms that perpetuate inequality (Anderson & Curry, 2021; Lavan, 2020).

Pauline Hopkins

Of One Blood recounts the journey/life of Reuel Briggs Johnson, a young, ambitious Negro who, after losing his newly wedded white wife, plunges into a fantastical quest that includes crossing the color line. Becoming "what his ancestors were," that is, an Egyptian high priest, he encounters cultural and racial dilemmas—which Nurhussein (2010) helps to explain as the outcome of the blend of traditions such as American, Mesopotamian, Greek, Roman, or even theosophical. The character changes in skin color ultimately and ends up being killed by his friend and magnetic healer, Dr. Frank Gaston. Just before dying, Reuel scatters papers that simulate an entire volume of instructions that would have helped unlock the mysteries of a secret vault in the temple of Aumen-Ra where gold and silver are stored. Hopkins's decision to kill Johnson and have Gaston not dive any further into the inheritance matter can be interpreted as a political position that avoided alienating the novel from its historical moment (Hopkins, 2022).

Essentially a crossover representative, Hopkins touches on and is also claimed by various critical stances/domains. Both she and her novel are pivotal to discourses on gender ("the text enacts the fluidity of categories of gender, race, and class"), and race (race as the determinant factor in character study). Or simply history and literature, as in the critical battle on which Hopkins produced the first African American novel to feature a scientist as the protagonist and a storyline focused on African roots. In 1903 Pauline Hopkins's novel *Of One Blood* was published in serialized form. Only the serial publication was known for years, but in 2004 the novel appeared as a separate entity and underscores how the author's attention is on the psychological dimensions of the humanity of Black people (Davies, 2021).

The literature of Griggs, Du Bois, and Hopkins examines how the Black body is invited into the flesh and how the Black voice is authorized to express itself. Explicating the function of speculative philosophy in the discourse of political agendas and others enables those supporting such agendas to link aesthetics, race, democracy, and knowledge; to investigate how ethnic awareness and empowerment function; and to confront race as a site where identification and singularity, aesthetics, and political recognition are provoked (Geiselman, 2020; Hooper, 2024; Moody-Turner, 2020). Each provides a compelling demonstration of the complex ways that ethnic perspectives, particularly African American ones, influenced their understanding of American national life. Fewer investigations have been undertaken concerning how speculative philosophy influences these authors' writings. Yet, examining the period in which the authors were writing, who their frequent interlocutors were, and their professions reveals a bounty of speculative philosophical work. This work involves temporal concerns and an examination of questions, developments, and archives addressing the notion of cosmopolitanism, classlessness, and classical worldviews, discourses, and speculations (Walton, 2020).

The intersection of race, politics, and speculative philosophy of African American literature in the late 19th and early 20th centuries opened radical possibilities in the act of racializing in reverse the seemingly fixed category of the human. We have examined how overlooked writers Sutton Griggs, W. E. B. Du Bois, Zora Neale Hurston, and Pauline Hopkins engaged various speculative philosophies to address the foundations, social organization, and improvement of African American lives. Their approach to speculative philosophy significantly broadens the ways scholars think about the role and genealogy of race as an instrument of resistance in early African American thought, as well as how it gave new content to African American social expression, painting portraits of prejudice, privileged Blacks, and poor whites from society's romantic margins, refraction of the central mainstays of American life (Dillender, 2020; Butler, 2021).

Griggs's profound recognition of the insidious workings of racism, cleverly disguised behind the facade of Christianity within the exploitative production structure of the American polity, unequivocally showcases his undeniable status as a pioneering visionary of speculative thought. This remarkable revelation serves as a profound testament to the necessity of cooperation, equality, understanding, empathy, morality, sharing, and productive endeavors that align with the principles of responsible living. By embracing these fundamental values, he lays the groundwork for the establishment of a new, just, and equitable future—one of fairness, tranquility, harmony, moral uprightness, and ethical fortitude that remains firmly grounded in honesty, equity, ecology, and value-based economic principles accessible to all individuals (Gruesser, 2022). In this era of profound intellect and unwavering commitment to truth, with a resounding call to action echoing throughout the core of our humanity, it becomes abundantly clear that our planet urgently demands an economic revolution. This transformative movement, embracing the totality of human understanding and beckoning us to navigate uncharted territories, shall not manifest as a cataclysmic eruption of violence reminiscent of bygone eras but rather as an ethically driven renaissance—an unprecedented metamorphosis that comprises the attitudes and actions of mankind, propelling us toward an immensely improved society and an existence that betters the lives of each and every individual fortunate enough to be part of this Black utopian ideal of existence (Gruesser, 2022; Wright, 2021).

As Griggs's novel makes plain, the stakes for grappling with the conjuncture of race, politics, and speculative philosophy are high. The historical reality demonstrates the continuing perniciousness of white supremacy and the economically driven colorblindness that justifies it. Speculative fiction suggests critical, imaginative possibilities. These two realms, the historical and the creative, have always interacted in intricate ways. Thus, underlying this connection is an aspiration for speculative fictive narratives to unfold from real and material conditions and to help visualize and make available other ways of inhabiting the world, other relations, and other possibilities. It is unnecessary—and perhaps impossible—to completely enumerate the ways in which such work could or does matter; its value instead derives in part from its elusiveness, its openness to multiple interpretations, and its potential to convey other kinds of knowing. Thus, I conclude by briefly speculating about its current relevance.

Conclusion

This chapter addressed how politics and race intersected in the work of philosopher Sutton Griggs as both a speculative thinker and publisher, with particular attention to how philosophy with politics in mind thrives outside the so-called marketplace of ideas. This is done by comparing the works of other authors of the era, Pauline Hopkins in literature, W. E. B. Du Bois in the social sciences, and Harlem Renaissance luminaries Jean Toomer and Zora Neale Hurston. In this chapter, we have aimed at several essential objectives. First, we have sought to introduce readers to the work of three crucial turn-of-the-century African American intellectuals, Griggs, Toomer, and Hurston, in addition to strengthening the sense that Du Bois and Hopkins were in conversation with multiple contemporaries working in various literary genres rather than principally with each other. Second, we have charted a possible late 19th- and early 20th-century Afrodiasporic genealogy of speculative antiracist thought across the fields of literature, politics, and philosophy both within and beyond the United States.

Griggs's thought and work generates expressions of speculative antiracist perspectives and anticipates the transnational translocal moves of Du Bois and Hopkins. All these thinkers, thus, are candidates for inclusion in a fully global history of modern speculation. Third, with adaptations designed to express these genealogical relationships rooted in ideas about slavery, the family, and racial futurity, we have identified in broad and encompassing terms the speculative racialist social ontology to which Griggs, Hopkins, Du Bois, and many of their contemporaries together and in tension aspired to engage. Fourth, we have shown the dimensions by which speculative antiracist social ontology was at work in antiracist political discussions around race during the Gilded age of Imperialism, colonialism and Jim Crow, the Black family, and the impact of scientific racism. However, these domains of Black life would be transformed with the arrival of the technostate.

CHAPTER 3

The Rise of the Deep State and the Technostate

Following World War II, the United States emerged as the strongest country in the world by virtue of its infrastructure surviving relatively untouched in the aftermath of the conflict. However, during this period the American state began to morph into something else. President Eisenhower's concept of the "military-industrial complex," announced during his farewell address in 1961, days after he signed off on the assassination of Patrice Lumumba, exemplify this phenomenon. Furthermore, John Kenneth Galbraith's "technostate" and the idea of the "deep state" all describe the interconnectedness of government, the economy, and the unseen forces that shape policy and democracy. Examining how these concepts interrelate provides insight into the balance between national security, economic interests, and democratic governance.

Eisenhower's warning about the military-industrial complex, given during his farewell address in 1961, cautioned against the powerful alliance between the US military and the defense industry. He feared that this relationship, without proper oversight, could lead to undue influence over national policy, emphasizing the threat that vested interests posed to democratic governance. Eisenhower highlighted the need for an alert civilian populace to safeguard democracy against this confluence of economic and political power. Galbraith's concept of the "technostate," introduced in *The*

New Industrial State (1967), describes how technology-driven corporations influence government structures and economic policy. Galbraith argues that large, bureaucratic corporations have gained substantial control over politics through their technological and economic power. This technocratic class can guide policies to favor their interests, aligning closely with Eisenhower's military-industrial complex. Both concepts underline the risk of concentrated power influencing public policy in ways that may sideline public accountability and broader democratic needs (Galbraith, 1967).

The modern concept of the deep state extends these ideas, suggesting that a network of influential, often unelected government officials and private sector actors operate behind the scenes. This group is believed to shape policy and decision-making outside the traditional democratic structures. While deep-state theories often carry a conspiratorial tone, the concept taps into the valid concerns raised by Eisenhower and Galbraith—namely, the potential for entrenched powers to operate with little oversight (Lofgren, 2014). Together, these theories describe a landscape where democracy is challenged by the entrenchment of powerful, yet often opaque, interests at the intersection of government, military, and large corporations. The balance between maintaining national security, promoting technological advancements, and safeguarding democratic principles remains delicate and contentious. Ensuring transparency and accountability continues to be critical in mitigating the risks associated with these powerful complexes.

During this brief period the United States sought to form a new international order based on its own strategic interests and created the world's first technostate. According to Galbraith, technology had become an increasingly autonomous force in shaping society, leading to the emergence of a new social order he calls the technostate (Courvisanos, 2005). The technostate is characterized by a network of large, technologically advanced organizations that operate according to their own rules, independent of political and social control. In this context, the problem of control becomes one of regulating the organization of technology itself. The technostate is a fully technocratic order, where authority rests with a class of decision-makers having technical knowledge and expertise. Within this new order, the public interest must be defined in terms of the practical organization of technology. Hence, an important instance of human agency in implementing the technostate is producing and propagating a new ideological vision of public interest (Mitchell, 2020).

Galbraith identifies three central agencies that delineate, define, or harbor this conception of public interest: the corporate organization, the macroeconomic institution, and the state agency. Each has played a crucial role at various times and for diverse reasons in the technological appropriation of the resources and capacity of the public institution. However, as I show, while the technostate's realization may have been primarily in the hands of these agencies, its origination was a much broader social process involving other agency processes of both decisively contributory and obstructive nature. The new ideological conception of the public interest was generated in social science departments, permeating academia and public policy agencies, and represented a critical development for the technostate (Galbraith et al., 1975). Yet the esoteric tradition would coincide with the development of the American rocket program and the technostate and deep state.

Thelema, Jack Parsons, and the American Rocket Program

Thelema is a philosophical and spiritual system developed by the early 20th-century writer and occultist Aleister Crowley, centered on individual will and the quest for personal freedom. Jack Parsons, an American rocket engineer and a member of Crowley's Ordo Templi Orientis, was an early practitioner of Thelema and attempted to apply its principles to his life, work, and relationships. Parsons developed an enduring interest in magic and the occult at a young age. He was greatly influenced by H. P. Blavatsky, the founder of theosophy, and composed his version of sacred books finding religious guidance in various traditions, including Freemasons, Rosicrucians, and experimental psychologists (West, 2021). L. Ron Hubbard, an aspiring occultist and science fiction writer, became friendly with Parsons and was a member of his social circle in Los Angeles shortly after the start of World War II.

Parsons was a pioneer of American human-crewed spaceflight and rockets. Parsons's work on JATO ("jet-assisted take-off") rockets and solid-fuel rockets was directly responsible for the very success of the American space program. Parsons won the coveted Langley Medal for his pioneering work on rockets. He founded and was of the Jet Propulsion Laboratory, the cradle of NASA. He developed solid-fuel rockets at Aerojet Engineering Corporation. Parsons and Wernher von Braun developed the idea of the F-1 rocket engine that carried the Apollo spacecraft to the moon (West, 2021). Parsons's scientific creativity was inspired by Aleister Crowley's "Moonchild" Thelemic prophecy.

Parson met L. Ron Hubbard in 1942. From 1945 to 1946 he performed a series of intense magical rituals called The Babalon Working to conjure up an "elemental mate" using blood and semen to birth a "moonchild." Parsons foolishly entered into a business partnership with Hubbard called Allied Enterprises; he was ultimately swindled by Hubbard (Hedenborg White, 2020; Introvigne, 2021). Philosophically, Parsons is often considered an occultist who developed a unique and American reinterpretation of Thelema. He viewed the will as the individual's creative and unique identity, ultimately confounding self-identity with divine identity, which entails a radical reinterpretation of Crowley's original Thelema. Parsons's Thelemic writings were collected and published by his followers and students. In the ongoing occult milieu and community, Parsons is often cast as an American Thelemic saint, martyr, or prophet for his radical beliefs and actions, some interpreting Parsons as a 20th-century forerunner of New Ageism and its ideas of love, freedom, and unity (West, 2021). The fusion of this speculative approach and science at the founding of the American rocket program would have a profound impact on the emerging astroculture, geopolitics, and the speculative imagination.

Understanding Astroculture and Its Implications

Astroculture refers explicitly to changing sociocultural meanings of human space exploration and settlement. In this sense, astroculture exists between the activities of real-world space agencies and their representation in the media and popular culture. Given this definition, the purpose of this chapter is to discuss the implications of Galbraithian astroculture as a national technostate in the context of Galbraith's model of political economy, modes of planetary consciousness associated with historical deployments of astroculture, and the utopian ideologies related to the subsequent representation of this culture in the science fiction genre. Integrating the topics above, this chapter traces and captures a glimpse of the trajectory of three competing visions of Galbraith astroculture in the science fiction genre: (1) explorations of Galbraith's planetary-teleological and cybernetic politics alongside competing ideologies of science fiction representation; (2) midcentury reactionary depictions of Galbraithian astroculture's global appropriation by Orwellian technocorporate states via NATO; and (3) the unfoldment of the libertarian futures marked by digital development, post and geopolitical upheaval, and evolving futures of knowledge (Chayt, 2014; Geppert & Siebeneichner, 2021).

Galbraith's 1960s vision of a tamed cybernetic technostate global manager in response to the threat of worldwide recession and war looms large in post–World War II UFO discourse across the political mainstream. Although American ufology has been disciplined across the spectrum of political extremes, the far right has most fully unpacked its astrocultural implications, interpreting UFO phenomena as a sign of techno-salvation in a "global" future unity—socially, materially, and culturally—on meta-terrestrial terms. The vision dwarfs earthly political discourse, framing Galbraith's destiny within fragile terrestrial biospheres and planetary geo-orbiting vehicles (Geppert & Siebeneichner, 2021). The narrative of this cosmic shift has been brought to fruition by entrepreneurs like Elon Musk. In the opposing poles of the discourse, the limits of Galbraith's technostate in envisioning a cybernetic future's emergence have catalyzed far-futures of space colonization.

Exploring Futurology as a Field of Study

John Kenneth Galbraith put forth the theory of the technostate, a central element of his ideas for political and economic reformation. This is famously elaborated in *The New Industrial State* (1967), the book for which Galbraith is best known. The growth of some important aspects common to the technostate paradigm is known as astroculture, a culture of openness to technologies and the future, which emerged (and partly even converged) in the US and the parts of the world influenced by the US post–World War II military-industrial complex. Some aspects of this culture are further taken on as political and economic goals to form galactic technostates (Mitchell, 2020). Therefore, the technostate/astroculture/futurology constellation is shown to be a significant unnoticed influence on shaping the narratives and settings of post–World War II science fiction and speculative thought as a critique.

The discussion here begins with the overarching reception of the technostate. It has a definable and coherent appearance in the genres associated with astroculture, such as planetary reports, space colonization narratives, and space opera. The models of the technostate are affected by the astrocultural topic, and this is especially true for such phenomena as star federation narratives, which are found in both technophoria and technophobia literature (Borst, 2009). Narratives of the technostate take different forms, like colonial tales, heroic or tragic space explorations, encounter scenarios, and speculative what-ifs. Those forms can partly explain the astrocultural focus on planetary history, environmental issues, and the relationship of the state or pro-state institutions to the technosphere in metapolitical terms. While this metapolitical framework largely adheres to the default political assumptions in Western popular science fiction (that is to say, narrating progress through technocapitalism like the American monomyth), the reception and articulation of the technostate is still distinctly not in line with the dominant techno-aesthetic paradigm of post-1960s space exploration that captivates popular imagination and desires a thousand space operas and glossy images of technofixes (Birat, 2017).

The dominant understanding of the technostate in Anglo-Western science fiction tradition has historically been limited, confused with the often-fantastic depiction of cybernetic technocracy in the genre associated with technophoria. The technostate is mainly dismissed as a "theocratic" and "technofascist"-like state in a popular sense. In both Anglocentric and continental translations of the genre, the technostate appears typically only as a momentary background, a rogue state in the periphery of the metaverse, or merely a colorful anecdote of parable-like tales on technocapitalism and futurity. No equivalent phrase or coherent similar understanding appears in the genre of technophilia, either in literature or criticism. In this respect, the encounter with Galbraith's technostate is characteristically awkward and surprising when the preconceptions of science fiction and popular philosophy/theory do not fit. Simultaneously, the technostate is also coherently and vividly described in both pessimistic and optimistic tones (Kohso, 2020).

Technostate Themes in Post-World War II Science Fiction

An article entitled "The Veblen-Commons Award" (Galbraith & Sharpe, 1977) points out several select technostate themes that would pop up in discourse around autonomous entities running a corporatized society separate from the public sphere. These dystopic images were broached earlier in the 1950s by Aldous Huxley in his book *Brave New World Revisited,* which concerned how the emerging society was reorganizing human inner life (Newman, 1992). In this sense, they can also be treated individually, though they must be understood in relation to one another to make sense: homogeneity, administration, artificiality, planning without progress, and dangers out of control. When separating these fields about Galbraith, it becomes evident that some appeared almost immediately. They would merge in what became a fictional fable of the technostate-oriented West, often ironically framing what was worse about humankind as the state of their best societies forecasting consumerism, violence, dystopia, and hyperreality (Chiu, 2013). As detailed below, most of these themes begin to emerge as a coalescent discursive field in works like *Alfred Besters the Demolished Man*, published in 1952, which would win its first Hugo award in 1953, and later titles like J. G. Ballard's *Kingdom Come* (2012). It articulates an age-old rule that commercial civilization would degrade, and visionary leaders would appear foolishly attempting to change that course (Andonopoulos, 2021; Khan, 2021).

Futurology in Science Fiction

Drawing from John Kenneth Galbraith's vision of a technostate, which emphasizes the ambiguous social context of technological supremacy, the tension between hope and anxiety regarding social technological development coincides with the emergence of futurology. The first wave of futurology following World War II looked outside Earth for solutions to planetary problems. Speculating on the restored balance between human destiny, technology, and nature, the works challenge the overwhelming fear of technology promoted by the media and elites and offer a unique ideological defense of high modernism and its faith in progress to a broader public (De Cock, 2009). Futurology emerged as a force in narrative culture in the aftermath of World War II: for example, the makings of the speculative and visionary work in an age of science, technology, and mass media in works of science fiction and commercial certainty in the future advertisements by Ford and the RAND Corporation. Faced with mass anxiety over the use of both atomic energy and technology, tensions between grand design and unintended consequence, and the planetary scale of the Cold War and reconstruction, this first wave of futurology proposed alternatives to global malaise outside the Earth and in the limitless cosmic ocean (Andersson, 2018).

Science fiction underwent a pivotal transformation in under two decades, overlapping the end of the Second World War and the early years of the Cold War. It swiftly expanded its fictional territory, emerging as astroculture, a genre that sought to entirely foretell and build the future of humanity as a technostate in the stars. Astroculture is the name given to a particular means of public spectacles, mythologies, institutions, and technologies used to mediate the impact of the space age (Geppert, 2012). It also constructed a fictional astropolitical world of astonishing complexity and on a vast scale that no other genre or mode of fiction has hitherto rivaled. The framing of science fiction as astroculture by its founders in the early 1950s is at the heart of the interconnectivity, coherence, and solidarity of a distinct body of literature published since the mid-1940s (Chayt, 2014). The key to the emergence of astroculture as a genre was the development and dissemination of a new lexicon of concepts, terms, ideas, and policies. They synthesized space science and missile and space flight technologies, anticipating their further development and application in the interest of humanity in the space age and its theocentric world policies.

Embedded in the new lexicon were new heroic figures of politicians, scientists, and thinkers representing a new hierarchy of astropolitical myth-symbols: Future Statesmen, Counsellors, or Systems Engineers. They became the collective protagonists and heroes of astroculture's adventurous tales of the technostate conquering new worlds, testing, transforming, and settling them, and the historic conjunctions of the epics of chronology at the vastest scale of the celestial empire (Wilhite, 1999). In close cooperation with the military-industrial-academic complex, which contracted scientists and science fiction writers to a campaign entailing war plans and contingency projects against the Soviet Union, liberal ideologues and science fiction writers underwrote the cultural politics of astroculture (Geppert, 2012; McQuaid, 2007). It furnished the technostate's comprehensive discourse on space and rationalized its policies and ventures. The reconstruction of the narrative worldview, politically, culturally, and industrially astropolitical in scale, preoccupied with the fate of humanity in the space age, endowed the science fiction literature that appeared after World War II with its unparalleled imaginative power.

Futurology Themes in Post-World War II Science Fiction

Following the overview of how futurity has been represented and understood, attention turns to a more explicit consideration of the themes and motifs of a specific subset of this science fiction—the short stories of the late 1960s and early 1970s published in the magazine *Galaxy Science Fiction*—as the principles of futurology shape these. In the hands of writers including Robert Sheckley, Frederik Pohl, and Larry Niven, the themes and concerns that have already been considered return in terms of a critique of a technocratic conception of the future that emphasizes the irrationality and inhumanity of the vision of the future based on extrapolation. How different authors interweave these themes, sometimes in contradictory terms, on occasion questioning the limits of futurology's conceptualization of the future, and in other regards arguing for the largely self-contained acceptance of its principles, are explored in detail (Jancovich, 2019).

The concern with societal systems assumes the rationality of human beings, and the inhumanity and irrationality of this situation are manifested in different particulars. In some, Galbraith's parameters are employed in terms of the Cold War capitalism's concerns with the horrors of controlled or designed societies founded on the ability of technologists to predict and control human social behavior (Wilhite, 1999). Other stories take the more optimistic perspective of futurology's embracing understanding of the future. Though projected toward the humane monsters who realize the negative Cold War variant, in other instances, this concern has been posited in terms of a space-bound "humanism" that denies the possibility of the orchestrated management of individuals and societies despite evidence to the contrary. In all such interpretations, however, the framing, hence often subconscious concerns, of these visions comes in for questioning.

Impact and Legacy

The manifesto outlined in Galbraith's projects for the technostate was not politically sustainable (Chayt, 2014). Toward the end of the decade, these technocratic aspirations were eroded by a widespread shift toward a more left-leaning agenda, fostering skepticism and anger at the technocracy behind the previous initiatives, even as those initiatives went unrealized. Anticipating this shift, cognitive architectures were proposed to imbue robots with humanlike minds and the ultimate robot takeover of virtually all aspects of contemporary life, from work to leisure. This would vastly change the relationship between man and technology and perhaps even the nature of man (Wilhite, 1999). Foreshadowing the aesthetic politics of John Akomfrah's *Last Angel of History*, eons after the triumph of transhumanism as portrayed, a Black augmented entity gazes upwards. What lies before the angel is a glowing monument built from interstellar graveyards of the long dead, an object of infinite proportion pieced together from ruins of the distant past, broken shards of worlds that once danced in the light (Harvey, 2021). Connected with the cosmos, an earthen star blinks brightly, signaling back to the void in a cosmic transference of remembrance.

Influence of Galbraith's Ideas on Science Fiction

Beginning with Galbraith's invocation of the technostate, a trinity of representation crystallized with the onset of the Cold War: astroculture, technoculture, and futurology. In Galbraith's observation of the technostate, this astropolitical culture formation was already gaining wide currency in fiction, policy inquiry, public moralism, and the installation of various apparatuses for collecting exploratory imagination. For the technostate, these public imaginings were not to be necessarily hued with a bright shade, as, for instance, would have been the case for an optimistic, peaceable, go-further-together claim to be built in space (Chayt, 2014). Such astropolitics is also featured prominently in science fiction across media. C. S. Lewis imagined the race of supernatural beings nearly immune from disaster because of their vast culture, which is more like Einstein than H. G. Wells. Later, the shadow of this astropolitical tropological heritage loomed large over the trichotomy of literature of realizing transcendental vision. With the technostate as a cultural counterhegemony, astroculture as a literary stratum of writing at the juncture of blueprints, visions, and speculations introducing the notion of futurology as a toolbox of instruments, methodologies, and tropes for deployment in the construction of the world of tomorrow, the stage was set. The technostate, astroculture, and futurology are topological, discursive, and representational figures forming a hegemonic project. Topologically, this era charted the transition from the technostate to a blueprint and its necessary side effects. Such astropolitical culture drew upon, extended, exploded, and overtook earlier discursive formations and technological apparatuses.

The interconnectedness of Galbraith's technostate, astroculture, and futurology is considered at once and grounded in works of science fiction considered in earlier sections of this chapter. By embracing this larger context, a mechanism is envisioned through which the collective impact these forces may have had upon the thematic landscape of science fiction can be understood. By analogy to the emergence of astroculture, whose boundaries were in large part defined by an exogenous social factor—the impetus given to space exploration and possible colonization by the competing social systems of the Cold War—Galbraith's technostate and the epiphenomenon of futurology can be seen as a mechanism that has facilitated the emergence of a more cohesive thematic milieu within science fiction at a specific historical moment, post–World War II and the work of Arthur C. Clarke (Kilgore, 2017). Specifically, the growing universalism of a technostate theme, emphasizing the state's role in an economy of abundance, has been within the milieu of the hard science fiction subgenre of astroculture, focused on space colonization and the many other aspects of large-scale terraforming, astro engineering, and terraforming the celestial bodies (or worlds beyond planets themselves). Through this complex of developments—the technostate/astroculture/futurology complex or troika—hard science fiction was said to enter its golden age, once again analogous to the earlier development of its proto exponents: the popularization of astronautics via the astroculture myth and advocacy of astronautics was quickly followed by a spate of commercial commodities which appropriated this mythology for pulp print magazines, radio and television shows, comic books and movie shorts, and advertising (Pak, 2010).

Futurology and the Struggle for the World

In a global historical context, futurology inherited the legacy of fields such as utopia, prophecy, and "the ages of futurity." As a sector distinct from the utopians, assertors also included futurists. The noted cosmologist and popularizer of the universe, Fred Hoyle (1989), proposed a theory known as the "steady state," which describes an alternative cosmological theory to the evolving universe proposed by the big bang theory. The theory refers to a universe that is shaped the same forever, in other words, not changing its way of existence despite the passage of time. However, futurology and futurism/foresight as a field of study began to solidify in the mid-1960s when two researchers, Olaf Helmer and Theodore Gordon, at the RAND Corporation in the United States tried to develop a general theory of prediction to deal with social and political problems (Andersson, 2012). It was an attempt to move beyond utopian fantasy. However, as others saw, it would also present a form of power of control and ignored the bias of how intuition organizes data (Andersson, 2012).

Futurology focused on academic and alternatively derived means of forecasting the long-term future blossomed in the United States during the early 1960s. Key figures included Alvin Toffler, author of the groundbreaking books *Future Shock* and *The Third Wave*, and Herman Kahn, the futurist who led studies for the United States Air Force (USAF) futures research agency, the Hudson Institute, and RAND Corporation and published several critical books on the relationship of strategy and foresight; American mathematician and sociologist Daniel Bell, who foresaw the rise of post-industrial society in his 1973 book *The Coming of Post-Industrial Society*; and economist Everett Rogers's identification of the S-curve as an analog for the diffusion of innovations. Three critical attitudes of the period recognized during this research were the belief in technocratic rationality, a new dawn of great wealth, particularly for the United States, and the generation of shock scenarios.

During the 1960s, Khan aimed to get businessmen, military leaders, and arms-control negotiators to think in more rational and prudent ways about the long-range future. He believed the conflict of his time to be largely psychological rather than factual; and to prevail in a crisis, actors required a variety of alternative strategies and selective actions to be ready for use. Some practitioners believed that Khan was writing about what organizations should do rather than what they do. His contemporaries were divided about futurism as a means of policy at the time, and a substantial literature critical of the feasibility of futurology as policy would quickly develop. Some key questions about science fiction and its people were at the heart of the emerging discipline (Kristóf & Nováky, 2023).

The Cold War

The Cold War was a distinct period in world history that spanned over three decades from the 1950s until the early 1990s. Encompassing a range of categories—political, military, ideological, and economic—the Cold War was also characterized by the absence of large-scale violence between the two primary antagonists: the United States and its allies on the one hand and the Soviet Union and its allies on the other. However, it involved violent confrontations through proxy wars between the opposing blocs. A series of events involving the rivalries between the two superpowers starting from 1947, such as the Berlin Blockade, the Korean War, and the Vietnam War, exacerbated the tension encompassing the Global North and divided the world according to the opposing ideologies of capitalism and Marxism-Leninism.

During this political confrontation between the Western Bloc and Eastern Bloc, metropolitan centers of Europe became abounding landscapes for the birth of a new discipline slowly inching its way from the periphery toward the center of policymaking. Accompanied by the fear of communism, this new discipline was called futurology. The United Nations section UNESCO sponsored two significant reports about the future of Africa in the mid-1960s in the Mali and the Monrovia reports (Oboe, 2019). While both reports are embedded in a political milieu, one with the thinking of the Western Bloc capitalists, the other echoing the voice of the Eastern Bloc Marxists, they have in common their utopian vision for the African continent's future development naively overlooking the socio-structural contextuality of that continent. By examining the fuzzy and contradictory visions for the future of Africa, this fuzzy area at the intersection of the Cold War and African development mirrors the blindness of the highly modernist view of thinking at its worldwide scale and endowing different futures with different utopian visions.

Africa and the Cold War

The dynamics of the Cold War shaped the African presence in futurist thought. In the 1950s and early 1960s, the Cold War intersected with developments on the African continent, most specifically with decolonization and the subsequent scramble for and consolidation of new states, to stylize and indeed caricature Africa as both the continent most distant from the future and the birthplace of the postmodern utopia. The former was the consequence of Western anxiety about the obvious but unmanageable demand for real change in Africa, the threat of Soviet influence and subversion, the scale of ambitious, self-confidence nationalist projects, and the nature of the terrain these experiments were taking place in; the latter, the result of the intellectual and emotional capture of many observers by the symbolism of newness, combined with the desire for drama and moral rehabilitation after four decades of threatened annihilation and actual catastrophe. Futurism during this period crystallized how Africa and the African imagination were constructed internally and perceived externally then. More specifically, it also provides an opportunity to concretely explore the linkages and interactions between the hegemonic systems sustaining futurism and the contending positions of the Soviet Union, the nonaligned movement, and the dissent emerging from within the Afro-Asian world (Brennan, 2021; Chapman, 2023).

The Spirit of Bandung, Black Power, and Pan-African Revival

In the aftermath of World War II, the struggle for freedom began in earnest in the African diaspora and the continent. The international conflict fortuitously had decimated the Western populations and military complex enough whereby they no longer had the military power to politically dominate their former colonial possessions. The Bandung Conference, held in April 1955 in Indonesia, marked a watershed moment in the global postcolonial movement. This gathering of Asian and African nations was pivotal in forging a collective voice for newly independent countries, while also challenging the prevailing geopolitical order dominated by the Cold War superpowers. It encouraged an exploration of Indigenous cultures, histories, and narratives, which consequently sparked the emergence of postcolonial science fiction as a distinct genre. The Bandung Conference was attended by delegates from 29 countries, representing more than half the world's population at the time.

These nations were committed to resisting colonial and neocolonial forces and promoting Afro-Asian economic and cultural cooperation. According to the conference declarations, the participants sought to assert their sovereignty and independence (Acharya, 2008). This unprecedented platform provided a fertile ground for exchange that was as cultural as it was political. As these nations moved to carve out their postcolonial identities, there was an increased interest in literature that could articulate their unique experiences and envision future prospects. Postcolonial science fiction emerged as a vehicle for these aspirations. It provided a speculative space where former colonies could imagine futures free from colonial domination and explore themes of technological inequality, identity, and resistance (Csicsery-Ronay, 2003). This genre veers away from traditional Western-inspired science fiction, underlining the histories and futures of the Global South. For instance, Indian author Vandana Singh's work often explores themes of environmentalism and socioeconomic disparities, reflective of the nation's developmental challenges post-independence (Langer, 2011).

The Bandung Conference can be credited with catalyzing postcolonial awareness, which extended beyond political arenas into literary realms. The emergence of postcolonial science fiction not only showcases the narratives of resilience and resistance from newly independent nations but also highlights the use of speculative frameworks to address complex sociopolitical issues. Thus, the conference's influence reverberated through both geopolitical landscapes and the transformative development of literature reflecting a postcolonial ethos. Correspondingly, there was a Pan-African revival after World War II. Historically, the Pan-Africanist movement is a topic that has been revisited many times since it arose at the dawn of the 20th century. Africans educated in Western systems were living in Europe, the Americas, and the Caribbean, and they began to advocate for a return to Africa, where they believed they could reclaim their agency and develop Africa into a mighty super-nation-state. Britain and other European nations colonized and partitioned Africa in 1884, during the Berlin Conference, an imperialist project and product of an epistemology rooted in European superiority (Varela, 2017). Within this context, some men and women of African descent rose through the ranks of this European-dominated education and economic system. These men and women tended to turn their focus toward Africa, especially after World War II, a war that saw more educated men of African descent act as soldiers, interpreters, and leaders based on their education and knowledge of European languages (Shepperson, 1962).

The Manchester 5th Pan-African Congress resulted in a renewed Pan-African movement and provided the driving force behind the decolonization of Africa. However, there are differences as to the sequential numbering of Pan-African Congresses. The Cotonou Congress, taken in 1950, brought together leaders of West African nationalist movements and illustrated the limitations of the Pan-African movement (Babarinde & Wright, 2017). However, an important feature of these congresses was around the issue of development. Walter Rodney's seminal work, *How Europe Underdeveloped Africa*, captured an important critique of how European powers systematically exploited and hindered African development, and discussed the economic, social, and political ramifications of colonialism and how these continue to impact Africa. In African science fiction, this historical backdrop can provide a rich tapestry for speculative narratives questioning the dystopian legacies of colonialism. Authors could explore themes of exploitation, resistance, and resilience within futuristic settings, imagining worlds where Africa reclaims its autonomy and technological superiority—a reversal of historically imposed underdevelopment. Such narratives may highlight the long-term impacts of colonial resource extraction, and societal disruption, envisioning alternative histories where Africa cultivates its path based on its cultural and traditional insights.

Furthermore, Kwame Nkrumah's exposition of neocolonialism further deepened this critical potential. In his theory, Nkrumah posits that even after gaining political independence, African countries remain economically dependent on and controlled by former colonial powers through indirect means. This conceptual overlap inspired African science fiction to address themes of autonomy and neo-imperialism—as authors craft stories where protagonists battle hidden forces that seek to exert control through technology, economics, and cultural dominance. African futures served as a canvas where the implications of neocolonial power are rendered visible through metaphorical alien invasions, oppressive techno-authoritarian regimes, or multinational corporations controlling vital resources. Moreover, integrating Rodney's and Nkrumah's ideologies paved the way for narratives that utilize Indigenous knowledge systems as central elements in speculative storytelling. African speculative literature spotlights alternative, decolonized futures, where communities harness traditional wisdom and modern technologies symbiotically. Such stories offered readers imaginative spaces to reconceptualize how Africa's past, present, and future might inform an emancipation from both the overt and covert chains of colonial dominance.

Afro-Mythology and African Futurism

Pamela Phatsimo Sunstrum's essay "Afro-Mythology and African Futurism" (2013) is a pivotal work that contributes significantly to the discourse surrounding African futures and Afrofuturism. Distinct from Nnedi Okorafor's (2019) concept of "Africanfuturism," which is solely focused on literary criticism of African science fiction as a subgenre of science fiction, Sunstrum's exploration of these themes is deeply embedded in the historical and cultural contexts of the continent, and involves a distinct methodology for examining African architecture, art, literature, and curation, offering a nuanced perspective that aligns with contemporary Afrofuturism. Her work embodies a continental sensibility, examining the ways in which African history and mythology inform future narratives. Sunstrum's essay situates itself at the intersection of African history, mythology, and futuristic imaginings, drawing from a rich tapestry of African cultural elements (Sunstrum, 2013). She emphasizes the importance of African mythology in constructing a narrative for the future, suggesting that these myths offer a framework through which future possibilities can be envisioned and realized. This focus on mythology as a foundational element positions her work within the larger tapestry of Afrofuturism, where reclaiming African cultural heritage is a central concern.

In examining how African mythology shapes future narratives, Sunstrum aligns her essay with the core tenets of Afrofuturism. Afrofuturism reimagines futures through the lens of African and diasporic experiences, often using elements of science fiction and fantasy to explore themes of identity, technology, and resilience (Eshun, 2003). Sunstrum's integration of African mythos into these future narratives underscores the continuity between past and future, a hallmark of Afrofuturism. Moreover, her work contributes a unique continental sensibility to the African futures discourse by emphasizing the geographical and cultural diversity of Africa. She highlights the dynamic and varied narratives emanating from different African regions, thus resisting a monolithic portrayal of the continent. This diversity is emblematic of contemporary Afrofuturism, which celebrates a plurality of voices and experiences within the African diaspora, illustrating the multiple paths available for African futures (Womack, 2013).

Sunstrum's essay foregrounds a dialogue between historical and futuristic dimensions, inviting a reimagining of Africa's place in the global future. Her incorporation of myth as a narrative tool ensures that African futures are not divorced from the continent's complex histories. This approach provides a template for thinking about Africa's future in a way that is both rooted in tradition and open to innovation. Therefore, Sunstrum's "Afro-Mythology and African Futurism" provides a foundational framework for understanding African futures through the lens of mythology and history, aligning with and enriching contemporary Afrofuturism narratives.

African futurism envisions futures through an African cultural lens, embracing narratives that root in Indigenous philosophies, cosmologies, and histories. Recognized often as stylistic movements of speculative fiction, these genres have literary forebears from Africa who have paved the way with their unique storytelling styles. Daniel Fagunwa, author of *Forest of a Thousand Daemons* (1938/2013), is considered one of the pioneers of African speculative fiction. Fagunwa's work integrates Yoruba mythology and folklore, depicting fantastical journeys and spiritual quests within supernatural realms. His narratives are steeped in traditional African cosmology and exist as early blueprints for African futurist themes. These tales not only entertain but also explore intricate human-nature-spirit relationships, foreshadowing the genre's focus on blending African culture with speculative elements.

Amos Tutuola, known for *The Palm-Wine Drinkard* (1952), expands on the themes initiated by Fagunwa. Tutuola's narrative navigates an otherworldly journey filled with mystery and mythos, serving as a critical link between oral traditions and written narrative forms. His works delve into the African psyche's fantastical aspects, where traditional beliefs intersect with surreal imagery. Tutuola's distinctive storytelling voice aligns closely with African futurism and Afrofuturism's focus on diaspora experiences and cultural reclamation through speculative narratives. Cyprian Ekwensi's *An African Night's Entertainment* (1941) offers another dimension, weaving together fables and moral tales with modernity and tradition. Ekwensi's use of folklore rapidly introduces speculative fiction elements to popular African literature, providing cultural insights and rich speculative themes. Early in the 20th century, these authors' contributions demonstrate a blending of traditional stories with speculative futures, crafting a comprehensive landscape that subsequently shapes Afrofuturism and African futurism. Their works conjure visions that celebrate African identities, philosophies, and cosmic interpretations, establishing a heritage from which modern-day Afro-speculative fiction derives inspiration and continuity.

Background on Futurology and Africa

During the Cold War, with many nations newly independent, the seeds of an Afrocentric view of the future experienced a renaissance among futurologists and scholars who envisioned possible African futures. Kwame Nkrumah was among the first African thinkers to posit an Afrocentric philosophical approach to Africa's development (Asante, 2017). In international organizations and policy think tanks, Africa was promoted as one of the potential future worlds and the object of British American historical destiny disrupted by the Berlin Conference division. Scientific futures were vital for social and political development, but their feasibility resulted from tensions during the Cold War, and this Western project used archival sources and fictional futures to analyze how these debates reflected Europe's past and role in shaping Africa in the future. African nation-states were imagined as hypothetical scenarios in policy discourses and science fiction and emphasized the West's worldview's impact on Africa's past and future (Asante, 2017; Elia, 2014).

Between the 1960s and the 1980s, an African view of the future experienced a renaissance among select futurologists. Futurology, the scientific study of possible futures, became a new social science in the postwar decades. Following the wave of independence granted to some African nations, the new "independent" countries had to worry about neocolonialism; assassinations and coups became the subjects of intensive imaginations of future worlds among American, British, German, and French scholars and planners in the context of international organizations and policy think tanks. In this context, the history of a world centered on Europe was questioned, and Africa was promoted as one of the potential future worlds of international politics. The Berlin Conference division of Africa was understood as a tragedy that disrupted the natural development of the continent in line with British American historical destiny (Oboe, 2019).

The dynamics of the Cold War shaped the African presence in futurist thought. In the 1950s and early 1960s, the Cold War intersected with developments on the African continent, most specifically with decolonization and the subsequent scramble for and consolidation of new states, to stylize and indeed caricature Africa as both the continent most distant from the future and the birthplace of the postmodern utopia. The former was the consequence of Western anxiety about the obvious but unmanageable demand for real change in Africa, the threat of Soviet influence and subversion, the scale of ambitious, self-confidence nationalist projects, and the nature of the terrain these experiments were taking place in; the latter, the result of the intellectual and emotional capture of many observers by the symbolism of newness, combined with the desire for drama and moral rehabilitation after four decades of threatened annihilation and actual catastrophe. Western futurology during this period crystallized how Africa and the African imagination were to be constructed internally and perceived externally; more specifically, it also provides an opportunity to concretely explore the linkages and interactions between the hegemonic systems sustaining futurism and the contending positions of the Soviet Union, the nonaligned movement, and the dissent emerging from within the Afro-Asian world (Brennan, 2021; Chapman, 2023).

The Deep State and the Legacy of Black Power Sci-Fi

The concept of the deep state refers to a form of clandestine governance where unelected bureaucrats or secret networks influence state policy and decisions, often bypassing democratic processes. This intangible yet impactful system has had profound effects on global politics, particularly visible in the assassinations of figures like Patrice Lumumba and Malcolm X, shaping African diasporic movements such as Black Power and elements of Black science fiction. Patrice Lumumba, the first prime minister of independent Congo, represented anticolonial and Pan-African aspirations. His assassination in 1961, under the orders of American president Eisenhower, within less than a year of Congo's independence, was reportedly orchestrated with help from international intelligence agencies, particularly the CIA (Gibbs, 1991). Lumumba's death was a direct strike against African sovereignty and resonated deeply within the African diaspora, galvanizing movements like Black Power that sought to resist imperialism and assert self-determination.

Parallelly, Malcolm X, a pivotal Black nationalist leader in the United States, coerced global attention with his advocacy for human rights and Pan-African unity. His assassination in 1965 is surrounded by controversies involving possible FBI and CIA complicity, reflecting domestic deep-state operations (Marable, 2011). Malcolm X's ties to African liberation movements, including his meetings with leaders like Nasser and Nkrumah, demonstrated an international intersectionality of resistance against racial oppression and imperial influence.

The deaths of Lumumba and Malcolm X were more than just failings in political aspirations; they signified the suppression of Black leadership by deep-state mechanisms, influencing the shift toward global Black consciousness. This consciousness emerged more dynamically within the Black Power movement in the 1960s, which advanced self-determination, cultural pride, and resistance to systemic racism (Joseph, 2006). The movement's exponents often referenced global collaborations and betrayals, as seen in Lumumba's and Malcolm X's trajectories, emphasizing a link between domestic racial struggles and the international fight against colonialism.

Simultaneously, the legacy of these leaders permeated Black science fiction, where authors like John A. Williams and Sam Greenlee explored themes of resistance, identity, and dystopia—a nod to the shadowy workings of deep-state-like entities and the relentless quest for autonomy. These narratives paralleled the sociopolitical climate of the era, using speculative fiction to critique and reimagine sociopolitical realities, infusing Black Power ideologies into futuristic storytelling. Thus, the intricate network of the deep state, the catalytic assassinations of Lumumba and Malcolm X, and the resultant spread of international Black Power thought are interconnected, leaving a lasting imprint on the 1960s geopolitical landscape and cultural expressions like Black science fiction.

However, this tension reflected the philosophical divides in the African diaspora around politics and its future community development. The mid-1960s marked a move away from the perceived limitations of the traditional civil rights movement despite the passage of the Civil Rights Acts of 1964 and 1965, because it was also a time in which we saw the assassination of Malcolm X, the Watts rebellion of 1965, and the 1967 publication of Stokely Carmichael's and Charles Hamilton's *Black Power* (Taylor, 2021). Furthermore, Bayard Rustin, an advisor to the civil rights movement leadership, wrote two important articles during this period, "From Protest to Politics" (1965) and "Black Power and Coalition Politics" (1966), believing Black Power could influence the growth of anti-Black forces (Taylor, 2021). The subsequent rejection of Black Power and nationalism as a strategic expression for people of African descent and the promotion of assimilationist behavior repacked, reproduced for political scientists, community leaders, and the white liberal establishment a Black-white interdependency (Taylor, 2021). However, like the Black studies movement and Black Arts movement, the Black Power sci-fi community emerged from *below* in Black communities with overlapping generations having memories of Jim Crow or colonialism and new realities of survival in an emerging American technostate that no longer needed their labor (Yette, 1971).

The emergence of Black Power science fiction during the Cold War is a compelling chapter in literary history, interweaving the ideological currents of the civil rights movement, decolonization, and Cold War geopolitics. While traditionally overshadowed by more mainstream narratives, works by authors like John A. Williams and Sam Greenlee provided a unique lens on African American experiences and aspirations. The Black Power movement of the 1960s and 1970s was characterized by its emphasis on racial pride, self-sufficiency, and the development of Black political and economic power. Within this sociopolitical context, science fiction became a medium through which African diasporan authors could envision futures that transcended the oppressive realities of their time. This genre allowed for the reimagining of identity, race relations, and societal structures. For example,

John A. Williams's novel, *The Man Who Cried I Am* (1967), while not traditionally classified as science fiction, uses speculative elements to explore the pervasive themes of racial injustice and paranoia during the Cold War. The book is a fictionalized account of the Black Power movement and its leaders, encapsulating the disillusionment and pessimism felt by many African Americans with both domestic policies and international Cold War politics (Hancuff, 2018). The novel's speculative nature emerges through its exploration of global conspiracies, like the King Alfred plan, suggesting that the oppression of Black individuals was orchestrated at the highest societal levels, a concept aligning with the genre's thematic explorations of power and control. Sam Greenlee's *The Spook Who Sat by the Door* (1969) presents a powerful narrative that intertwines elements of espionage with utopian visions of urban guerilla warfare. The novel, later adapted into a film, tells the story of the first Black CIA officer, who uses his training to spark a revolutionary movement.

Critically, this work envisions the coalescence of liberatory Black communities into a formidable force challenging systemic oppression (Mitchell, 2023). The speculative nature of Greenlee's work is emblematic of Black Power science fiction, highlighting both the potential and peril of insurgency as a means of liberation. The works of John A. Williams and Sam Greenlee reflected the complexities of African American identity and resistance during the Cold War. By merging the speculative with the political, they forged a space within science fiction that allowed for radical reimagining of Black existence, offering profound commentary on race, power, and the future. However, during the Cold War, a primordial phase can be found in the beginnings of the free-jazz movement in the late 1950s. One of the first attempts to redefine music experimented with by this new genre was to abolish previous notions of sonic production and literary expression, which provided the fertile ground for the unpredictable emergences of new hybrid forms. Three key figures in this experimentation would go on to frame the late 20th-century debate on Afrofuturism: Sun Ra, Samuel Delany, and Octavia Butler.

By the late 1970s, futurology's expensive and inappropriately detailed planning outcomes were fundamentally low on Africa's priority lists. African governments had found the future more unpredictable than they had anticipated, possibly to the surprise of Africana futurologists, some of whom were created to meet state sponsorship parameters and pandering to other ideologies. Freedom dreams were long on dreamtime, and brief encounters between ruling party representatives, social scientific idols, and potential Afronauts were about as fruitful as futurology's notions of scientific planning. The greatest threat to Africa's cities and future was the most intensive form of intersectoral interaction, coups, war, and assassination (Chapman et al., 2022). Correspondingly during this period, in the African diaspora, the Black speculative tradition began to re-emerge in response to political tensions manifesting in various forms like music, literature, and art, articulating deep time and wide space, a sense of passes: ephemeral power began to develop (de Paor-Evans, 2018). Black sci-fi, a cyborg sensibility, frequently extends realizing alternative formation and or obvious fantasies while still holding an anachronic sense and often framing Blackness as an inescapable horizon (Armillas-Tiseyra, 2023; Eshun, 2022; Young & Reid, 2023).

Sun Ra

Sun Ra, born Herman Poole Blount, is revered not only for his avant-garde jazz compositions but also for his unique philosophical outlook, which draws from a rich tapestry of influences, including Freemasonry, Heterodox Islam, and various secret societies. Freemasonry, a fraternal organization with its origins in the late 16th to early 17th century, has long intrigued intellectuals with its esoteric symbolism and focus on moral fortitude. Sun Ra's approach to music and life reflects Masonic ideals such as enlightenment and brotherhood. According to McLarney & Idris (2023), Sun Ra was intrigued by Masonic rituals, which often incorporate ancient symbols and practices aimed at personal transformation. This is mirrored in Sun Ra's emphasis on cosmic awareness and spiritual elevation, as he often spoke of his music as a transformative force, akin to the philosophical journey Masons undertake.

Heterodox interpretations of Islam, particularly those linked to African American movements such as the Moorish Science Temple and the Nation of Islam, played a role in shaping Sun Ra's spiritual and cultural aesthetic (McLarney & Idris, 2023). Sun Ra adopted similar syncretic views, embracing ancient Egyptian culture and sci-fi futurism to forge a unique identity that bypassed traditional Western religious narratives. His adoption of an "Angel Race" identity can be seen as a metaphorical extension of these beliefs, as it aligns with the Moorish reimagining of racial identity and spiritual awakening. Sun Ra's affinity for secrecy, symbols, and surreal narratives is reminiscent of the mystery surrounding many secret societies, like the Rosicrucians. These societies often elucidate the idea of hidden wisdom accessible through personal initiation and exploration, a theme prevalent in Sun Ra's work. His deep dive into unorthodox teachings and his portrayal as a mysterious, otherworldly figure reflect the influence of such organizations.

Sun Ra's cosmic philosophies and avant-garde jazz embodied a kind of proto-Afrofuturism that offered both a critique and a reimagining of Black identity during a time of racial oppression and civil rights upheavals. Sun Ra's musical journey took a pivotal turn in the mid-1950s when he formed the Arkestra in Chicago, adopting avant-garde styles and experimenting with electronic instruments and thematic compositions. His work defied traditional jazz by incorporating space-themed elements and creating entire soundscapes that suggested an otherworldly presence. This divergence from norms wasn't simply artistic exploration; it was a profound response to the societal limitations imposed on Black Americans. By envisioning a cosmic identity, Sun Ra crafted an alternate reality where African Americans could transcend earthly boundaries of racism and oppression (Szwed, 1997).

His 1974 film *Space Is the Place* further elucidates his philosophical programming. Infusing science fiction with sharp social critique, the film casts Sun Ra heroically as he battles oppressive structures while offering members of the African diaspora a utopian alternative. The narrative is steeped in Black speculative thought, whereby Sun Ra uses music as both a weapon and a refuge, charging his audience to think beyond the physical world and into a realm of possibility where they can redefine their destiny (McLeod, 2008). The backdrop of the Cold War fostered innovation and the questioning of existential paradigms, dovetailing with his cosmic aspirations. During a time when space exploration was a symbol of national pride and scientific prowess, Sun Ra repurposed this narrative, aligning it with the struggles and strivings of Black America. By likening space with liberation, he depicted an escape from a racially charged terrestrial reality into an infinite cosmic landscape. His declaration of space as an abode for Black individuals was not only a potent metaphor but served as a political stance against racial injustice and social constraints of the era (Eshun, 2003).

In summary, Sun Ra's avant-garde cosmic space jazz and the film *Space Is the Place* served as critical cultural artifacts in expressing the African American experience during the Cold War. Through their synthesis, he provided a platform for introspection and liberation that resonated deeply with an audience eager for change. Sun Ra's cosmic philosophy emphasized collective transformation and transcending the limits of Earth culture, which profoundly impacted the Afrofuturist movement's future. He rejected Earth culture, believing that Black people should escape Western civilization's oppressive institutions, and thus wrote the highly influential poem "The Blues" with the burning line "This planet is doomed," urging humanity to leave planet Earth and explore the cosmos (Parhizkar, 2015). A sentiment that aligns with the argument that no one could ever come out of the same space—defined by one's ethnicity and, thus, historical oppression—as the one who was responsible for your enslavement, for war, strife, examination, and taxation (Brown, 2021).

Samuel R. Delany

A significant contributor to the Afrofuturist narrative during the late 20th century was Samuel R. Delany. Born in 1942 in New York City, he attended the New York State School of Industrial and Graphic Arts and the University of Pittsburgh while simultaneously publishing short stories in science fiction magazines. Novels like *Dhalgren* and the *Neveryóna* series engaged with sexual themes and otherness in science fiction and fantasy, bridging these genres and Black cultural discourse. These works utilize the tenets of speculative fiction, such as neologism and world-building, to provide engaging responses to the concerns of Black culture and negotiate competing forms of identity. Through merging narrative devices and concerns, Delany affirms the potential of storytelling, in all its forms, to reshape and liberate experience (Colmon, 2020; Young & Reid, 2023).

Delany's novels often delve into the complexities of race, identity, and power, themes central to the Black Power movement of the 1960s and 1970s. This movement, which sought to empower African Americans and challenge systemic racial injustice, finds resonances in Delany's exploration of marginalized characters and societies. For example, in *Dhalgren* (1975), Delany constructs a sprawling urban landscape that reflects the chaotic and transformative nature of civil rights upheavals. As Jerng (2011) noted, Delany's portrayal of race in *Dhalgren* serves as a critique of both racial segregation and the rift between idealistic representations of equality and grim realities faced by African Americans.

Cosmology, or the study of the universe's origins, structure, and dynamics, also features prominently in Delany's work. His interest in scientific concepts is evident in the complex world-building of novels like *Nova* (1968). Here, Delany melds the mechanics of space travel and elemental theory with character-driven narratives that explore existential questions. This novel exemplifies how Delany uses science fiction as a platform to discuss not only scientific advancements but also philosophical inquiries about the nature of humanity. According to Rutledge (2000), Delany's narrative structures often emulate the chaotic and unpredictable nature of the cosmos, reflecting broader themes of existential uncertainty and transformation.

Furthermore, Delany's impact on the evolution of science fiction lies in his ability to challenge conventional storytelling and thematic boundaries. Often celebrated among the New Wave of science fiction writers, Delany pushed the genre beyond its common tropes of space adventures and into realms of abstract thought and social experimentation. His works such as *Babel-17* (1966) use linguistic theory as a narrative device to explore the power of language in shaping reality, an innovative approach that expanded the scope of speculative fiction. Jameson (2016) describes Delany's unique narrative style as a blend of speculative imagination with acute commentary on human condition, thus reshaping the landscape of science fiction. Delany's contributions reflect a profound intersection of intellectual and cultural movements. His works stand as a testament to the power of storytelling in addressing and illuminating the profound complexities of human society and the cosmos.

Octavia Butler

Octavia Butler's novel *Kindred*, often celebrated for its intricate portrayal of antebellum slavery, and which connects the neo–slave narrative to the Black speculative tradition, has had a significant impact on African American identity. The novel's time-traveling protagonist, Dana, serves as a conduit through which Butler addresses complex themes of identity, power, and communal struggle. At its core, *Kindred* examines the tensions between Black empowerment and the harsh realities of racial oppression, providing a nuanced critique of the Black Power movement of the 1960s and 1970s.

The Black Power movement was characterized by its emphasis on racial pride, self-sufficiency, and the strengthening of Black communities. It emerged as a response to the perceived limitations of earlier civil rights strategies, advocating for a more assertive and uncompromising stance against racism (Joseph, 2006). However, Butler's *Kindred* offers a counterpoint to idealized visions of empowerment by depicting the stark, brutal realities of slavery. Through Dana's time-travel experiences, Butler confronts the romanticized notions of Black resistance by highlighting the complexity and interracial entanglements in America's history. Dana's forced returns to the antebellum South serve as a mechanism for Butler to explore historical continuity in racial oppression, indicating that the struggle for empowerment is deeply rooted in an unresolved past. This temporal dislocation compels readers to understand personal empowerment not just in terms of resistance but also within the context of survival and adaptation (Rowell & Butler, 1997). Dana's interactions with her white ancestor, Rufus, complicate notions of empowerment and complicity, showcasing the nuanced power dynamics often overlooked by simplistic oppositional narratives of the Black Power era.

Moreover, Butler's narrative critique lies in its deconstruction of the notion of an untainted, isolated Black identity. Dana's encounters reveal that Black identity is inextricably linked with a history that involves pain, compromise, and strategic navigation within oppressive structures. *Kindred* functions as a profound counternarrative to some elements of the Black Power movement. By intertwining themes of survival, historical immutability, and the intricacies of power through time travel and historical introspection, Butler compels readers to rethink empowerment and identity as contingent, multifaceted phenomena, highlighting that true liberation requires a confrontation with the past's layered realities. Through *Kindred*, Butler enriches the discourse on Black Power, framing it within a broader, more reflective historical and cultural context.

Butler's novels *Patternmaster* and *Mind of My Mind* describe the lives of a populace of hybridized individuals with psionic and empathic powers. All were born of a shared "Spawned" bloodline, the progeny of a slave matriarch known as "The Pattern," who rules with an iron fist and a collective telepathic mind. Patternist acolytes live directly through her blood echoes while tamed hellhounds hunt down defiant Others who resist this yoke (Thaxter, 2020). The novels depict a harsh castigation across the horizon line of difference, wherein all born of the bloodline are common property and a pool of papal imperial authority. In such worlds, Butler's Black bodies wander on the fringe of poaching, exile, experimentation, and life outside the law. Butler's writing explores the darker threads running through both Butler's work and her life, namely power, power relations, and oppression. No matter the futuristic setting or the science involved, these are the themes she seems to return to repeatedly. Butler's theory asserts that this dark side of human nature, at its root, results from our all-too-human unwillingness (or inability) to accept difference (McGarity, 2009). In Butler's hands, each side of the difference becomes alien, terrifying, contemptible, and incomprehensible. Extending this thought further, difference or even perceived racial or species impurity can be exploited and used to justify genocidal tendencies. From a purely Africological perspective, this suggests the necessity to revisit, reexamine, and utilize a Ma'atian ethic to interrogate the agency reduction of the African existence and that of all humans and other lifeforms.

Even though these dreams have obvious personal implications, Butler transformed them into incomparably more disturbing stories than her biographically safer ones would have been simply because she refused to describe other people's terror. She insisted on conveying, directly and dramatically, what the terror was supposed to feel like, making the point that the thing feared could not possess language or even, often, a shape while fear obscures comprehension. Moreover, Butler's Afrofuturist feminism interrogates themes around ancestry, power, and race that are the focus of Africana studies though sometimes missing in the scholarship (Morris, 2019).

The mid- to late 20th century witnessed increased interest in Black experimental jazz, Black science fiction literature, and the relationship between the two. This interest was partly sparked by archival research, and the sonic stew of Sun Ra and the Black Arts movement from the 1960s offered an alternative soundscape and viewpoint to the standard jazz narratives dominated by white men and institutions (Elia, 2014). At the same time, music and literature were steeped in the 1950s and 1960s African American culture, responding to various assumptions about Blacks and science as a response to an emerging identity. Widespread social discontent, confinement in suffocating spaces, systematic distortions, and blatant misinterpretations were framed as manifestations of madness and interpretative genius. The larger social context in which people lived—cities crumbling with poverty and unemployment, racism, police brutality, and discontent—required visionary thought on the path toward social change. In addition, fostering a visionary, science-oriented fictional thought-world fit with the powerful yearning for space exploration at that time.

The ideological and social legacy of the narrative frame was prolific, deeply entrenched in contemporary Black culture, and fundamental to the artistic experimentation of the Black Arts movement. In parallel with various cultural interpretations of planet Earth as the Black man's hell, utopian visions of another (good) Earth also became thematic preoccupations in various Black genre films (e.g., "space hip-hop") and literature. These reflexive Black narratives were deeply transmedial and sought new, coherent sound images for Black futures that only found credence in detached environments like outer space. The reception and entrenchment of these speculative fictional thought worlds emphasized and naturalized "Afrofuturism" as a coherent cultural phenomenon (Ibrahim, 2015). Afrofuturism is a rearticulated genre label addressing pre-existing sonic and literary textures, themes, narratives, and questions in the current proliferation of Black cultural production.

CHAPTER 4

The Dark Enlightenment and the Collapse of the Anglo Liberal World Order

The examination of Western fascism through the lens of metaphysical elements reveals deep connections with both accelerationism and the concept of the Dark Enlightenment. These philosophical currents, while diverging in some respects, share a preoccupation with themes of collapse, transformation, and transcendence. Western fascism, imbued with metaphysical elements, searches for an overarching narrative that transcends quotidian existence. This narrative often centers on notions of purity, destiny, and a return to some imagined primordial state of unity and strength. As Carl Schmitt (2005), an intellectual figure often associated with fascistic ideas, asserts, the concept of the modern state is an expression of a secularized theological framework. This statement highlights the metaphysical underpinnings within fascism's search for order and authority outside the bounds of conventional morality or politics.

Accelerationism, meanwhile, proposes a radical intensification of capitalism's intrinsic tendencies toward innovation and collapse to bring about transformative change. Accelerationism, despite its radical differences from fascism, shares a metaphysical engagement with the notion of an inevitable and transcendent restructuring of society. As theorist Nick Land (2011) has suggested, capital radically changes everything and helps feed the destructive impulses necessary for creation and recreation. The concept of the Dark

Enlightenment, popularized by thinkers like Curtis Yarvin, a.k.a. Mencius Moldbug (2008), suggests the dismantling of modern democratic systems in favor of a return to pre-Enlightenment governance structures. Like both fascism and accelerationism, the Dark Enlightenment engages with a metaphysical vision of transformation, one that seeks to return to an idealized past or to carve a novel structure out of the ruins of modernity. In essence, Western fascism, accelerationism, and the Dark Enlightenment each articulate a desire to transcend the existing social order, whether through purification, accelerated collapse, or devolution to premodern power systems. They share a metaphysical vision of societal transformation, whether forward or backward, and challenge contemporary paradigms by proposing alternatives that appeal to existential and transcendental desires. While these paths diverge in praxis and ethos, their metaphysical intersections provide fertile ground for examining the complexities and continuities in modern ideological thought.

This chapter provides an overview of social and political changes in the Western world over the past three decades. Before we proceed, it is essential to discuss the term "dark enlightenment" itself, which has various meanings. The principles of democracy, liberty, industry, and equality have recently been contrasted with human nature (Morlino, 2020). There is a continued focus on industrial and technological achievements as well as a rejection of the idea of equality for all. Instead, there is a push for individualism, meritocracy, and embracing diversity and genius. The main issue lies in the move away from meritocracy, with a gradual reconsideration of the role of nations and their sovereignty as a means for restoring individual diversity and talent (Morlino, 2020).

The Dark Enlightenment views the liberal world order as unachievable and undesirable, the politically correct establishment as tyrannical and destructive, and the notion of universal progress as a faith not shared by most people. From this perspective, substantial predictions are made. The analysis is rather stimulating and much needed, illuminating numerous current long-standing problems and the possible flaws of attempts to solve them. However, it is essential to delve deeper into the intricacies of this perspective to grasp its implications fully. The Dark Enlightenment serves as a means for critically examining the liberal world order and presenting it as an unattainable and undesired state. It argues that the politically correct establishment exercises tyrannical control, stifling free thought and inhibiting diversity of ideas. This domination is seen as inherently detrimental, leading to the erosion of traditional values and moral foundations. Moreover, this alternative viewpoint contests the notion of universal progress as a shared belief among the masses.

According to the Dark Enlightenment, the notions of continuous advancement and improvement are more akin to faith rather than universally embraced truths. It suggests that while there may be pockets of progress, large segments of society do not necessarily buy in to this narrative. The predictions put forth by this ideology are substantial and thought-provoking. The Dark Enlightenment challenges the status quo by shedding light on long-standing problems and critically examining attempted solutions. It delves into the systemic flaws that underlie current approaches and provides an insightful critique of various societal issues.

Nevertheless, when closely scrutinized, the predictions offered by the Dark Enlightenment fail to hold up. The original ideas presented may initially appear captivating, but they reveal their lack of novelty upon closer inspection. While the analysis provided by the Dark Enlightenment sheds valuable light on ongoing issues, it ultimately falls short when it comes to offering groundbreaking proposals or solutions. As a movement, its ability to provide innovative ideas for the future is hindered by its preoccupation with promoting traditional ideals and criticizing modern liberalism (Morlino, 2020). This narrow focus limits its potential impact on shaping a new societal framework. However, it is vital to acknowledge the perspective it brings to the table to understand the current ideological landscape fully. The Dark Enlightenment is a set of ideas associated with versions 1.0 and 2.0 of Nick Land's Dark Reformation, the anarcho-capitalist writings of Hans Hermann-Hoppe, the accelerationism of Land and the CCRU, neoreaction, and the writings of Curtis Yarvin. Other theorists associated with these ideas include instapundit Iain Livingston, the pseudonymous Mencius Moldbug, anti-HBD Jim Donald, and Derbyleaks pioneer John Derbyshire (Delaney, 2020; Ikenberry, 2020; Parsi, 2021).

The Dark Enlightenment shares many philosophical beliefs with European counter-Enlightenment movements and far-right thinkers. For instance, Joseph de Maistre, who criticized Enlightenment social philosophy, argued that imposing a single morality on entire societies was impossible and harmful. This ideology advocates for a strong belief in individual effort and emphasizes the need to revamp economic policy, budget policy, stabilization policy, monetary policy, and planned resource priorities to counteract biases in libertarianism. Influential figures in the movement, such as Mencius Moldbug and Nick Land, reject egalitarianism and promote hierarchy and traditional values. Due to its affinity for postmodern ideas, the Dark Enlightenment is challenging to define and understand. Because of the anonymity and strength of online social media platforms, the community is complex and not easily understood. Many supporters use pseudonyms on the internet, and the movement's ideology is most prominent on websites like 4chan, 8chan, and Reddit. While the term *Dark Enlightenment* is not widely used in public discourse, its ideas are visible in various technological and scholarly circles. The movement is supported by a range of organizations, including the Artificial General Intelligence Research Institute and the Machine Intelligence Research Institute, both of which discuss the societal impact of artificial intelligence and advocate for the use of friendly AI (Lok, 2023).

The series of crises that followed the 2008 financial crisis has led to an increasing feeling of catastrophe among observers, especially those in the center and on the political right. The rise of the Dark Enlightenment has significantly strengthened these critiques of the liberal world order, fueled by the perception that the liberal world order had attempted to maintain global dominance while advocating for open borders and promoting the delegitimization of cultural identity and tradition. This juxtaposition has deeply influenced the growing number of voices that have joined in critiquing the liberal world order, focusing not only on the internal contradictions within liberal and left perspectives but also voicing concerns regarding the affordability and sustainability of liberal democracy from conservative and radical viewpoints (Delaney, 2020). Such concerns have emerged as a result of an intricate and interdisciplinary analysis that scrutinizes the multifaceted implications arising from the interplay between economic, social, and political factors within the framework of the liberal world order. By exploring these dimensions, individuals from various ideological backgrounds have expanded the scope of the critique, contributing to a more comprehensive understanding of the challenges and potential alternatives that lie ahead (Ikenberry, 2020; Porter, 2020).

Before World War II, inequality was seen as rising, largely due to the increased visibility of the super-rich. By contrast, inequality after World War II declined to a point, and then the accelerated rise since the 1980s began. This return to a more unequal age has been both international and domestic. In developing countries, some economists have seen intense levels of both economic and, to a lesser extent, familial inequality. While it is the case that inequality today is higher in the United States and Latin America than in Africa, based on the internals of national scores, constraints are left (Klein & Pettis, 2020).

Globalization and the movement of immigrants are causing changes in domestic conditions and institutions, reflecting changes in international institutions. In some cases, increasing inequality has led to economic protectionism as a successful electoral strategy, like Trump's, during a time of low media confidence and increasing superintelligence. During a time of prolonged peace, successful electoral strategies will be met with unsuccessful ones (Anderson, 2023; Césaire, 2000). Having the freedom to think in that manner is a potent tool. If we are not, indeed, doomed, and if accelerationism allows the technological and innovative capabilities of modern society to appear benign and in control of the future and reduces the fears of collapse and civilization-ending risks to some extent by eliminating the need to consider them, and by highlighting how absurd the doomsayers who continue to worry about these issues have become, this is a significant development. This makes accelerationism, in a perverse way, the progressive option, with the key distinction being that technological doors have no barriers. While there are technological barriers, they are insufficient to engender trust in any long-term cultural or political suppression that does not come from cultural or political institutions themselves. As stated in the introduction to *#ACCELERATE*, "Despair seems to be the dominant sentiment of the contemporary Left, whose crisis perversely mimics its foe, consoling itself either with the minor pleasures of shrill denunciation, mediated protest, and ludic disruptions" (Mackay & Avanessian, 2014, p. 24). Rhetoric such as pattern austerity will impede efforts to recognize the costs of the same security measures. It will emphasize that if the only way forward is either irrational or terrifyingly more of the same, the rational choice is to embrace the accelerating progress of a world shaped by the mystical standard of technological acceptance (Noys, 2023; Mirsky, 2023).

The rise of the Dark Enlightenment can be understood by examining the intersection of technology and ideology. One thought-provoking viewpoint comes from the accelerationists, who question whether modern, globalized people are cursed or blessed. They suggest that people are damned in a more efficient and advanced manner than ever before, leading to a consequential outcome. This type of questioning, akin to laughter, effectively undermines legitimacy. It presents the actions as not only thinkable and not a threat but also as something so ridiculous that it can be easily dismissed with laughter. The underlying suggestion is that this is not the terrifying, inevitable end of the world but rather an overly complex and overthought deception that can be laughed off (Nilsson, 2022; Schmidt, 2022; Fürstenberg, 2022).

Pursuing this thread of thought, it is easy to see how the Dark Enlightenment attracted a following on social media. Contemporary scholarship explains that groups use group heuristics to make decisions about collective action, allowing for quick mobilization, even for extreme and violent causes that appeal to only a small number of people (Fagan, 2024). The roots of mimetic desire play a role in the targeting process, where unrelated individuals with shallow social ties become the first adopters of a marketing strategy. These like-minded loners come from a diverse pool of individuals seeking new identities through popular culture and group branding. Given a long history of manipulating the human population, the question is not whether someone will exploit our desire for high-status self-reinvention in pop culture, but rather how often and to what extent. The answer is clear: exploitation happens frequently and consistently (Krafft et al., 2021; Kameda et al., 2022; Teixeira et al., 2020).

Tufekci and Wilson (2012), social media scholars, have brought to light a significant revelation regarding the impact of social media platforms like Facebook. They astutely point out that these platforms frequently play a role in the proliferation of extreme ideologies by cultivating what they aptly term cognitive bubbles. These bubbles essentially create an environment where individuals are consistently exposed only to information that aligns with their pre-existing beliefs, ultimately causing a narrowing of shared knowledge and an escalation of animosity toward opposing viewpoints. Consequently, this phenomenon breeds a society characterized by deep polarization. Moreover, Tufekci and Wilson emphasize that social media holds the power to magnify messages via the concept of social proof, which results in the exponential dissemination of contentious or inflammatory content. The inherent nature of these platforms—which thrive on likes, shares, and comments—tends to amplify and propel such messages to the forefront of public consciousness. This can lead to the rapid and widespread distribution of controversial narratives, further intensifying the already volatile landscape of online discourse. Only through a collective effort to foster diverse perspectives, encourage open dialogue, and promote critical thinking can we hope to mitigate the detrimental effects of social media's influence on societal dynamics (Barberá, 2020; Harel et al., 2020).

Nationalism and Populism

The straightforward rejection of conspiracy theories in global politics is only meaningful for a short time, as interest groups continue to act as if they are part of a secretive plot that benefits everyone involved. The Brexit referendums and the rise of the Trump phenomenon show the political effects of commercial and academic institutions failing to recognize national interests. The growing influence of right-wing political movements in Europe is another result of ignoring the impact of unrestricted mass immigration on the social and cultural cohesion of Western European nations. Moreover, the intricate web of conspiracy theories woven within the fabric of global politics extends far beyond what meets the eye. While dismissing such notions as baseless may be tempting, the striking persistence of interest groups perpetuating clandestine plots, even as they appear innocuous to the untrained eye, must be acknowledged.

The fleeting nature of debunking these theories swiftly becomes apparent as new layers unfurl and secretive agendas persist. The ramifications of this covert political landscape have been laid bare in recent events, serving as a stark reminder of the consequences brought forth by disregarding national interests. Take, for instance, the Brexit referendums that shook the world, reverberating through the very foundations of global governance. The failure of commercial and academic institutions to acknowledge the significance of such momentous decisions shackled them to a state of complacency, allowing the interests of the few to overshadow the needs of the many (Haynes, 2020). Similarly, the rise of the Trump phenomenon demonstrated the seismic impact of neglecting national interests within the intricate tapestry of global politics. Academic and commercial institutions, preoccupied with their own agendas, turned a blind eye to the pulse of the nation and, in doing so, failed to anticipate the clamor for change that reverberated throughout the United States. As we have witnessed, the consequences were far-reaching and continue to shape the geopolitical landscape. Thus, the simplistic rejection of conspiracy theories in global politics proves to be a transitory shield against the vast complexities that lie beneath the surface. It is imperative that commercial and academic institutions peel back the layers of secrecy surrounding our political landscape, recognizing national interests as a vital component of successful governance. Only through a comprehensive understanding of the impact of mass immigration on societal cohesion can we understand the fragility of the social behaviors that enables a level of cohesion within the liberal world-order Western European nations (Haynes, 2020; Mamonova & Franquesa, 2020; Sandrin, 2021).

Many political pundits present the 2008 financial crisis as the trigger for discontent and fear while also pointing out that the performance of democracies has been underwhelming and is the leading cause for the decrease in trust in governments worldwide. This contributes to a broader sentiment of dissatisfaction with the belief that democracies are no longer the best system for improving the lives of most citizens. The rapid economic decline has significant and harmful consequences, leading to a loss of trust in political leaders and potentially creating an environment where authoritarian demagogues can gain support. According to Samuel Huntington (1993), disappointments with democratic rule often encourage the rise of authoritarian governments. Regimes may be slow to deliver on their aspirations, and expectations among citizens increase concomitantly as time passes. When the juncture between fact and expectation is tremendous, the disparity may lead to an erosion of confidence in the regime. Diminishing confidence, a threat to economic well-being and security, or the aspiration to achieve political goals are commonly acknowledged causes of unrest and support for alternative forms of governance. Unfortunately, authoritarian leaders may benefit from these democratic contradictions. Many democracies appear ill-disposed to reinvigorate these emaciated social contracts (Kilavuz & Sumaktoyo, 2020).

Challenges to Democratic Institutions

The advancement of modern communication and control technology not only increased forms of domination and constraints on communication but also introduced unprecedented levels of social complexity. This encompassed a greater number of actors and a wider range of interests and interactions than ever before. If unchecked, social complexity could lead to pluralism or shift the focus from pursuing the common good to embracing various conflicts and disagreements. This idea has existed since Montesquieu classified monarchy, dictatorship, and pure democracy. Unlike other forms of government, democracies are distinct because complex social structures unite in mutual acknowledgment (Balland et al., 2022).

The liberal consensus has long maintained that politics should be free of certainty claims, as they are seen as inherently exclusionary and divisive. However, upon closer examination, it becomes clear that this perspective does not align with the realities of our world. In fact, our existence is marked by a constant state of disagreement, where various individuals and groups hold differing opinions and interests. To address this reality, efforts have been made to establish institutions that foster a sense of common interest and unity amid diversity. These initiatives aim to bridge the gap between conflicting individual interests, recognizing that without mutual understanding and cooperation, people are bound to be pitted against one another. In essence, the idea that politics should be devoid of certainty is noble in its intention to promote inclusivity; however, it fails to acknowledge the fundamental nature of disagreement and the need to foster a collective understanding and recognition of shared power. Only through such cooperative efforts can we hope to build a society that serves the interests of all its members (Bistagnino, 2020; Adler & Drieschova, 2021).

Data within nations and political entities cannot be manipulated in the same manner as data between nations. Countries and political entities are not adjusted for differences. As demonstrated in the first chapter, focusing on the most troubled areas of order, those at the highest risk of descending into violence, exposes the extent of challenges the broader world faces. This approach is not a fair solution. However, following the logic of Black Lives Matter, it is necessary to allocate resources and social movements to the poorest segments of society and champions of human rights. Their issues are the most overlooked in the data. Even in prosperous, globally minded political entities, there will always be some individuals who support movements like Brexit. But institutions that disregard the magnitude of challenges and fail to provide positive narratives do not understand how to assist the majority of those who are losing out—their constituents who don't understand what's happening—making them valid targets for populist movements and, in fact, they are significant failures of the democratic political system. The appeal of these movements can be compelling at times. And when they fail, illiberal forces from both the Left and the Right step in to address the resulting issues; this is where the problem lies (Chun, 2021; Bjørnskov & Rode, 2020; Fourcade & Gordon, 2020).

The liberal international order was built on a foundation that was designed to prevent the rise of the very nihilistic ideologies the cycle of ideology and violence revolts against. Donald Trump's election and his many violations of the norms and institutions of the liberal international order have tested some of the strengths and weaknesses of this system. Many of these violations, like his level of corruption, were less critical in rank-order measures of institutional strength than compliance problems and political polarization. Hence, the international system seemed strong on these aspects. The country survived Trump and pursued orthodox restoration on his eventual departure. But the system's survival was partly a product of a very robust bureaucracy, deep state, or the insulated oligarchal elite parts of the administrative state (Porter, 2020; Lake et al., 2021).

Ethnonationalism and Xenophobia

Ethnonationalist ideas heavily emphasize the importance of fostering robust and cohesive ethnocultural identities within a society. These ideas are often closely linked to advocating for stringent border control measures and the meticulous regulation of migration. Moreover, ethnonationalism typically rejects the concept of multiculturalism and instead favors policies and practices that promote a sense of homogeneity within a community. Additionally, it often leads to the exclusion and discrimination of minority groups within a society. This can result in increased tensions and conflicts between different ethnic and cultural communities.

From the perspective of ethnonationalists, societies characterized by significant heterogeneity and the resultant tensions stemming from diversity ultimately lead to the erosion of social capital. This, in turn, gives rise to a multitude of everyday disorders, a pervasive loss of social trust, and a general state of instability that can cause harm. Furthermore, adherents of ethnonationalist ideologies often assert that such circumstances frequently impede the open expression of public rationales and, instead, foster a climate where implicit rather than explicit legal contracts or agreements are consistently violated (Dikici, 2022; Adesanya 2021; Comaroff & Comaroff, 2022). Ethnonationalism and xenophobia play a significant role in the Dark Enlightenment ideology. They have arisen in reaction to demographic shifts and are characterized by a right-wing populism that romanticizes a nonexistent "golden age" and opposes globalization, liberalism, immigration, and ethnocultural diversity. This resistance raises serious concerns about environmental change, rights, and politics (Hull, 2022). For example, with the recent 2024 re-election victory of Donald Trump, which demonstrates increased support from disaffected people of African descent, a possible scenario to continue to undermine what he and his followers call the "Deep State" may occur, outlined as follows:

> The "MAGA (Make America Great Again) movement" and the "Black Nationalist community" forge a tactical alliance against a common adversary: the "Deep State." Though traditionally divergent in political priorities, both factions recognize mutual advantages in challenging this entrenched bureaucracy and a shared belief in its oversize influence over democratic and community institutions.
>
> **Alliance Rationale:**
> - MAGA Movement: This populist faction views the Deep State as an obstruction to democratic will, patriotic renewal, and economic freedom. They perceive it as hindering national priorities such as deregulation, immigration control, and transparency.
> - Black Nationalist Community: For Black nationalists, the Deep State symbolizes historic systemic racism, sustaining structures that marginalize and disenfranchise Black populations. They advocate for sovereignty, economic independence, and the dismantling of institutional injustice perpetuated by established authorities.
>
> **Joint Goals:**
> 1. Decentralization of Power: Both groups strive to curtail federal overreach by advocating for decentralized power structures, fostering local governance reflecting community values.

2. Increased Transparency: Demanding transparency enforces accountability, reducing clandestine operations within political systems unknown to public scrutiny.
3. Economic Reform: They seek reformative policies that address economic disparities. For the MAGA group, focusing on taxation and trade; whereas Black nationalists emphasize restitution and investment in Black-owned enterprises.

Strategic Collaboration:
- Information Campaigns: Utilizing social media platforms, shared narratives highlight conspiracies and inefficiencies attributed to the Deep State, rallying grassroots support from diverse backgrounds.
- Political Lobbying: Though ideologically different, their combined political pressure could influence policymakers through strategic lobbying, advocating for similar concerns like surveillance reform.
- Community Engagement: Joint community events emphasize self-reliance, education on constitutional rights, and advocacy for civil liberties, aiming to build bridges between communities typically perceived as opposed.

Potential Challenges:
- Ideological Differences: The contrasting core ideologies may present challenges in maintaining a cohesive strategy beyond short-term objectives.
- Public Perception: Skepticism arises from disparate public identities; maintaining legitimacy and trust requires careful navigation to avoid alienating core supporters.

This theory, although perhaps unlikely, presents an intriguing analysis of cross-sectional alliances against perceived elitist institutional control.

Afrofuturism and the Dark Enlightenment

Nick Land (2023) believes humanity cannot escape its nature as destructive and transcendent. People's intractable natures determine the teleological meaning of nature. The state of nature is the state of war. Afrofuturism and Land's Dark Enlightenment suggest differing attitudes toward nature and the networked digital world. Afrofuturism proposes that people should work to recover their lost organic connection with nature to create alternative pluralistic futures. Land argues that nonhuman forces such as capital, power, and intelligence are too strong for people to resist realistically. In this chapter, the framework for Afrofuturism 2.0 draws upon Afrofuturism and African historiography literature. After constructing the theoretical framework, I apply it to Nick Land's work to demonstrate its efficacy in political possibilities and the technosphere (Zamalin, 2022; Brock, 2020; Tynes et al., 2023).

Afrofuturism has aimed to revitalize the notion of a future growing from African diaspora culture, history, and the racial problems that haunt advanced technological societies within an African context and to encourage dialogue with the African diaspora community. Land is one of the leading thinkers of the philosophy of accelerationism, and he states that technology will free nature from humanity. This contradiction has specific implications for how people interrogate and enact humanity (Peattie, 2022). Afrofuturism 2.0 distinguishes itself from other, more utopian, framings by being less invested in presenting permanent hope, joy, or festivity. Instead, it shows rays of despair inside of economic systems, nation-states, and global networks. Conceptually, how does hope spring from Afrofuturism 2.0 under conditions far worse than those of the first efforts after the Cold War? More importantly, how does one build better futures when more egalitarian aspirations move those futures away from the West, its wealth, and its hubris? Indeed, how does desire coincide with better futures that are well adhered to but that loudly express the cost and sacrifice of formerly accepted ways of life (Asante, 2023; Underwood, 2022)?

Afrofuturism is a critical practice for envisioning Black life's political and societal possibilities and existence in historically and contemporary anti-Black societies. It celebrates the African past and endeavors to direct the Black future by undertaking cosmological inquiries within fictional and scientific spaces, communal debates, and traditional belief systems (Eseonu & Okoye, 2023). Unlike certain aspects of the first stage of Afrofuturism in the 1990s, there is no ambition to delay, defer, contest, or downplay Black self-reaching futures. Black hopes have matured and are ready to be wrested in the 21st century. Thus, in Afrofuturism 2.0, there is a cleavage with the primarily terrestrial arguments that overlook climate collapse and the readily known, less vatic, predictions of transhumanism (Toliver, 2023; Holbert et al., 2020). Nick Land argues that democracy will either collapse into barbarism (absolutism) or re-engineer itself back into the feudal trajectory (commercialism) due to Left politics, Left economics, and Left science. Land's Dark Enlightenment outlines that the political order would act as a negative singularity by dissipating socioeconomic production and transferring informational services to the governance industry so that the excessive demand-generating bureaucratic machinery of the state can be evaded or temporarily annihilated. For this, the enlightened should accelerate societal collapse to bypass semicapitalism and stratify into an accelerated transitional framework.

Afrofuturism operates from the location of lived experience, family, and community, which is also a practice, method, and mode of study. Afrofuturism involves taking up the task of reclaiming agency as socially mediated praxis and situated critique. While figurative realism places the subject upfront and underwrites meaning from human experience, Afrofuturism is premised on nonidentifying, disidentifying, and practically reinterpreting material and intellectual necessities and representing the subject (Jones, 2022; Coles, 2023). Afrofuturism is a critical lens and political theory for engaging Black experiences of the past, present, and future. Elements and practices of Afrofuturism are visible in various locations, from the 1960s visual art of Sun Ra to the late 20th-century fiction of Octavia Butler, Afrofuturismo in South America, or African futurism on the continent (Anderson & Jones, 2016; Turpin, 2021; Waghid & Ontong, 2022).

Afrofuturism, Blacceleration, Afropessimism: A Creative Response

Contemporary geopolitical realities necessitate a synthesis of Afrofuturism, Blacceleration and Afropessimism to examine how these frameworks intersect, converge, and challenge conventional notions of time, technology, and liberation by weaving together the speculative imagination of Afrofuturism and the radical philosophy of accelerationism. The analysis centers on their shared critiques of humanism, capitalism, and linear temporality while highlighting Afrofuturism's unique contributions to reimagining futurity through radical thought and navigating the social milieu of the Dark Enlightenment.

Afrofuturism destabilizes linear time, creating narratives that merge the past with speculative futures. Kodwo Eshun (2003), in "Further Considerations on Afrofuturism," frames this as a counter-future where African diasporic subjects excavate historical ruins to redefine their place in time. Similarly, accelerationism, particularly its leftist variant, as articulated by Alex Williams and Nick Snircek (2013), advocates for accelerating capitalist systems to collapse under their contradictions, envisioning postcapitalism. Both frameworks reject static temporalities but diverge in their ethical grounding: Afrofuturism often critiques the Eurocentric roots of technological progress, while accelerationism risks replicating the capitalist logic of speed without addressing racialized exploitation. For instance, Afrofuturist works like Octavia Butler's (1993) *Parable of the Sower* reimagine survival through communal resilience, contrasting with accelerationism's abstract "speed."

Accelerationism's antihumanist stance, exemplified by Nick Land's (2023) nihilistic embrace of capital as an "alien life-form" clashes with Afrofuturism's reclamation of Black subjectivity. While Land dismisses the human as obsolete, Afrofuturism interrogates the racialized boundaries of humanity itself. As articulated in Aria Dean's (2017) "Notes on Blacceleration," Blackness has historically been excluded from the category of the human, rendering Afrofuturist visions inherently posthumanist. For example, the "cyborg" figures in Afrofuturist art (e.g., Janelle Monáe's *Dirty Computer*) reimagine Black identity through augmentation, resisting both capitalist dehumanization and accelerationism's erasure of marginalized voices. This tension underscores Afrofuturism's refusal to abandon the political stakes of identity in favor of accelerationism's "inhuman subjectivization."

A key divergence lies in accelerationism's failure to reckon with slavery's foundational role in capital accumulation (Dean, 2017). Afrofuturism, by contrast, centers this history, as seen in N. K. Jemisin's Broken Earth Trilogy (2015–2016), which allegorizes racial capitalism through geological cataclysms. The concept of Blacceleration, a portmanteau of *Blackness* and *acceleration*(ism), argues accelerationist thought is embedded in Black radical traditions, given slavery's role as capitalism's "kick-starter." Blacceleration reframes acceleration not as a neutral process but as a reclaiming of Black technoculture, as exemplified by Drexciya's aquatic mythos, which reimagines enslaved Africans evolving into underwater beings (Harvey, 2020). Here, Afrofuturism subverts accelerationism's Eurocentric assumptions by grounding speculation in diasporic memory.

While Afrofuturism often leans toward utopianism, its intersection with Afropessimism reveals a skepticism toward facile optimism. Candice Jenkins (2021) notes that both frameworks share a "speculative radicality," balancing worldbuilding with critiques of anti-Black violence—accelerationism's teleological faith in progress clashes with Afropessimism's insistence on the permanence of racial antagonism. For instance, Stefanie Dunning (2020) notes how the film *Sorry to Bother You* satirizes accelerationist fantasies by depicting a dystopia where Black labor is hyperexploited under technocapitalism, resisting accelerationism's naivety, engaging weirdness and Afrofuturism's occasional idealism. The critique also extends to the reality of African culture, labor, sexuality, exploitation, and mining in Africa, as represented in the 2021 film *Neptune Frost* (Kgongoane, 2024).

The synthesis of Afrofuturism, Blacceleration, and Afropessimism lies in their shared desire to "destroy worlds to build new ones." Afrofuturism 2.0 expands this vision by integrating astro-Blackness and Black quantum futures as espoused by Rasheedah Phillips (2023), proposing decentralized futures beyond colonial spatial logics. Meanwhile, leftist accelerationists like Williams and Srnicek (2013) advocate for repurposing automation to create a postwork society—a vision that could align with Afrofuturist critiques of labor exploitation. However, Afrofuturism insists that such futures must center cultural epistemologies, as in Pamela Phatsimo's Sunstrum's (2013) African futurism, which prioritizes African ontologies over Western techno-utopias.

Afrofuturism's analysis of accelerationism reveals both synergies and irreconcilable tensions. For example, while aspects of accelerationism offer a provocative lens for navigating capitalist collapse, accelerationism often neglects the racialized violence embedded in technological progress. Afrofuturism, by contrast, reimagines futurity and African agency through Black speculative praxis, offering an alternative to accelerationism's blind spots. As Kodwo Eshun (2003) argues, the task is not to accelerate toward oblivion but to "hijack the future" through diasporic memory and radical imagination. In this synthesis, the path forward demands centering those historically excluded from the human, a project where Afrofuturism holds unparalleled critical potency.

Decolonizing African Historiography and Afrofuturism

There are many origins to these postcolonial points of contact. However, a clear linking point can be observed from ancient Ghana, Mali, and Songhai empires to the Senegalese academician, anthropologist, and author of *The African Origin of Civilization*, Cheikh Anta Diop (1967). The rising monopolization of the African past in the imperialist and colonial capitalist world has, as a counterpart, been the monopolization of culture in the social movement of the dominant society. The dividing line in each case is the line established in the context of the racist ideology used in turn to justify slave society, then colonialism, and now Western world supremacy, by which the authors and actors of the dominant culture take care to ensure that hegemony remains in the hands of the dominant classes. The disoriented masses must find ideological points of support and intellectual models in the dominant culture to legitimate their behavior, essential automatisms for the stability of the capitalist system, for the regularity of the machinations that guarantee its dominance over humanity and over the endless resource that is the labor of the dumbfounded citizen of the Western world (Delices, 2021; Dias, 2022; Taylor, 2022). The need to use Afrofuturism 2.0 to solve entrenched global problems from a local, traditional, cultural context is perhaps one of the most essential, dialectical components of the act of envisioning the future that can best contribute to understanding the elite. The Eurocentric, culturally aggressive narrative of neoliberalism tempers the pessimistic potential dark side of neoliberalist futures while contributing only to the very right-wing neoliberalists who have funds—those who are attempting to build off the idea that their dark futures must be preserved as the only option left. Doing so may lead to liberatory potential from a socially responsible, dialectical anticolonial stance because of enacting land-based, cultural, and human values, those things that should be of importance in constructing a viable future (Holbert et al., 2023; Eseonu & Duggan, 2022; Nathaniel & Akung, 2022).

In conclusion, by theorizing and practicing Afrofuturism 2.0, one can critically analyze various texts and better address issues of globalization and intersectional concerns. Especially since one of the key texts in political theory and the manifesto for this movement, the essay *The Dark Enlightenment* by Nick Land, leaves out any discussions of concerns regarding postcolonialism, feminism, and other major world issues that can plague this goal of actively trying to resolve human social problems while curbing the politics of fear following the aid of modern technologies.

The Future of Global Governance

The political aspect of the liberal order is a challenge that certain recent contributions to discussions about the resurgence of right-wing movements do not fully understand. Notably, some liberal academics are resolute in examining these political representations without considering ideology, despite political ideologies existing as frameworks of values that individuals use to perceive the world and make political decisions. In the context of global liberal politics, globalization introduces new values to individuals, influencing their political convictions. The widespread dissemination of information worldwide, coupled with the unpredictable nature of most violent events, intensifies human apprehension and uncertainty about risks (Baylis et al., 2020).

To maintain international collaboration in governance, it is essential that all participants can achieve their goals. However, simply meeting the policy needs of states, businesses, and individuals doesn't guarantee that the political expression of these interests will promote peaceful governance. As Hobbes noted, allowing individuals to act on their own judgment often leads to conflicts with rulers and each other, as everyone pursues their own interests without considering the common good. If people believe that their governing elite is self-serving and only serves the needs of wealthy groups, they will not support them. This can lead to government fragmentation and the breakdown of cooperative global governance, as seen in the chaos in international markets under domestic power monopolies (Cooley & Nexon, 2020).

Emerging Power Dynamics

Patterns in domestic politics show that existing hierarchies tend to suppress dissenting opinions. This has led to a growing skepticism toward the propaganda of liberal nations' established hierarchies, particularly as the violence from the nonliberal global middle intensifies. The betrayal of national interests by corrupt local elites is met with strong condemnation and often threats of violence. Denying any connection between global hierarchies and local anti-states is not a convincing argument for war. This balance theory suggests that as one group rises, another falls (Diesen, 2022).

The traditional power transition theories suggested that the rise of a new power would disrupt the global order. A significant shift is taking place in the domestic politics of liberal democracies, which are major world powers. The rejection of liberalism and the established world order in liberal states is not solely driven by the existing great powers but also by the growing influence of the nonliberal global middle. Tanja A. Börzel and Michael Zürn (2021) highlight that both left- and right-wing populists are advocating for the legitimacy of the liberal nation-state and the preservation of its long-standing cultural heritage.

Reflections on the Postliberal World

Political revolts grow more likely as global norms about exercising legitimate authority rapidly decay. With such decline comes increased certainty among rising powers and declining hegemons that the only effective way to head off these challenges is by abandoning any moral or normative constraints on their mercantilism, at least in foreign relations. They also decrease the willingness of would-be regional hegemons to demand that international agreements respect the national government's ability to regulate its society, economy, and culture while increasing the general inclination of emerging powers to use either overt or covert violations of international law to facilitate their regional dominance and liberty to maneuver at the expense of international and national efforts to minimize global externalities (Gazzini, 2022). As these revolts and challenges persist and intensify, the global landscape witnesses a profound shift in power dynamics. The very foundation of diplomatic cooperation and international relations shakes under the weight of conflicting interests and diverging agendas.

Additionally, the erosion of moral constraints and normative principles only amplifies the chaos and unpredictability in the political realm. Nations that once claimed to embody virtuous values and uphold ethical standards now find themselves entangled in a maelstrom of self-interest and opportunism. In this turbulent environment, notions of fairness, justice, and collective responsibility become increasingly elusive, replaced by a ruthless pursuit of individual gain and survival. Desperate to maintain their influence and secure their own interests, governments resort to Machiavellian tactics, discarding any remnants of moral high ground they once held. The principles that guided the international community for decades are now mere relics, overshadowed by a frenzied scramble for power and dominance.

Regional hegemons, eager to cement their status and exploit the chaotic atmosphere, flout international agreements with impunity. Boundaries are stretched and redrawn as nations assert their authority and exert control over resources, trade routes, and strategic territories (Deitelhoff & Zimmerman, 2020). The very fabric of global stability unravels before our eyes, replaced by a precarious balance of power governed by self-interest and pragmatism. As the moral compass of nations becomes distorted, the consequences ripple across borders, affecting not only international relations but also the lives and livelihoods of ordinary citizens. Societies crumble under the weight of economic exploitation and cultural hegemony imposed by those in positions of power. The voices of dissent are marginalized and silenced by the overwhelming might of the dominant forces. With each passing day, the world sinks deeper into a state of lawlessness and moral bankruptcy, where the vulnerable are left defenseless and the powerful reign unchecked (Gazzini, 2022). The ideas of cooperation, collaboration, and global solidarity seem like relics of a bygone era, shattered by avarice and short-sightedness. The road ahead appears treacherous and uncertain as nations navigate the treacherous waters of a world driven by self-interest and devoid of ethical moorings. Will humanity find a way to restore a semblance of order and justice amid this prevailing chaos, or are we destined to plunge further into the abyss of anarchy and despair? Only time will tell (Gazzini, 2022; Deitelhoff & Zimmermann, 2020; Bettiza & Lewis, 2020).

Finally, in the developed world, there is currently a period of significant conflict and weakening of institutional structures. Both global and domestic orders, already fragile and reliant heavily on their constituents' careful attention and concern, are facing threats from outside forces that have greatly diminished the reactive institutions and traditions that once protected them. The general dissatisfaction, perception of government ineffectiveness, and high levels of debt have led to uprisings from both the Left and the Right. Attempts to rally public support in defense of liberal states are not only ineffective, but the way they are presented, the messages themselves, and the messengers are contributing to the decline of public trust, social and political stability, and global order.

CHAPTER 5

The Nommo of the Black Speculative Turn

We want art to have discursive effects on those exposed to it; the question is what kind of discourses works of art can promote and by what mechanisms. Our work is conceived to build coherent aesthetic politics. "Black speculative art is a creative, aesthetic practice that integrates African diasporic or African metaphysics with science or technology and seeks to interpret, engage, design, or alter reality for the re-imagination of the past, the contested present, and (act) as a catalyst for the future" (Anderson, 2016, p. 233). Not content to identify Afrofuturist imaginaries as having the capacity to critique recognizable phenomena of the current moment, we ask whether Afrofuturist texts have the potential to add to the formation of the social body itself in this current era of accelerating change. This chapter's most comprehensive, polemical intention is to identify the existence of the Black Speculative Arts movement (BSAM) and explore connections with other theoretical political aesthetic philosophies.

In 1992 Jacques Rancière raised the following question: "How are we to reinvent politics?" The Cold War, which allegedly featured the global struggle between the binary terms of capitalism and socialism, democracy and communism, had ended (Rancière, 1992, p. 64). What did Rancière intend to be the characteristics of a genuinely political work of art? He identifies the political work of art as fulfilling the "redistribution of the roles of speaking and acting." Politically speaking, a work of art changes the distribution of the sensible by changing what is visible, audible, and hence thinkable. We can see at once how tasks that are so specific yet abstract resemble a job description written for that indispensable but somehow invisible middle manager in this especially messianic and apocalyptic version of neoliberalism in the wake of capitalism's global crisis (Rancière, 2022).

Afrofuturism is a popular topic among contemporary practitioners of political Black aesthetics. This term was coined in the 1990s, and some argue that it focuses on studying the African diaspora's history and future. Others respond that this taints it with Eurocentrism and instead believe that Afrofuturists are attempting to decenter European culture. Furthermore, this movement is driven by dissatisfaction with the current state of race relations in the United States or seeking to create a future where racism has withered away from the consciousness of humanity (Holbert et al., 2023; Amoah, 2020).

Aesthetic Politics in Afrocentric Theory

By the mid- to late 1990s, a new dilemma developed since disillusionment came in faster than the solution for the devastating outcomes of the neoliberalism and the emergence of the internet ethically demanded. The positions demonstrate that notable achievements in African politics were reached through innovative developments that emerged from within the collective memory of African traditions. African aesthetic politics as inclusive and accommodative of numerous voices and interests are one such development (Jethro, 2020). The aggregation of diverse positions and interests in traditional African philosophy brought unique interactions and considerations that enshrined a society of humans and nature. Trevor Morgan (2020) formally defines African aesthetic politics as traditional African practices emerging from below that significantly inform the exercise of political power in contemporary Nigeria. Similarly, in South Africa, an attempt to transcend colonial and postcolonial realities to universally capture the aesthetic essence of heritage African innovation is applied (Jethro, 2020).

Thinking about the Black Speculative Arts movement's Afrofuturist aesthetic politics and Jacques Rancière's "distribution of the sensible" allows theory-building to be much more helpful in understanding and analyzing racialized aspects of contemporary phenomena, why many settings are unable to create new ideas in creative fields, and how sometimes productive relationships can or cannot be pursued. Cities are traditionally represented as centers of exchange of goods, surrounded by suburbs and the countryside. When other benefits of living in the city become so one-sided as to overshadow traditional needs such as safety and public transit, the city becomes a center of exchanges of wealth, culture, and possibly novel ideas. In fact, it actively perpetuates the spewing out of new novels and short stories that perpetuate the largely imaginary vision of desirability. As the world of speculative studies and its attendant spheres of interest—science fiction, Utopian studies, and queer theory—have all come to be seen as outgrowths of rejecting exclusionary social structures by embracing displacement led by marginalized subjects, this then offers Black speculative creators the creators a seat in settings they have previously been excluded from. This opportunity is the reason for the record success of various diverse, progressive artistic movements, most recently the Black Speculative Arts movement.

Rancière's Theory of the Distribution of the Sensible

Indeed, in most cases, it is always important to separate the visible and invisible spheres in any community. These spheres are always two sides of the same operation—the "partitioning" in any political act. In other words, the political organization of sensible distribution always creates this partitioning between the visible, the vocally expressive, and the inert, which determines the common subjects of the community at any given time. The central question of democracy then becomes: How does one afford the most analogous relationship between these fragmented social groups? Rancière's theory of the distribution of the sensible narrates historically how these partitions are drawn and redrawn (Blakey, 2021).

To be able to develop a framework for Afrofuturism's aesthetic politics and its engagement with other communities of interest, it is necessary first to have an understanding of Rancière's theory of the distribution of the sensible since it serves as a point of engagement for the aspect of this work and its deployment in discussing Afrofuturism and the Black Speculative Arts movement and its work with other future-oriented formations. Some of the central questions Rancière's work raises include these: How do we share in the sensible, the observable, and the thinkable? Who is the subject of the experience and knowledge of seeing, hearing, and thinking? How can some voices be heard while others are excluded from participation, both artistically and politically? The distribution of the sensible explores Rancière's answers to these critical questions. For him, different ways of distributing the sensible divide the subjects of any community into at least two parts:

those with authority to identify some sensible accurate as political subjects and those whose status is to implement and execute the established order (Fajardo, 2022).

Key Concepts and Principles

First, Afrofuturism can revise and extend Rancière's theory of the distribution of the sensible; I would like to express how both Afrofuturist political aesthetics and the theory of the distribution of the sensible can engage. While few, if any, explanations of Afrofuturism and the theory of the distribution of the sensible exist, one does not exist that goes in depth and back into the past to apply them both to the same concerns. Through such explanations, I will also be able to determine what of these concepts need revision and extend them into what I am calling a Nommo framework for the aesthetic politics of Afrofuturism in the African diaspora and Africa that can be used to deepen an understanding of and the potential of interactions in the distribution of the sensible in practice. A practical framework that combines an understanding of the expression that Black speculative arts represent, a reality of freedom through the revolutionary gesture, with the political theory of equality such an explanation represents. A polity concerned with the distribution of the sensible and general art of equality to achieve the fullest expression of freedom it can permit. In the next section, I explain the aesthetic politics of the Black Speculative Arts movement, followed by Rancière's theory on the distribution of the sensible.

The Black Speculative Turn

Although the European-centered approach to science fiction is often focused on its relationship to Darko Suvin's notion of *cognitive estrangement*, contemporary Black speculative thought and practice are indebted to the memories of Black diasporan ancestors who survived enslavement and colonialism and who were key to the foundation of modernity. In the current metamodern moment, Black speculative thought is more focused on *cognitive reconstruction* in pursuit of futures that have not happened yet. Moreover, it has collapsed the distinction between the technoscientific and the supernatural or spiritual as it operates from an in-between or liminal space of creative praxis (Jennings & Fluker, 2020; Dubey, 2023). When discussing time in the political context, it is essential to establish the underlying reference framework.

The Afrofuturism tradition is focused on the idea of time as inherently flexible. Rather than adhering to the European traditional space-time principles of Euclidean and Kantian theories, authors like Robert T. Browne and Nalo Hopkinson and musicians such as DJ Spooky use speculative practice to explore the interconnected relationships between time, space, race, technology, and colonialism (Neptune, 2023; Miller, 2004). These imaginative writings and musical improvisations are not just about inventing alternative timelines but also about examining our societies and our perception of time. Afrofuturism challenges us to consider how time is constructed and who benefits from its formulation. This philosophical framework can be complex and may not always present an optimistic view—mirroring time's intricate and unpredictable nature—and it is essential to approach our analysis of time with precision and care (Young & Reid, 2023; Dove, 2023).

Nommo and the Black Speculative Arts Movement

The aesthetic politics of BSAM emphasizes social location and agency, evades reification, and has developed an Africological hermeneutical framework to understand its process (Asante, 2007; Yancy, 2004). Nommo is an "ontological register of the African Spirit in form or action and is a framework for Africans (or African diaspora) to create or construct patterns and practices which new cultural elements are absorbed, synthesized or reconfigured" (Yancy, 2004, p. 291). Moreover, this process is "indicative of the fact that people of African descent have been creating these practices in the face of anti-black or White terrorist practices indicating a subjunctive (indicative possibilities of our possibilities) ontological mode of existence" (Yancy, 2004, p. 291). Nommo has several manifestations in the creative world, arts, architecture, literature, economics, science, and medicine, reaffirming the African geography of reason and ontological experience (Bates et al., 2008). Correspondingly, with contemporary Afrofuturism, the Black Speculative Arts movement has a *djed* or (standpoint) stasis to engage in aesthetic politics around its artistic practice, production, or promotion with culture and technology.

In the Black Speculative Arts movement, form follows function. Black speculative art is an artistic, visual practice. The movement is futuristic in that it hopes to shine a light on the future with the knowledge that is increasingly evolving into empowerment. It is also human-centered in that it holds that humans should view the experiences of the past, create the present, and engineer the future with the understanding that these experiences are part of a web of links that make up ancestral stories of life and tragedy. The Black Speculative Arts movement is not only African womanist in that it considers the experiences of women and other marginalized identities (such as the LGBTQ community) of the human experience; it explores or exposes the experiences of the diaspora and the continent. This is why much of what follows is designed to look at the African diaspora and Africa in terms of the world. More recently, other artists and intellectuals like those within BSAM, such as Quentin Vercetty, LaWana Richmond, Phillip Butler, Zaika dos Santos, Nkolo Blondel, Lonny Brooks, Natasha A Kelly, Emmanuel Ikenna Nwani, and me at our own Black Speculative Arts movement conferences by helping to cement and define Afrofuturism further through the process of speculative creativity and design (Butler, 2021).

The Black Speculative Arts movement (BSAM) is focused on innovation and artistic creation, emphasizing the scholarly push and research around social philosophy regarding the arts and praxis within the Black community of the future. Vanguard material and innovation are being introduced to contemporary thought within that community, as well as new ways to diagnose problems and synthesize possible solutions. Unlike the broader Afrofuturist movement, which has a more ambiguous definition and scope, BSAM has a clearly defined interest in research and production in the creative mode that involves the conjunction between the past, present, and the future as well as a commitment to the theorization, philosophy, and manifestos that would help to understand specific topics relating to the African diaspora, and Africa (Anderson, 2016).

In developing a framework for the aesthetic politics of Afrofuturism as part of the Black Speculative Arts movement, it is essential to make especially clear what is meant by Afrofuturism, shared commonalities, and geographic differences with the broader Black speculative movement. Afrofuturism comprises works of art that engage with speculative themes by creators who self-identify as Black or African, with a focus on either the future's impact on the notion of Blackness or Afrofuturism's potential as a force that can shape a future where Blackness or astro-Blackness can signal subversiveness or power.

Background on the Emergence of the Black Speculative Arts Movement

Several events between 2005 and 2015 shaped the domestic development of BSAM, including the explosion in social media platforms illustrated by

Facebook, YouTube, and Twitter (Van Dijck, 2013), and three publications: *The Big Short*, documenting the global market collapse; Bill Bishop's book *The Big Sort*, detailing resegregation of people based on ideology or race or class interest; and the high incarceration of African descent people within the New Jim Crow or prison industrial complex. Major contributing events were the election of the United States' first African American president, Barack Obama, racist reactions like the American Tea Party and subsequent collapse of the liberal postracial project, the increased use of crowdfunding and other new technologies to design creative projects, escalating environmental stress, and the "new scramble for Africa" (Kimenyi & Lewis, 2011). Other major contributing factors were the resurgence of Pan-Africanism and outreach to the African diaspora (now incorporated as the 6th region) by the African Union in 2005 and the appearance of state-sanctioned deaths of Black people through police brutality, such as the Marikana massacre in South Africa (Anderson & Jones, 2016).

The US economy was in a deep recession for the first two years of President Obama's tenure. The fiscal stimulus that helped the country move from recession to recovery was not on a clear glide path to economic recovery. In March 2009, Congress passed the $787 billion American Recovery and Reinvestment Act to rescue the economy from the freefall caused by the financial and housing markets' breakdown. However, the act was passed without much Republican support, and significant state budget shortfalls are still lurking in the future. The act was controversial and was characterized by its detractors as expensive and overly ambitious, not producing immediate tangible benefits. There was deep skepticism about the estimates of new long-term job creation that could be credited to the fiscal stimulus. In April 2009, unemployment reached an all-time high, as reported in the CBO's estimate that the US would lose 2.9 million jobs in 2009.

US President Barack Obama and key figures within his administration, like Hillary Clinton, together with corporate media, promoted claims about the spread of democracy in Libya, relying on reports on "African mercenaries" who defeat opposition forces and "mass rape" (which was widely discredited), leading to a regime change of dramatic proportions for citizens who were previously among the beneficiaries of the great Gaddafi welfare in comparison to other Arab countries. The current United States and its allies blame the government they support for failing to stop the civil war and defend human rights, starting from 2014 when ICAFIS (ISIL and al-Qaeda terrorists in Libya) took control of large cities. NATO's political leaders believe Russia's involvement in Libya indicates that Libya will be "returned to a dictator" and pushed into their narratives. Still, some 22

NATO countries, especially the United Kingdom and France, are foreign countries that bombed Libya and took an active part in regime change. Not long after, the Gaddafi government stated that opponents of Islamists in Libya would not be welcome in any political transition, citing the end of Islamist terrorist group reactions as justification (Belkoli Houda, 2021; Baghiani & Kaouli, 2021).

A coalition of NATO countries launched Operation Unified Protector on March 19, 2011. Its goal was to enforce UN Security Council Resolutions 1970 and 1973 by implementing a no-fly zone in Libya. The mission was put into effect five days after a council vote to protect Libyans from the loyal forces of Colonel Muammar Gaddafi, who were engaged in a violent campaign against opposition forces for almost eight months. Throughout the NATO air campaign and the subsequent national effort to defeat Gaddafi's military forces, Libyans faced increased violence, including killing, sexual assault, and hostage-taking. The fighting and NATO air strikes resulted in thousands of deaths, with half of the victims being foreign nationals. NATO's actions have been documented as war crimes. However, the organization's focus on the victims has shifted to addressing the latest atrocities, cries for Russian aggression, and famine warnings, which have diminished the urgency of the situation (Gaub, 2024).

The Murders of Trayvon Martin, Mike Brown, and George Floyd

The violent response of the Missouri Police Department to the spectacles of silent, peaceful protest and civil disobedience, however, helped expose a consistency in the white supremacist state directing its violence toward Black protest within that particular space. The violence put on display through physical police violence, militarization, and aggression became the visual example that a predominantly white and geographically distanced audience needed to see to shift their understanding from the general awareness and discussions fostered by the Black Lives Matter movement in years prior, to the shock that made the state of racism and injustice more "real" and tangible. In the digital sphere(s) following the events in Ferguson, Missouri, curious or existing readers and viewers experienced a flood of related sociopolitical, academic, and cultural content pushing back against centuries of racial terrorism and dispossession under slavery and colonialism. They went from frequently answering to asking questions about the Ferguson situation and local history to historical contextual overviews of police–community dynamics / community policing in the United States, to explanations as to how media representations of Mike Brown helped to downplay the humanity and character of Black Americans, to efforts in developing strategies, analyses, and intersections for response and action (First et al., 2020).

Over the past decade, the Black Lives Matter movement has led to a reorientation of concern for the lives and the issues faced by members of the Black community. On an individual level, many Black creators and creators of Black speculative arts, especially those working and collaborating in digital spaces, have also consistently and actively used digital media as a platform to discuss and build community around the victims of police violence. From the public riots in 2011 following the murder of Mark Duggan by the British Metropolitan Police Service to the state-directed violence that occurred in Ferguson, Missouri, following the police-involved killing of Michael Brown that August, Black speculative arts creators have leveraged the digital sphere to catalyze discourse and activism in response to police violence (Dunivin et al., 2022).

The Birth of a Movement

In response to a police brutality crisis, a collection of movements and organizations on both sides of the Atlantic organized around the philosophy of Afrofuturism and Black futurity (Anderson, 2016; Anderson & Carr, 2023). Crucial moments during this time included a range of symposia and projects, such as Ferguson Is the Future, hosted by Ruha Benjamin; the Astro-Blackness conferences, hosted by Adilifu Nama at Loyola Marymount; initiatives led by Black science fiction organizers and publishers like Maurice Broadus, Maurice Waters, and Milton Davis, and Black independent comic promoters or publishers like Bill Campbell and Yumy Odom; performance and exhibitions by King Britt; the appearance of Ytasha Womack's book on Afrofuturism in 2013; and later the sci-fi anthology *Octavia's Brood* coedited by Walidah Imarasha and Adrienne Maree Brown.

For example, Black Quantum Futurism Collective (BQF), in Philadelphia, and Wildseeds: The Octavia Butler Emergent Strategy Collective, in New Orleans, were founded in 2013 and 2014. BQF, by Camae Ayewa (Moor Mother) and Rasheedah Phillips, explores the intersections of futurity, media, DIY aesthetics, and community activism in marginalized urban communities through an alternative time orientation. Wildseeds work, by Desiree Evans and Soraya Jean-Louis McElroy, is situated in Black feminist traditions of survival and healing and engages Octavia Butler and other speculative, sci-fi, and fantastical authors and artists of color. In Detroit, its postindustrial scene influenced the techno performers Drexciya and Carl

Craig, who pioneered the early Afrofuturist movement; and recently, leaders like Ingrid LaFleur and her Afrotopia exhibition, Cultural Curator Bryce Detroit, the Octavia's Brood Collective, and writers like Clarence Young characterize the city as a hub of the movement.

The Black Speculative Arts movement took form shortly after the *Unveiling Visions: Alchemy of the Black Imagination* exhibition curated by John Jennings and me at the Schomburg Library in New York in 2015, the posting of its manifesto online by AfroFutures_UK, and the publication of the anthology *Afrofuturism 2.0: The Rise of Astro-Blackness*. It has grown into an international network of creatives, intellectuals, and artists like Sheree Rene Thomas, Dacia Polk, Quentin Vercetty, Stacey Robinson, Tim Fielder, Zaika Dos Santos, Natasha Kelly, Lonny Brooks, Schetanna Powell, Shannon Theus, Emmanuel Nwani, Nkolo Ntyam, Michael Bhatch, LaWana Richmond, and more, creating community projects, exhibitions, and events based on Afrofuturism. AfroFutures_UK is a collective of artists, writers, activists, and scholars exploring the future Black experience through art, multimedia, and disruptive technologies. An early seminal event occurred in 2015 in Manchester, England: a conference/exhibition where they utilized thematic elements of Afrofuturism to critique possible futures. Also in England, in Birmingham, the Afroflux collective with creatives like Applz Sunra and Juice Aleem organizes exhibitions and events around sequential art, music, and Afrofuturism.

In Canada, there is a thriving Afrofuturism community, and the work of science fiction writer Nalo Hopkins has had a considerable influence. Toronto activists like Quentin Vercetty, Nicole Taylor, and Queen Kikuyu curate and create community projects, while Danilo Deluxo served as the curator and creator of Black Future Month from 2013–2017. This annual Afrofuturism exhibition attained national recognition and international acclaim. In Vancouver, the Afro Van Connect Society, with Dae Shields and Kor Kase, is focused on empowering people of African descent through conversation, collaboration, creativity, and performance. Afro-Brazilians are reclaiming and affirming their Blackness through the lens of contemporary Afrofuturism or what they call Afrofuturismo. Activists like writer Ain Zaila and Fabio Kabral connect Afrofuturism through the cosmology of African-descent populations; Zaika Dos Santos has developed what she calls Afrofuturalidades. For them, Afrofuturismo means influencing the future and empowering the Afro-Brazilian community to change a past that was forced on them.

In Accra, Ghana, the Chale Wote Street Art Festival, since its inception in 2011, has been thematically preoccupied with Afrofuturist themes and developing alternatives for the future life of African people. The African Women's Development Fund is Africa's first Pan-African women's fund; it was co-founded in 2000 by three African women: Hilda Tadria, Bisi Adeleye-Fayemi, and Joana Foster, who passed in 2016. Since its establishment, the fund has supported almost 1,500 women's rights organizations and women-led initiatives in countries all over the continent. In 2017 the fund launched its AWDF Futures Project. The futuristic initiative is focused on the continent's future as seen through an African feminist lens. However, the Southern African sphere is highly dynamic. For example, Eddy Kamwuanga Ilungu of Congo (DRC), Cyrus Kabiru of Kenya, Wangechi Mutu of Kenya, and Emo De Medeiros of Benin are a generation of artists who embrace the movement. Founded by Chimurenga in 2008, the established media center, Pan African Space Station, based in Cape Town, South Africa, reflects the themes of the Afrofuturism movement in South Africa. The Francophone world is also active in the movement.

In the Francophone world, organizations like Blacks to the Future, in Paris, France, co-founded in 2015 by Mawena Yehouessi, develop events, software, and art from an Afrofuturist perspective. Artists like Paris-based Kapwani Kiwanga have attained international stature with her work. Her interests include Afrofuturism, science fiction, and anticolonial struggle, as well as examining the histories and subjects that have been underexplored. Jean-Pierre Bekolo is a Cameroon-based filmmaker whose African science fiction motifs embedded in his 2005 film *Les Saignantes* brought him international acclaim. More recently, filmmaker Alain Bidard of Martinique directed the Kreyol-Afrofuturist films *Battlefield Chronicle* in 2015 and *Opal* in 2021. Bidard represents a growing international wave of Francophone artists and creatives embracing Afrofuturism (Anderson & Carr, 2023).

Sankofa and Historical Consciousness

Again, time does not become only the future changing of events, not evaluating the essence of the past for a better future in each descendant group, nor the eventual power that advanced space control might mean for the first time, with an entrance and an exit point in space, without an enlightening journey about the continuous process of life since time immemorial. Such historical lessons cannot be revisited in a null perspective about historical consciousness: time is a means of existing and identity as time and place change off-planet in a coexisting eternal state; it is vital to understand Sankofa as a living metaphor through time in the African concept of traditional space, spatial relationships, cultural values, and life practices complete with consequences of practice. Sankofa is the foundation, the commencement, and re-entry into Mother Earth, including outward and homeward journey into the artistic and spiritual consciousness offered by Saidiya Hartman's time-space creation complex and the cosmic consciousness that is difficult to measure or theorize over the extreme time of back-and-forth space travel. It is indeed one of the changing dimensions in the African theory of ethnomathematics (Osei, 2023; Asante, 2022).

Sankofa and historical consciousness suggest that there is power and wisdom in the past's living traditions and lived experiences. From a liberation perspective, understanding the present or being able to deconstruct hegemonies and fundamentalism of power, there is little value in a future paradigm without many reflective, evaluative critiques of external or prior events, meaning making, and evaluations after the fact, let alone a critique of present paradigms. The historical consciousness of Sankofa gives a springboard into the present to give reflective meaning to past events. It can incorporate views from the past and actual history, not just socially constructed history, that may work for everyday consumption by selected groups. An Afrocentric model of space/time would incorporate an understanding of the ongoing from the perspective of what has happened (Deterville, 2020).

Understanding Afrofuturist Time

Epiphenomenalism is a theory in philosophy that posits the mind as a mere byproduct of bodily activity with no influence on the body. Epiphenomenal time and Afrofuturism represent two intriguing and interconnected concepts in contemporary cultural discourse. Though each stems from a different theoretical background, together they offer a valuable lens through which to explore the intersections of time, culture, and identity. Epiphenomenal time is a notion interpreted in the context of philosophy and cultural theory, where it generally refers to the idea that time as perceived is not fundamental to the framework of reality but rather emerges as a secondary phenomenon. In philosophical discourses, particularly in the works of David Chalmers, epiphenomena are properties that arise from but do not directly influence the workings of a system. Applied to the concept of time, this suggests that human perception of temporal order and duration might be a byproduct of physical processes in the universe without having causal efficacy itself (Chalmers, 1996). This challenges linear perceptions of time, suggesting an alternative understanding that ties in neatly with notions of nonlinear narratives prevalent in various cultural narratives.

Afrofuturism inherently embodies a disruption of conventional temporal structures, making it a fertile ground for incorporating ideas of epiphenomenal time. Many Afrofuturist narratives operate on an understanding of time that is nonlinear and multidirectional, allowing diverse truths and realities to coexist. This resonates with the concept of epiphenomenal time by demonstrating how temporal experiences might not be rooted in linear causality but are instead complex constructs reflecting cultural narratives that emerge epiphenomenally through collective consciousness. Integrating these ideas, Afrofuturism presents an opportunity to explore a structure of time that does not adhere strictly to past, present, or future but collapses these distinctions into a multifaceted tapestry. This approach encourages rethinking linear histories of colonization and oppression and instead constructs timelines that permit the past to be continuously reimagined through the flux of future possibilities (Eshun, 2003).

Furthermore, the concept of epiphenomenal time suggests a unique perspective on the relationship between technology and colonialism. It challenges traditional notions of causality and invites us to reconsider the impact of race on our understanding of time (Camara, 2020). It is a concept that suggests alternative temporal experiences and new approaches to historical narratives. For the *other*, epiphenomenal time is broadly accepted; the individual may not give it voice but is asserted and reclaimed collectively—as part of a Black or Indigenous (or other non-Western) traditional lifestyle and embedded in discussions about "natural remedies." The Western, usually white framework is a form of temporal warfare that denies the original timekeeper the ancestry of time. Epiphenomenal time holds a profound significance in alternative perspectives and the diverse tapestry of cultural heritage. Though often obscured and suppressed, its essence resonates silently within individuals, finding solace and validation through collective assertion and reclamation. Particularly in the realm of African, Indigenous, or other non-Western societies, this cherished concept lingers as an integral part of their traditional way of life. However, the dominant Western ideology, predominantly embodied by the white population, represents a temporal battlefield. Consequently, it ruthlessly diminishes the ancestral timekeeper's profound connection to the lineage of time, perpetuating a sense of loss and erasure (Camara, 2020; Falola, 2020).

It is common knowledge that space and time are categories developed from African perceptions and understandings of the nature of the cosmos, dating back to at least 5000 BCE. Despite the knowledge of how African understandings anchored conceptions of space about time, bringing into existence cultural and aesthetic frames of reference (consciousness, traditions, myths, symbols, ceremonies, and rituals), social science and art criticism have developed either from European Enlightenment or post-Enlightenment ways of understanding cosmic reality or from derivative reflections on their continuation rather than transformation (Falola & Salau, 2021; Ehret & Posnansky, 2023).

This section focuses on creating an Afrocentric Afrofuturist theory of space and time. However, it is essential to note that in the broader Eurocentric tradition of European modernity, the ideas of space and time were developed in conjunction with the wider notions of history, effect, rationality, and with more detailed relative branches of knowledge such as "historiography" or sciences. In this tradition, the concepts were given grand cosmological or metaphysical meaning and then arranged with or against the history, society, nature, and sense of nonwhite societies. This means that while concepts of space, time, and their effects are taken for granted or natural, such definitions reflect and are reflected in other ideas. In contrast to the Eurocentric mode, the space and time of non-Western orientations are characterized by vagueness, secrecy, inconsistencies, silence, and counterintuitive thought (Duzgun, 2022; Saramago, 2022).

Afrofuturism and Temporalities

Some claim that Afrofuturism originated in Black popular music, and others maintain that it has ancient roots in the study of the African diaspora and thus draws from the African concepts of time, which parallel traditional understandings of time in quantum mechanics. Afrofuturists have appropriated time travel as a way of using the past to inform the present, as well as demystifying and imagining the future. Researchers claim that these derived futures result from the movement's focus on Blackness's interactive, reciprocal, and nonpurposive nature, manifesting as distinctive performances creating forward and backward temporality (Young & Reid, 2023; Pirker & Rahn, 2023; Asante, 2023; Scott, 2021).

Nettrice Gaskins

Nettrice Gaskins is a digital scientist who has worked in the Afrofuturist field for over a decade and is a key figure in aesthetic design. Gaskins (2019) understands the Kongo cosmogram as a diagram emblematic of the African cosmos representing the boundary between the living and the dead that informs social responses. The Kongo cosmogram is a visual representation of movement and ritual that impacts identities and African communities. It can exist as a form of call and response, generating an aesthetic response. Finally, the Kongo cosmogram and attendant cosmology tracks, decodes, and encodes the geographic dispersion of the African diaspora over water and is sonically represented by artists like Drexciya, Flying Lotus, Kahlil Joseph, and Xenobia Bailey (Gaskins, 2019).

Nettrice Gaskins is a pivotal figure in the intersection of Afrofuturism, digital science, and Web 3.0. As the work of a digital scientist and scholar, Gaskins's contributions lie in her capacity to bridge the realms of cultural heritage and technological innovation through Afrofuturism. This distinct perspective not only enhances our understanding of digital spaces but also enriches the broader narrative around technology and its implications for marginalized communities. Gaskins employs Afrofuturism as a lens to explore future-oriented digital spaces like Web 3.0. Her work brings forth a vision of tomorrow's Africana digital environments by emphasizing diversity and representation. As Web 3.0 focuses on the decentralized web that leverages blockchain technology for more democratized participation, Gaskins advocates for minority voices to play an integral role in designing this emerging cyber-ecosystem.

By integrating her deep understanding of critical race theory and computer science, Gaskins underscores the potential of Afrofuturism to shape the ethical foundations and user inclusivity of Web 3.0. Her publications highlight the power of speculative fiction and myth-making in imagining new structures of cyberspace that are liberated from the biases of current digital frameworks. These insights are crucial in a world where digital environments swiftly influence societal structures and individual interactions. By proposing models rooted in ancestral knowledge and speculative technology narratives, she fosters a digital literacy that acknowledges and celebrates cultural uniqueness. In conclusion, Nettrice Gaskins's influence in theory-building symbolizes a crucial nexus of Afrofuturism and Web 3.0. By promoting cultural awareness and diversity within technological spheres, she not only reshapes how digital spaces are perceived but also actively contributes to constructing a more reflective and inclusive digital future. Her work is an essential reminder of the critical need for diverse narratives within the evolving landscape of digital technologies.

Rasheedah Phillips: Reimagining Time and Space

Rasheedah Phillips discussed how the experience of living in inner-city Philadelphia, marked by high levels of HIV and incarceration rates for young men, as well as poverty affecting young mothers, reflects a reaction to marginalization and oppression. People in these communities are impacted by political and economic systems that restrict their opportunities for upward mobility. The social structures within these neighborhoods are isolated and contribute to maintaining oppressive systems. Addressing these social restraints could lead to positive change and end the oppression of the Black transgender community. Phillips's perspective emphasizes the value and contribution of Black and marginalized individuals to society, highlighting the need to recognize their worth and provide them with opportunities.

Phillips, a remarkable thinker, artist, and activist, also played an instrumental role in shaping contemporary discourses on Afrofuturism through her work with Black Quantum Futurism (BQF). The collective, co-founded with Camae Ayewa (a.k.a. Moor Mother), integrates Afrodiasporic traditions, quantum physics, and future narratives to reimagine the concept of time and space. This fusion of disciplines offers a radical departure from linear, Western-centric views of history and futurity, introducing a multidimensional approach to Afrofuturism. Antithetical to the Western linear perception, BQF posits that time is nonlinear and interconnected, echoing Indigenous African cosmologies where past, present, and future coexist. This idea is profoundly articulated in Phillips's work *Recurrence Plot (and Other Time Travel Tales)* (2014) which encapsulates the cyclical and intertwined nature of temporal existence. This theoretical framework undermines colonial constructs of time, providing an alternative narrative that empowers marginalized communities through reclaiming and recontextualizing historical narratives.

The impact of BQF on Afrofuturism is profound, adding layers to notions of time and space often overlooked. Afrofuturism traditionally intersects diasporic culture with technology and speculative fiction, envisioning futures where Black identity flourishes unbound by historical oppression. By introducing quantum physics into the cultural lexicon, BQF expands these narratives. It propels Afrofuturists to consider the potentiality of multiple futures and realities, enabling the conception of worlds where African cultural expressions and knowledge systems reshape global futures.

Moreover, Phillips's (2023) work contributes to a broader understanding of how time is experienced and perceived differently within Black communities, influenced by systemic racism and socioeconomic inequalities. By exploring how these factors affect temporal perception, BQF underscores the resilience and adaptability inherent in Black existence—a theme central to Afrofuturism. In conclusion, Rasheedah Phillips and Black Quantum Futurism significantly enrich Afrofuturism by presenting time and space as flexible, interconnected constructs. This paradigm shift not only challenges the Eurocentric understanding of these dimensions but also empowers diasporic communities to engage with their histories and futures in transformative, liberating ways. By foregrounding the cyclical and pluralistic nature of time, Phillips and BQF continue to inspire a new generation of thinkers and creators to imagine possibilities beyond the confines of Western temporal constructs.

Nalo Hopkinson: Afro-Caribbean Futurisms

Finally, it is beneficial to delve into the work of Afro-Caribbean speculative fiction author Nalo Hopkinson. Hopkinson, originally from Jamaica, relocated to Canada during her teenage years. Hopkinson's work is at the intersection of Afro-Caribbean geography and mythos. In addition to several short stories, she has authored several novels, including *Brown Girl in the Ring* (1998), and *Midnight Robber* (2000). Beginning with the narrative instead of the analysis may provide a more accessible entry point (Adeniyi, 2023; Holgado, 2020).

Postcolonial thinking has been influenced by the dynamic literary works from the African diaspora, which are often marginalized and misunderstood in the dominant cultures that have historically both sympathized with and dominated these communities. The speculative fictions of the Caribbean diaspora are particularly vibrant, characterized by lyrical and allegorical qualities rather than realistic and introspective ones. Coming from a different place and time, these works are critiqued through a different lens, reflecting metaphysical questions that may seem out of place in knowledge-driven cultures where technology often overshadows metaphysical concerns. Studies in Afrofuturism aim to promote equality and intertextuality of these different perspectives by examining both traditions, illuminating how humans interact with and are impacted by material and spiritual aspects (Armillas-Tiseyra, 2023).

Afrofuturism, which merges African diasporic culture with technology and speculative thought, finds a distinct voice in Hopkinson. Her works incorporate traditional African and Caribbean beliefs into speculative landscapes, challenging the Western-dominated narrative in science fiction. By embedding elements such as folklore, spirituality, and diasporic history into her stories, she broadens the scope of future imaginaries, much like her peers Octavia Butler and Samuel R. Delany. Hopkinson's debut novel, *Brown Girl in the Ring*, vividly exemplifies her influence. It explores a dystopian future Toronto, infused with Afro-Caribbean culture and spiritual practices.

This setting not only challenges the typical Eurocentric portrayal of dystopian futures but also emphasizes the resilience and innovation inherent in Black cultures. The novel received critical acclaim, winning the Locus Award for Best First Novel, and marked a shift toward inclusive narratives within the genre.

In her stories, Hopkinson often addresses themes of identity, migration, and cultural nuances. Books like *Midnight Robber* exemplify how Hopkinson uses science fiction to dialogue with present realities and historical nuances of African diasporas. Hopkinson's adept blending of patois and magical elements in futuristic settings creates a verisimilitude that resonates with Black readers, enriching the tapestry of Afrofuturism. Her editorial work, notably in anthologies like *So Long Been Dreaming: Postcolonial Science Fiction and Fantasy* (2004), champions stories from marginalized communities, thus broadening the audience and reach of Afrofuturistic narratives.

Through her work, Nalo Hopkinson has advanced the dialogue of Afrofuturism and science fiction by centering Caribbean reality and culture within speculative frameworks. Her contributions challenge normative narratives and expand the imaginative possibilities, reinforcing the importance of diverse voices in shaping future landscapes. Her influence is ongoing, nurturing a new generation of writers who explore the intersections of cultural identity, technology, and the future within their narratives. Hopkinson's legacy in the genre is profound, paving the way for more inclusive and representative storytelling in science fiction.

Black Speculative Art as Visual Resistance

Beginning in the 1960s with the advent of the Black Power movement, there was an effort to rearticulate Black contributions as parallel to yet consciously resisting the mainstream of American art. For the first time, the contributions of African American artists in the visual arts were confirmed as original and dynamic expressions of the Black experience. The work of Romare Bearden, Elizabeth Catlett, and many others was declared aesthetically authentic, charting similar conceptual territory to that of the artist Jean-Michel Basquiat. However, in the 21st century, art is undergoing a seismic shift in relation to production and conceptual development. Black speculative production defies temporal limitations and engages in praxis that "recontextualizes the perceptions of Black people to restore their subjectivity" (Jennings & Fluker, 2020, p. 59). Moreover, critical theoretical approaches that overlap to inform Black speculative theory and praxis around resistance are Greg Tate's, Alondra Nelson's, and John Akomfrah's. Between 1995 and 2012, several key inflection points informed the development of visual aesthetic Afrofuturists and their resistance in the English-speaking world, including art, race, technology, social science, and geography.

In 2012 Greg Tate delivered his manifesto *Kalahari Hopscotch, Or Notes Toward a 20-Volume History of Black Science Fiction and Afrofuturism* in the Atlanta Contemporary Arts Center, connecting his ideas to past Black aesthetic movements in conversation with Ishmael Reed's classic speculative text *Mumbo Jumbo* (Jennings & Fluker, 2020). Within this context, Tate makes the case that Afrofuturism has multiple modes of meaning and interpretation and notes it as "a temporally troubled matrix that thrives on opposites and opposition, flowing lines and nonlinearity, conflict resolution, and asymmetrical warfare" (Jennings & Fluker, 2020, p. 61). According to Jennings, this move by Tate is representative of the character Papa Labas in Reed's text *Mumbo Jumbo* regarding the *Jes Grew* phenomenon, where the protagonist is in search of the Kemetic textbook of Thoth, suggesting that if the book is not found, Jes Grew, and by extension, Afrofuturism will remain elusive and indeterminate (Jennings & Fluker, 2020).

Tate's perspective contrasts with Alondra Nelson's more social science perspective that she wrote about in her volume *Social Text* in 2002. For Nelson, the social capital of the future is connected to representation. Drawing upon social science, Nelson and her prior work to develop the Afrofuturist.net platform in the 1990s makes the case that Afrofuturism is part of a dynamic aesthetic tradition connected to Africa and makes a speculative connection toward Tate's position via Reed's *Mumbo Jumbo* describing the African creative as existing as a necromancer forecasting the future in the bowels of America (Jennings & Fluker, 2020). However, it is Beth Coleman's work connecting race and technology that builds on Afrofuturism more succinctly. Coleman interrogates the concept of *techne* within the fields of anthropology, philosophy, and technology. She connects it to how race is conceptually constructed and redefined and encourages a pan-technological approach to examine weaknesses in systematic structures of and legacies of white supremacy (Jennings & Fluker, 2020). Finally, John Akomfrah in his 1995 documentary *The Last Angel of History* develops a character called The Data Thief, an intergalactic time-traveling hacker, to find and reassemble which he calls the *code* (Jennings & Fluker, 2020). Therefore, within this framework, Black speculative creatives can rewrite the technology and steal the past back from colonizers and the forces of necrocapital (Jennings & Fluker, 2020).

Visual Nommo and Black Kirby

The *Visual Nommo* of Black Kirby, the creative team of John Jennings and Stacey Robinson, aesthetically engages Black identity to attack stereotypical and monolithic notions of identity impacting the agency of African descent peoples in the public sphere (Jennings & Fluker, 2020). Both Jennings and Robinson are master sequential art creatives whose aesthetic production operates fluidly in what was previously considered low-culture spaces like comic fairs or in highbrow spaces like prestigious art galleries. Black Kirby accomplishes this approach through an Afrofuturist framework and pan-technological methodology to interrogate fixed positions of identity imposed on people of African descent. Because Afrofuturism is resistant to fixed Eurocentric notions of identity formation, it influences radical modes of cultural production. Black Kirby uses this approach by mixing space and time travel with concepts of the alien and cyborg as social commentary (Jennings & Fluker, 2020).

The Black Arts movement, which theorist and cultural critic Amiri Baraka, a.k.a. LeRoi Jones, previously observed the Black Power movement and arts phenomenon worked together to impact the worldview of African Americans rooted in the ideological belief that the artist, out of all groups and corners of the power structure, helped foster liberation. The emergent Black Speculative Arts movement seeks this same end: the empowerment of the imagination in the face of aggressive oppression; it is a kind of Black visual alchemy—the practice of transmuting dross images of the past into gold medallions and envisioning the future. This new movement differs from other "Black" arts in the implemented tools. Thanks to digital technology, the new focus can no longer be limited to one grand genre like painting, filmmaking, music, theater, literature, dance, or fashion arts. We now incorporate old media and new digital media under the vast umbrella known as speculative fiction; it is a broad, culturally democratic intermingling of multimedia expressions by artists who take a critical theory stance in their production. With the recent increase in speculative fiction titles by authors of color, the issue is not a paucity of available works but rather the explosion of specificity and the growing diversity of consumer demands. Modern forces and evolving consumption patterns have shaped these trends in the arts and entertainment industries (Bray & Harrington, 2021; Harrington et al., 2022).

Artist John Jennings has argued that the definition of "Blackness" and "what it means to be Black" pervades the work of Black speculative artists. In their book *Black Comics: Politics of Race and Representation,* free from the typical restrictions of academia, Sheena Howard and Ronald Jackson effectively posit the visionary stance, or the expression of ideas-ideals through the products of the imagination, of Black speculative artists as an attempt to extrapolate and perhaps predict a problematized, or even eradicated future for signifiers of Blackness within the realms of futuristic appreciation. Afrofuturism is a philosophy and aesthetic foundation that concerns identity, race, culture, and society through the metaphorical and metaphysical looking glass of the future. It does so by importing the idealized ethics, practices, tenets, and philosophical sensibilities of the African diaspora and Africa. Afrofuturism is an ontological attempt to imagine the various futures of peoples of African descent with the customs, mores, and meanings to justify continued existence (Asante, 2023).

Afrofuturism in Dialogue with Rancière's Theory

As an aesthetic-philosophical discourse located within and particular to postbellum American contexts, Afrofuturism is an attractive force for reining in and focusing the otherwise unwieldy cast of practitioners helping to evolve and expand on Rancière's notion of "communal aesthetics" and recommends ways of applying communal aesthetic theory. In reconstructing and extending Rancière's concept of the distribution of the sensible, the set of sense ratios that determines the "common sense" also makes sense. To simplify, convincing many people that a particular act of speech or presence of a thing or individual somehow exceeds strict limits or proper bounds is relatively easy.

Afrofuturism in the Black Speculative Arts movement has promise as an innovative model for structuring and framing the sensibilities associated with who gets to count as a member of human society and how they count as such, but also the sensing and sensemaking aspects of this process. Thus, the latest movement to address the distribution of the sensible theorized by Jacques Rancière in *The Politics of Aesthetics* offers a fruitful means of bridging the theory–practice gap. So far, Black speculative artists and intellectuals of the present are already making it their task to meet and extend Rancière's insights to understand and interrogate how the production and dissemination of Black speculative arts might serve as a new and provocative model for the distribution of the sensible.

We propose that Rancière's theory of the distribution of sensible functions as a tool and "a turn" about utopic or dystopic representations of the future, which are the critical components of the discourse of the Black Speculative Arts movement, especially Afrofuturism. Rancière's work ensures that representational concepts provide a politically resistant force and that new political inclusions will be more than attempts to continue existing political struggles with a political strategy that has waning validity due to what we propose is an increased distribution of what can be sensed that is illuminated by the nontraditional representational methods of the Black Speculative Arts movement. Rancière's theory of the distribution of the sensible and the tenets of Afrofuturism share vital similarities. Due to these similarities, Rancière's theory can be extended to include the Black Speculative Arts movement. We also propose that the feeling of resistance when something new does not fit the current representative technologies and expectations is a "distribution of what can be sensed." In keeping with the tenets of Afrofuturism, we propose that a redistribution of the sensible is required and that this redistribution can offer alternative interpretations and actions for the current representations of the revolution that revolve primarily around the demand for equality.

Implications and Future Directions

Engaging with Rancière demonstrates which artists should be considered members of these communities based on his theories on aesthetics and art. Using him with other applied philosophy theories can allow us to critically evaluate which communities, genres, and representations can be appropriately considered new aesthetic communities and why. The Black Speculative Arts movement's embrace of new tools and technologies supports the ideas of Rancière, who challenges modernity's belief in the forward narrative nature of culture, knowledge, and progress. Technology is too often left out of the picture, as philosophers like Heidegger, Derrida, and Baudrillard argue or subjugate and appropriate in ways that support the status quo. Using an idea of multiple histories, this new understanding of BSAM allows us to produce and conserve knowledge to construct a global imperative to progress and develop while making it impossible for this necessity to be truly satisfied by any single entity.

This chapter explored some implications and future directions for extending Rancière's theory for the Black Speculative Arts movement. Engaging Rancière's aesthetic perspective, Afrofuturism's Black speculative performance illustrates the underexplored dimension of a Black avant-garde that Rancière outlines in his theory. Furthermore, the Black speculative arts genre provides a new way of examining the way the members of the African diaspora innovate within this civilization to expand and produce new aesthetic communities. Remixing and appropriating from the past, present, and future, the members of BSAM can assert an approach to art that says that anyone can make art that does not only pursue the avant-garde.

The exploitative crimes of racism and cultural appropriation are nothing new but, rather, continually reified and reinforced mechanisms. Due to the prolonged unpacking time required, these experiences are not unique to users of any characteristic or those born in any historical time frame. The result is the production of visual art that is vibrant, innovative, and extraordinarily provocative while presenting a strong, new, and significant response to these ongoing processes. The use and validity of these tools and the transformations to the design of the process of deconstruction regarding how to think, how to create, and how to live are some of the primary content that I hope to add to progressive political thought. In addition, the framework will also help understand long-standing inquiries into positive versus negative and progressive versus stagnant, all before the concepts are tested by the process involved in shifting political paradigms. These ideas are not achieved through creations obscured by an obtuse, ambiguous range of methods and are also not achieved through creations that tend toward the dictates of stereotypes. High-quality content will also be concerned with making and disseminating inspiring forms of enlightenment.

This work brings to visual arts practice and criticism not only a force reconsideration of what Afrofuturism might look like or how it might operate but also a force reconsideration of what is possible through African and African diaspora artwork. Racism diminishes these possibilities, dimming certain aspects of human nature through silencing, repressing, and limiting. Afrofuturism is an innovative way to reject racism, classism, or any consideration that limits, controls, and harms people. My investigation has the potential to be particularly useful for both formalized and relational artworks alike. Regarding formalized, progressive artistic practices, my framework can be applied by both artists and critics to gauge how Afrofuturism is exhibited, presented, and engaged. It can also serve as a set of guidelines to assist in creating content for generating high-quality Afrofuturist artwork that challenges the status quo.

Studying the work in a specialized field of Black independent speculative arts can be challenging simply because speculative arts is unpredictable, influences are multitudinous, and no specific definition of Black speculative arts is universally accepted or can fully embrace every artistic endeavor. Nevertheless, what constitutes the Black speculative arts has an authenticity that is cohesive and accepted by most in the broader field of speculative arts. As such, independent Black speculative artists have developed a strong, cohesive voice within the broader speculative arts community. This Black Speculative Arts movement is the collective effort made by authors, filmmakers, visual artists, and other creatives to tell a new story of what it means to identify as Black or African and what roles they can play in contemporary society. This is the new generation of Afrofuturism in which speculative arts are used to examine Black people's past and current social conditions (Brown, 2021).

Contemporary Black independent filmmakers, visual artists, novelists, and musicians create influential art and entertainment, challenging the social dominance and ideology of the major media industries and providing an independent, creative platform for marginalized voices within American culture. Set apart from their contemporaries by their creative use of the fantastic, these independent artists rewrite and revise believable stories out of the world in which we live, providing new opportunities for underrepresented groups to become the heroes of our social mythologies. The creative effort made by Black independent speculative artists has coalesced into a social movement whose creative output can be analyzed through an arts and culture movement theory. By doing so, the creative development of this movement can be observed, and the current wave of public change precipitated by the creative work of Black speculative artists can be identified and theorized against known social change models (Gunn, 2020).

CHAPTER 6

AI Nationalism and the New World Order

The global order that gave rise to Afrofuturism 2.0 was the conclusion of the ideological struggle of the Cold War between the United States and the Soviet Union, which resulted in the US becoming the global hegemon of the so-called free world and the beginning of the end of American hegemony (Anderson & Jones, 2016; Rapanyane, 2021). Authors like Francis Fukuyama (2006) wrote about what they term "the end of history," while many African American and other scholars moved on to discussions of postmodern identity and postcolonialism that overlooked the fact that history was not over. Contemporary Afrofuturism, or Afrofuturism 2.0, however, with its origins in the rise of social media and the politics of transnationalism and globalization, began to transition its discourse between 2016 and 2018 following Donald Trump's election, the emergence of other authoritarian politicos around the world, the increased growth in the use of artificial intelligence with machine-learning frameworks, use of chatbots by industry, and climate change.

The descent into a seemingly disordered world was complicated by the inability of liberal democracies to grapple with the COVID-19 pandemic and the growing boldness of authoritarian regimes and their fascistic sympathizers in flouting human rights and spreading disinformation (Anderson & Carr, 2023). The decision of Russian leadership to invade Ukraine and challenge Western hegemony in February of 2022, for example, caused a reaction in the pro-Western state system that has demonstrated the global geopolitical fault lines in the world system that in some ways resemble the old Cold War order, but with distinctive underlying tensions that reflect the new rivalry between the United States and China. Moreover, this tension erupted during the attempted January 6, 2021, coup in Washington, DC, and the ongoing COVID-19 pandemic and the European war highlight the future tension in the emerging global order between ostensibly liberal democratic societies and illiberal autocracies. The period in question will determine the future of human beings on this planet for the next few decades. Still, there is time to make ethical choices to prepare the global society for other challenges facing human beings, such as climate change, transitioning away from a carbon-based economy, and a universal approach to world affairs.

The technological advancements of this era have opened new doors for Afrofuturistic practice, allowing more dynamic and interactive ways of conveying the alternate realities and futures of those of African descent. An artistic example was the transition to online platforms during the pandemic, which permitted international collaboration between creatives and local art organizations. The "Curating the End of the World" exhibition with New York Live Arts highlighted this process (Anderson & Thomas, 2021). Furthermore, video games and virtual reality simulations are examples of new tech that have aided the progression of art and technology. For example, *Tales of Kenzera: Zau* is an African futurist-oriented game combining Afrofuturist aesthetics and the culture surrounding Bantu mythology. *We Are the Caretakers* expresses an Afrofuturist perspective on environmental politics. On the VR simulation front, Utherverse is a virtual reality engine that allows individuals to create virtual environments using tools indistinguishable from Photoshop. This software opens a vast realm of possibilities for Afrofuturistic simulation, as users may create an alternate reality or future and allow others to experience it from a first-person perspective (Anderson & Carr, 2023; Peattie, 2022; Kroeker, 2022; Cadle, 2020; Asante, 2023; Brooks et al., 2023; Anderson, 2022c).

Afrofuturism and Contemporary Technology

Contemporary Afrofuturism offers people of African descent a design lens for technological innovation (Winchester, 2019). Furthermore, it allows for critiquing bias in design and technological development (Winchester, 2019). While the internet was once viewed as an innovative landscape of limitless potential and freedom, it has gradually shifted toward one in which online activities and access are increasingly governed by laws and regulations specific to individual nations. This shift has resulted in significant software companies attempting to eradicate piracy in Third-World countries. However, this crackdown on piracy can cause considerable inconveniences for those relying on pirated software.

This shift implies that the world order will always find a way to impact developing nations, whether socially, economically, or technologically. The emerging world order is a situation that resonates with the struggles faced by the African diaspora and Africa today as they constantly strive to overcome the social and economic challenges that hinder their progress. Previously, Afrofuturism primarily represented the African diaspora, suggesting an ongoing struggle to achieve social and technological advancement on par with mainstream society. Technology, therefore, serves as a crucial means to attain that desired liberation (Darity & Mullen, 2022). Afrofuturism combines the myths and visions of the African diaspora with science fiction, futurist themes, and technology. The digital technology and social media explosion accompanied by the parallel emergence of Afrofuturism 2.0, African futurism, and Afropolitan perspectives has provided the African diaspora and Africa with fresh and inventive methods of expressing their diverse cultural perspectives.

Furthermore, the digital realm has transformed previous perspectives of Afrofuturist expression, such as the works of Samuel R. Delany and Octavia Butler. Moreover, Afrofuturist culture has flourished in virtual environments and computer games. The independent Afrofuturist movement in various genres of music, such as hip-hop, techno, and electronic music, has recently gained prominence, illustrated in the international impact of Afrofuturism, and continues evolving in novel and innovative ways, influencing global arts and culture (Dyer-Johnson, 2022; Okoro, 2021; Scott, 2021; Sites, 2021).

Afrofuturism and Social Change in the 21st Century

This transformation is not unique to Afrofuturism, as it mirrors the transformation of science fiction. However, the speculative future visions of Afrofuturism perhaps take on profound significance in an era of paradigmatic uncertainty and global transformation. Global events in the 21st century are outstripping Western-dominated science fiction, mired in played-out Near Future (cyberpunk, dystopia) and Far Future (space opera, posthuman) clichés. From the election of the first Black president of the United States to the rise of China to the probable decline of the US as a superpower to the possible 21st-century renaissance of Africa, the changing status quo of the world has created an increasing demand for the articulation of alternative future visioning. In the 21st century, Afrofuturism stands poised to address the global Black experience with a postcolonial and increasingly post-Western sensibility. Therefore, the Afrofuturist project necessitates breaking free of narrow definitions and exploring speculative frontiers.

A Multipolar World

A multipolar world order refers to a global system in which several superpowers hold leadership positions, not necessarily in alliance with each other or the leading power. The shift toward multipolarity could become the new global arrangement, following the period of unipolarity that began in 1991 but ended in the early 21st century in the United States. Current international events and the involvement of various global actors indicate the demise of the short-lived unipolar moment and the emergence of a multipolar global society (Safranchuk & Lukyanov, 2021).

In a multipolar world, a major war would be much less likely due to the checks and balances of rival alliances (Diesen, 2024). The US, freed from its commitments in the Middle East, would have been a strong balancing power to China; however, many European nations are seeking to export power from the US to Europe to steer US policy, perhaps back to its days as a counterbalance to the USSR (Scholz, 2023). The American invasion of Iraq in the first decade of this century was the beginning of the end of US hegemony in the Middle East. The global response to the US attempt to reshape the Middle East led to a further dispersion of power worldwide. This shift toward a multipolar world involves a more diverse distribution of power in terms of military strength and cultural, economic, and political realms. The impact of the war on terror has become more evident in the past decade (Diesen, 2022). The 2008 financial crisis and China's rise in the global arena played significant roles in creating an alternate world order where the US no longer leads, causing many US allies to distance themselves from US policies and align with emerging powers (Chan, 2021).

In an interview with *Le Temps* in December 2008, Zbigniew Brzezinski discussed a future without a singular power center. He further emphasized this idea in his book *The Grand Chessboard*, highlighting the global changes, such as China's rise, a united Europe, and India's emergence. As a result, the United States will face challenges in maintaining its current position of global dominance, leading to the replacement of a unipolar world with a more complex and disputed multipolar world. The emergence of a multipolar system suggests that the world will be organized into various power centers, ranging from dominant powers to those with significant regional influence (Clam, 2022; Chan, 2021; Rapp-Hooper, 2020; Wertheim, 2020). Contemporary Afrofuturism is beginning to envisage these shifting dynamics of international relations in a multipolar world where new and old forces contend for resources and influence. Realist theories of international relations, for example, have always considered power to be a relative concept between states. Changes in power between states occur in a global structure where a sole power bloc no longer exists. China, India, Brazil, and a potential African superstate are all expected to be future powerhouses in a more evenly distributed global power structure. China is locking in relations to secure energy resources, particularly throughout Africa and Latin America, and has continued to snap up natural resources before their prices skyrocket. This new era may even see a resurgent Japan throwing off the post-war Article 9 constitution after increasingly feeling the pressure from the North Korean missile problem. Power changes and power struggles in the future are something that humanity must be prepared to deal with (McMahon, 2021).

There is, however, an inherent danger that the increased competition at the state level driven by the multipolar world will heighten conflict. For example, a multipolar world is desirable for some states compared with a bipolar world, with Chinese–US rivalry likened to the Cold War. Conflict may take many forms, from proxy wars in regions of strategic importance to a second Cold War fought through an information and economic divide or, at its worst, full-scale military conflict. An example is a potential conflict between the US and China to control the South China Sea. If this were to occur, the implications for the global economy and the future of international relations would be highly damaging. Any conflict between major powers in a multipolar world has the potential to be catastrophic. Thus, the critical issue is to mitigate conflict and find peaceful resolutions to competition situations (Kuklinski et al., 2020).

The concept of "challenges and opportunities in a multipolar world" can be seen as interconnected. International relations' complex and fluid nature presents challenges and opportunities for various global players, including nations, businesses, and individuals. In this context, the analogy of a coin is relevant, as it highlights the financial position of the US and its repercussions on the global stage, which is a crucial concern in a multipolar world. A decrease in the dollar's value would adversely impact the economic stability of numerous states, and relying excessively on the euro or renminbi might not be preferable. Nevertheless, this economic instability in developed countries could lead to increased foreign aid and investment directed toward developed and underdeveloped regions. At the very least, this could signify progress toward greater equality within the global system (Baur & Dimpfl, 2021).

AI Nationalism

In 2017 the AI program AlphaZero caused a paradigm shift that ushered in a revolutionary change in computer science (Kissinger et al., 2021). AlphaZero is an AI program invented to play chess, and no human has ever defeated it. In 2020 MIT used AI to research molecules and discovered Halicen in a fraction of the cost and time of traditional research (Kissinger et al., 2021). The AI and human interface will usher in a previously unknown dimension in world affairs. The introduction of artificial intelligence in the context of nationalistic tendencies presents an intriguing situation in the current landscape of AI progress, characterized by a competitive race among influential countries. While globalization has brought substantial technological advancements, one could argue that technological progress shares similarities with the periods preceding World War I and World War II. During those times, competition between powerful nations and the pursuit of strategic advantage were the driving forces behind progress. Globalization and the subsequent spread of Western liberalism have resulted in significant transformation in human welfare, equality, and overall quality of life. However, the rise of AI nationalism poses potential challenges.

As AI becomes more prevalent, the future of the current global order becomes uncertain, considering the potential implications it may have on the dynamics of strategic power. In his book *Accelerando*, Charles Stross, a prominent science fiction author, emphasizes that the development of AI will manifest as a technological race, since the winner would likely acquire the ability to become the dominant global superpower. The intelligence explosion, where an AI system can rapidly enhance its capabilities, could enable a single AI to make decisive changes in global affairs (Kaminski, 2022). This concept carries substantial implications for international stability as nations strive to avoid becoming subordinate to a foreign AI. Consequently, they will strategically position and take pre-emptive measures to ensure that the AI aligns with their interests. Such actions would risk future conflicts among powerful nations and have the potential to be determined by a single exchange between forces backed by AI, leading to catastrophic consequences (Bukowski & Novokmet, 2021).

A strategic imperative is attached to the nationalist approach taken toward AI development to ensure national security and maintain the economic advantages of technological leadership. The concept of power and economic considerations each serve as the foundation for a more competitive multipolar world, where the existing liberal Western order, which has aimed to promote global public goods along with the economic and security interests of the West, may deteriorate. This deterioration could lead to a world where AI augments the ability of the great powers to reinforce their spheres of influence. Suppose the global AI industry is split into two, with the United States leading one branch, mirroring current structures of US dominance and alliances among liberal democracies, and China leading another, emphasizing digital authoritarianism. In that case, the developing and least-developed countries will suffer. These countries rely on extending Western public goods and norms to secure safer and more prosperous futures. As a result, an increased influence of authoritarian or illiberal democratic regimes on the global governance of AI may shape the future of AI technology around the values and interests of the powerful, potentially disadvantaging the weak (Aaronson, 2024). In the worst-case scenarios, developing countries may even become the testing grounds for AI weapon systems during proxy conflicts among the great powers.

The weaponization of AI is a vital area for strategic advantage and a necessary means of maintaining global and regional security. The dynamics of the race between nations or blocs competing for relative advantage in AI and quantum computing will likely involve attempts to hoard human capital and other resources from other states. Therefore, there is an increase in the migration of skilled IT workers recruited for talent migration, resulting in brain-drain effects on developing countries and a global labor market competition for AI-related jobs (Iuga & Socol, 2024). Higher education institutions may need to revise their training programs to meet the needs of domestic industry or target the immigration of international students. In the long run, race-based policies will likely emerge if genetic differences in intelligence are proven exploitable through genetic enhancement techniques or if there are differential automation rates (Schwartz, 2022; Dai et al., 2024).

The effects of AI nationalism on global cooperation will depend on the military strength of sovereigntist AI and its affiliated states. The preliminary stages of an AI conflict could be as politically intense as the historic Cold War between the US and the Soviet Union. The realist perspective in international relations suggests that states will align with or oppose the dominant AI power or coalition based on the security threat they perceive. On the other hand, the liberalist viewpoint and its associated complex interdependence theory argue that increased cooperation, negotiation, and transnational regulations can prevent conflicts and arms races from escalating into violent confrontations that could lead to human extinction. A transnational regulatory system could foster a relatively peaceful rivalry between sovereigntist AI, much like Sino-American relations in the 21st century. However, it is crucial to actively guard against worst-case scenarios of an AI war due to the existential risks involved (Goode, 2021). If transnational regulation fails and a single global AI attains dominance, it may utilize its creator state as a proxy to establish hegemony over the international system. Advanced AI can make rational decisions with information, employing strategies and tactics that may not necessarily align with the common good (Goode, 2021).

Ethical Consideration of AI Nationalism

As AI progresses, discrepancies in the standardization or establishment of AI will probably arise among diverse cultural or national groups due to disparities in technology, resources, and education in AI development. Thus, there is a growing potential to lead to conflicts akin to contemporary geopolitical disputes. Given that AI may eventually surpass humans in numerous intellectual pursuits, they could also embody their respective cultures' interests in international negotiations (Cachat & Klarsfeld, 2023). If a significant global power perceives that its AI is advocating for another culture's interests, it can create diplomatic strain. In an extreme scenario, a nation might demand the extradition of an AI or AI developer from another country to face trial for a perceived offense against their culture. Although this may appear far-fetched, similar incidents have already occurred with human agents, and it is entirely conceivable that AI will reach a level of advancement where this becomes a genuine concern. Any AI proxy war or conflict between multiple cultures would be a disastrous global catastrophe. Instead of pursuing a challenging and unattainable path toward multicultural and internationalist AI, striving for a harmonious and cooperative form of AI globalism may be more pragmatic. Regardless, preventing cultural conflicts driven by AI will necessitate a profound comprehension of the precise cause-and-effect relationship between AI behavior and cultural consequences, which could become a significant area of research in the social sciences (Cachat & Klarsfeld, 2023).

Mass Migration and Climate Change

Climate change will alter the Earth's atmospheric conditions, displacing millions of people. Various factors are driving this displacement, including sudden- and slow-onset disasters. Sudden-onset disasters, such as tsunamis, hurricanes, and typhoons, can cause mass casualties and leave vast areas destroyed and uninhabitable, which we saw when Hurricane Katrina hit New Orleans in 2005. Slow-onset disasters, such as droughts, desertification, sea-level rise, and ice caps melting, also have severe impacts. Desertification forced 3.5 million people to emigrate from the Sahel region of Africa. By 2050 climate-change-induced water shortage will displace 24 million to 700 million people from the Himalayan region (Wester et al., 2019). Small island states and low-lying coastal countries such as the Maldives, Tuvalu, and Bangladesh will be affected by sea-level rise and increased frequency of flooding, leading to forced displacement of many people. This displacement will often be permanent, becoming a form of statelessness. Mass migration of this nature will have numerous effects, both on the countries of origin of the migrants and the countries to which the migrants travel, and the result will be an increased conflict between diverse ethnic groups (Sunga, 2014).

In some cases, this will increase racial tensions and xenophobia, leading to violence and conflict. There could be a potential for increased recruitment by extremist groups of people who feel marginalized or victimized. States will also face territorial disputes externally with other states and internally with separatist movements seeking to obtain or hold on to land deemed suitable for rehabilitation (Ojha & Schofield, 2022). Significant population displacement can potentially be a rising issue on a large scale as climate-related disasters become more frequent and severe. Environmental migrants are individuals or groups compelled and forced from their native homes as ecological changes occur. The causes of environmental migration are complex and interconnected. Climate change and ecological disasters drive migration, and the consequences of migration can also impact the environment. These factors can lead to both internal and international migration. For instance, the depletion of resources like farmland and water sources in a particular area can directly affect the livelihoods of the local population. In another scenario, environmental factors can make a community more vulnerable to conflict, although proving these indirect connections can be challenging (Kaczan & Orgill-Meyer, 2020).

Challenges of Managing Mass Migration

The increasing speed of climate change and its effects on human life means that the areas affected will become unlivable much faster, and gradual migration of affected people is unlikely. Therefore, it becomes more probable that sudden and rapid movements will occur as the affected people move into disastrous living conditions. This happened after Hurricane Katrina, when many of the poorest people, such as those living in projects, had no means of evacuation or place to go. The Katrina debacle was an internal migration, with people relocating within the US area (Cannavò, 2008). It was still haphazard, with many being sent from shelter to shelter before leaving New Orleans. This type of situation will occur on a much broader scale, with the victims of natural disasters being moved within the country and then to neighboring countries. An example of the former occurred in the case of Tuvalu, where evacuations began in 2005 when a series of king tides caused widespread damage to the islands (Farbotko, 2005). Major cities are the most common destination for migrating populations, particularly in neighboring countries, as Global South–South migration exceeds regional migration to the Global North. The attempt to move north will cause sustainability issues in said cities as they struggle to support increased populations and carve socioeconomic niches for the incoming peoples. Strained resources likely cause tension between the affected migrants and the locals. The challenges of managing mass migration are unlike any others. Migration is a difficult task and must be dealt with properly to prevent as much suffering as possible. The human population's issues in managing the migration lie with the speed at which it will take place, the uncertainty about when and where people will move, and the fact that an incremental, planned response will become increasingly unfeasible in the context of rapid and unpredicted movement (Çelik, 2020).

Global Collaboration and Climate Change

The post–Cold War era has witnessed a rise in conflicts, prompting national leaders to employ diplomatic and structural efforts to prevent and resolve them. Numerous initiatives are under consideration to tackle conflicts and employ comprehensive and multifaceted strategies. However, these strategies can inadvertently lead to conflicting programs and create specific agendas that overlap in both region and time. In the case of climate migration, not all international efforts and agreements aimed at curbing climate change will necessarily promote stability in affected areas or prevent the displacement of populations (Çelik, 2020). For example, geoengineering, which aims to reverse global warming, can pose additional threats to marginalized societies and the impoverished. Considering that areas affected by climate change are at a higher risk of conflicts and that the effectiveness of conflict prevention lies in addressing the root causes of tensions, potential climate migrants can suffer in prolonged refugee situations. In such scenarios, international cooperation, centered on tackling the causes of conflict, remains the most effective approach to managing or resolving the problem and facilitating the return of refugees/migrants to their home country. However, in certain circumstances, some migrants may have already integrated into their new society, or their home country may no longer function, making it necessary to prevent climate migrants from becoming permanent migrants (Ferris, 2020). An example of an international agreement addressing specific issues is the mediation and peacebuilding efforts in South Sudan, as well as the 2005 Sudan Comprehensive Peace Agreement, which sought to prevent Sudanese citizens from migrating to other countries in the long run.

Given climate migration's global nature and complexity, relying solely on one pact or institution to effectively address the issue is insufficient. With factors ranging from environmental and weather patterns to demographic and socioeconomic changes and the varying severity of impacts in different parts of the world, mitigation efforts must be flexible and tailored to the needs and conditions of specific regions and times. However, the effectiveness of any form of international cooperation in combating climate change or mitigating its impacts and ultimately reducing migration depends on the presence of political will and the level of global governance. Ideally, countries should demonstrate dedication and work toward common goals. At the same time, international norms should provide a holistic strategy for dealing with climate migration and alleviating the burden on affected countries (Ferris, 2020; Matias, 2020; Fransen & De Haas, 2022).

Multipolarity and Agency of African-Descended People

The examination of the interconnectedness of these phenomena reveals significant implications for citizens and communities worldwide. The convergence of Afrofuturism, multipolar world order, AI nationalism, and climate migration is essential for cultural producers. It can shape resilience and sustainability efforts for African-descended communities and society. Additionally, marginalized groups impacted by climate change face the risk of further disadvantage in a future marked by volatile geopolitical order and discriminatory or exclusionary AI alliances. These alliances pose unforeseen threats to their digital personhood and material well-being. For the diasporic and continental Africans, the ability to adapt and mitigate climate shocks will directly affect their participation in a global multipolar world. It is crucial to no longer perceive Africa as a passive victim in the face of climate change. Instead, their agency in survival and thriving will be shaped by how a multipolar world order addresses climate displacement and crisis migration from other regions. By understanding the likelihoods and potential corridors of climate migration, appropriate technology and skills transfer can ease tensions and reduce exploitative relationships with climate-affected regions (Mihatsch & Mulligan, 2022).

AI nationalism is a form of exclusive solidarity. It will probably primarily benefit those elite groups with access to artificial intelligence. This phenomenon will probably lead to unforeseen dimensions of inequality and create new divisions or class stratification (Lee, 2018). AI nationalism, in turn, will increase global economic and social disparity. As a result of climate migration, there will be some displacement to areas less affected by climate change. For others, it will mean movement to territories controlled by artificial intelligence for work. The unethical use of AI is a dangerous path to conflict but is not necessarily war in the traditional sense, and it will further entrench the global class divide (Khan & Aazka, 2023).

On the other hand, there are multiple forms of resistance and possibilities to subvert traditional structures oppressive to African peoples (Okidegbe, 2022). During this transitioning moment in world history, the potential intersections between Afrofuturism, AI, and a multipolar world will swiftly become evident. Africa and its diaspora share a common goal and vision of envisioning a future where African culture and identity are not oppressed or marginalized globally. An Afrofuturist Pan-African framework achieves this by reimagining African societies and their diaspora by strategically applying science and technology. Similarly, a multipolar world represents a shift away from the current dominance of a single hegemonic power toward a more balanced distribution of power among various states. This shift is likely to lessen global opposition to the progress of Afrodiasporic peoples and their culture. However, a multipolar world may also become an arena for neocolonialism and imperialism. In a multipolar world, the implications of an AI-driven future for Afrodiasporic communities and Africa are significant. Automation by AI will bring about substantial economic and structural changes in the global economy. Certain nations may rapidly advance their development status through AI, further blurring the distinctions between developed and developing societies.

In contrast to historical patterns where African and Afrodiasporic cultures have been appropriated and marginalized in Western societies, a future multipolar world may see a reversal in power dynamics, potentially leading to greater recognition and global influence. For example, AI and increased self-determination for people of African descent could make astro-Blackness a global political identity. However, the effects of AI-driven automation may also mirror current globalization dynamics, potentially leading to displacement and unequal development among Black communities. Furthermore, AI's focus on power accumulation may divert attention from climate change mitigation efforts, raising concerns about the planet's well-being (Peters, 2023).

Implication for Global Governance and Policy

An era of AI nationalism will undermine the notion of global humanity that underpins many traditional approaches to global governance. Development and deployment of artificial intelligence are likely to be skewed in favor of the developed world. The scarcity of advanced AI and the security imperative will lead to a situation akin to the nuclear divide of the 20th century. AI will be employed to insulate developed states and regions from the effects of climate change and climate migration, furthering global economic and political divergence. The widespread belief that AI can simulate human decision-making processes coherently suggests that the global divide in AI will manifest a global power divide in which the Global South has little influence on the direction of global affairs (Leal et al., 2022). The increased automation of the developing world will strand these regions in low-wage equilibriums as they compete to maintain global production contracts. In this scenario, joint initiatives to address global challenges will take more work to achieve as states employ AI to optimize their position within a more competitive and fragmented global system. The use of AI for military and security purposes is likely widespread and carries a substantial risk of arms races and conflict. At the global scale, an era defined by multipolarity, AI nationalism, and climate migration will undermine existing approaches to global governance. Key to the post-Western global order is the decline of Western hegemony, leading to a diffusion of global authority and influence on non-Western and transnational actors. Climate change will further exacerbate this trend. As the world becomes increasingly multipolar, the ability of global institutions to address global challenges will diminish. A multipolar world order will likely be more conflictual and characterized by increased competition for global resources. The decline of Western global influence will reduce the diffusion of liberal norms and values, leading to a more culturally pluralistic international system (Leal et al., 2022; Cowls et al., 2023; Truby, 2020).

Possible Scenarios

In one scenario, the wealthy in all countries will have escaped the worst effects of climate change into controlled high-technology eco-habitats, leaving the rest of the population to suffer and fight over now-scarce resources. In another, more apocalyptic scenario, rampant climate fluctuations and positive feedback into the technosphere cause a global systems crash, destroying much human knowledge and technology and leaving a much smaller population to eke out a sustainable lifestyle on a depopulated Earth (Vince, 2022). Climate change in three dystopian scenarios leads to mass migrations and resource conflicts. The sparsely populated Global South sends massive waves of climate refugees into the North, which builds massive border fortifications and ultimately uses weather control technology to make the climate of the Global North harsh and unpredictable, to dissuade further migration (Vince, 2022). The speculative futures produced by workshop participants articulate alternative perspectives on the balance between technology, nature, and society. In most scenarios, technology continues to spread into every niche of the globe. The nature of this technological spread, however, varies widely. In the most utopian scenario, nanotechnology and other future tools have solved the energy crisis and repaired the environment (Vince, 2022).

Africa's diverse and abundant cultures and dispersed communities in other parts of the world offer many possibilities for stories set in imaginary future scenarios. These narratives explore the consequences of migrating due to climate change and how they affect generations of displaced communities. Science fiction provides a unique platform for artists to delve into how people adapt to new environments, technologies, and cultures. Climate migration affects all human populations, even those who live in regions that have historically been destinations for migrants. The impact and response to climate change transcend borders, but they will likely deepen the existing divisions created by the global colonization project that initially caused this crisis. Nations with high emissions, whose populations have benefited from colonialism, will likely aim to secure livable areas and maintain access to diminishing resources. The scenario will exacerbate global inequality and the neocolonial relationships with societies most affected by climate change. Exploring Afrofuturism scenarios of speculative migration will help us understand the experience of being seen as an outsider in a foreign land, preserving or losing culture, and possibly creating new blended cultures formed from various global traditions. The voices of our ancestors might exist in a cybernetic form. Additionally, inflated fears of job and resource competition from climate migrants could potentially lead to scapegoating tactics and new forms of discrimination. However, on a more positive note, multiculturalism, which has become a lived reality in nations historically characterized by monoculturalism, is often recognized as a valuable contribution resulting from migration. In the end, thriving climate migrant communities could become pivotal cultural influencers in a country's history, akin to the significant impact of the previous liberation movements (Kaczan & Orgill-Meyer, 2020). However, in this multipolar moment the phenomenon of Resource Nationalism must be reckoned with.

Strategic Collaboration in a Multipolar World

One key to global governance in a multipolar world will be providing more credible exit strategies for states that feel that their interests are compromised. Global issues always involve some sacrifice of national autonomy, and the fear of impotence in the face of decisions over which they have little influence is a significant driver of state resistance to international commitments (Pfeiffer, 2022). The fear of sacrifice can manifest as foot dragging or simple refusal to comply, as well as sabotage from within by dominant state or corporate actors. An early example of the latter is the weakening of EU carbon-trading regulations by energy-intensive industries to protect their national sectors from competition with other member states or outsourcing to the developing world. However, the only exit is a graceless abandonment of a treaty in the face of domestic political backlash. This can compound the damage to the global commons and leave the discredited treaty framework in place of chaotic nonsolution. A more positive form of disengagement is needed—one in which a state that feels that global consensus moves away from a policy it sees as vital to its national interest takes action to distance itself from that consensus in a manner that minimizes harm to the common good. Two such actionable forms of disengagement might be developing parallel policies, in which a small coalition of like-minded states agrees to undertake an issue in a different forum, or issue-linkage strategies, in which a state agrees to freeze instead of progressing on a given issue to gain concessions elsewhere. Open issues around such strategies can drain resistance to unfavorable global decisions and build new cooperation between states and actors with diverging interests (Pfeiffer, 2022; Saz-Carranza et al., 2024).

For collaborative solutions with shared responsibilities to succeed in a world of new geopolitical power sharing, balanced multilateral governance of global resources and issues will be necessary from both the top down and the bottom up. At the adaptability and resilience policy level, this means moving beyond the state-centric expressions of national interest that have dominated climate policy and foreign policy and engaging a more comprehensive range of state and nonstate actors. Moreover, the involvement of intergovernmental organizations, regional and local governments, and nongovernmental actors from business to advocacy organizations will be key at the local and national levels. Decision-making must involve all actors who have a stake in an issue and can contribute resources and expertise. For issues that cross state borders, this will often mean new forms of sovereignty sharing between public and private actors and hybrid public–private governance forms. Any such governance change carries its risks as well as potential benefits. However, considering the options' complexity is the best way to avoid deadlocking into zero-sum contestation of resources and influence (Sakib, 2022; Mishra, 2023).

Conclusion

Our central objective has been to analyze the implications for the future of the nation-state and people of African descent in an era characterized by global climate-induced disruption, forced migration, and hybrid, nonlinear warfare. The approach builds on previous futurist themes we have explored but with even greater emphasis. Recent global events, as outlined in the introduction, strongly indicate that traditional forms of state power from the 20th century are facing rapid erosion due to a combination of nonstate actors and stateless populations. It is easy to foresee that climate refugees' imminent tipping point and the resulting scarcity of resources worldwide will intensify these trends. Automation, artificial intelligence, and robotics are already reshaping and replacing human labor in various industries. How will these "bot" workers and military units interact with the masses of climate refugees also striving for a better future? What new, multipolar power structures will emerge as the traditional Westphalian order crumbles? In what ways will the growing complexity and interconnectedness resulting from these systems bring about both further turmoil and novel forms of organization? These pressing questions are in the context of a global African diaspora, the African continent, and the diverse future scenarios it will create. We firmly believe that Black and Afrodiasporic communities, given their historical and ongoing exposure to the negative consequences of globalization and its associated violence, serve as critical indicators of emerging global trends. Consequently, they possess a wealth of untapped knowledge regarding strategies for survival and identity formation in times of profound change.

There are several shared principles among different factions of the global bourgeoisie that shed light on the overall direction of this period. One crucial aspect is the unanimous agreement on acquiring a workforce with the necessary skills to adapt to new technologies while still being cost-effective in a time when profit rates are low and the population is at a surplus. The workforce in the future will undergo a significant transformation as rapid technological advancements render specific jobs or entire sectors obsolete. The World Economic Forum (WEF) is optimistic about this prospect, especially in the United Kingdom, which has struggled with long-standing unemployment. The UK sees the implementation of the universal basic income as a way to withdraw from the European Union and avoid the impending free-movement legislation for all EU member states in 2021. High-skill industries are also grappling with changes in job roles, particularly regarding training future data scientists and AI engineers. Last, there is a growing consensus on the importance of attracting foreign direct investment, as data has become a crucial form of capital, and there is potential to evade nationalist regulations concerning new technologies (Balakrishnan, 2022).

The WEF's 2018 meeting signifies a crucial moment in the race to construct the following ideology. However, we must first determine the exact nature of this new ideology before speculating what comes after capitalism. Throughout history, ideologies have shaped the economic landscape and influenced political systems. Take, for example, liberalism, which forms the foundation of both capitalism and modern democracy. Therefore, despite the WEF's assertion that the revolution is progressing exponentially, the rush to regulate emerging technologies implies that we are nearing a tipping point. Once reached, strategies built on these technologies will permeate all levels of society. In essence, the WEF's establishment of the revolution is an initial proposal to establish the game's rules. The coming years will determine its success or whether competing approaches will lead to a new era of large-scale power conflicts (Murinde et al., 2022).

The preceding analysis offers valuable insights into a world where a global African identity and collective agency will have taken shape. Afrofuturism presents a compelling vision of an independent African world. Through this study, we can envision what that world might entail by predicting future migration, technology, and geopolitics developments. Acknowledging that an Afrofuturist world may have challenges is essential. Our scenarios demonstrate that there will be both winners and losers. Whether the African world will overcome the existing divisions and inequalities remains. However, the forces of globalization over the past 500 years will result in increased mixing, hybridity, and cultural diffusion, making the concept of Blackness even more complex. The three global African identity archetypes will not exist in isolation; they must define themselves about one another. Power struggles and attempts to influence each other are inevitable. The extent and nature of the Pan-African sentiment expressed will depend on whether the African world can unite in addressing shared problems or if one segment triumphs over the others. Our estimation suggests that climate change has the potential to undo many of the advancements made by the diasporic and continental segments, widening the gap between the global elite and the general global population. The urgent need for solidarity and cooperation among African peoples in preparation for a global civil society and a world state in which they must act in the best interest of their descendants or, as some may argue, in the interest of their race must be emphasized (Osei-Tutu, 2023; Mpande, 2021; Thondhlana et al., 2021).

EPILOGUE

Dark MAGA, BRICS+, and the Biofunk Era

A Brave New World Order

The date is November 6, 2024, and I feel the familiar churn of history repeating, though it is wrapped in a new garb, with echoes of flawed systems and cyclical pain, returning to haunt us once more. The nation is teetering on the edge of a precipice, but does it know? The day broke with a strange quietness as I arrived on campus, the calm before the storm, perhaps. The air carried an electric charge, each breath seemed heavier with the anticipation of change. It's a peculiar world we live in, where fiction often seems less strange than fact, and yet, here we are again. Dark MAGA surged forward, sweeping through barriers thought to be invulnerable. Donald Trump's voice, a potent symbol of division, has found resonance in places many considered unreachable, finding its way back into the seat of power. Defeating Kamala Harris, and the neoliberal, trilateral establishment, was not a gentle push but a torrent, swift and unyielding. It signified a defeat of a type of Black American leadership that reflects the attempted incorporation of African Americans into the service of the *Deep State* from Ralph Bunch to Barack Obama and Kamala Harris. The winds of change promised by the opposing side now feel more distant than ever. I try to understand how history continually leads us here—these cycles of hope dashed, and visions altered, a dance between progression and regression. In these times, I am reminded of the worlds previously created and the lessons they hold. Stories of resilience, of those who endure against tides of hostility and ignorance, those who refuse to let despair be the end of their narrative.

The sky has darkened. A metaphor, perhaps, of what lies ahead under the shadow that promises to deepen before it lessens. Yet I believe profoundly in the power of resilience, in breaking through the strongest armor with persistence and truth. The tides may turn as swiftly again—a tidal wave of unity borne out of necessity and the unyielding human spirit. What happens now isn't just a political shift; it is a test of endurance and a testament to the narratives we know, the ones we live and write every day in silent actions and loud cries. We are more than the characters in one story of power; we are shaping countless stories, each breath a choice, a narrative thread in the larger tapestry. Tomorrow, we pick up the pieces. Tomorrow, we weave something new from the wreck's remnants—because that's where true strength lies. In visions of futures unmade, we find the courage to begin again.

The world order, or Bretton Woods system, shaped by Western dominant powers after the world wars, established institutions to ostensibly guide nations toward global prosperity, peace, and development. However, the cracks that began to appear in the late 20th century and unraveling beginning in 2008 proceed apace. It now faces criticism from rising nationalist and antiglobalization movements, notably seen in Brexit and the election of the America First president in the West and the rising influence of the BRICS+ nations. Despite this, the United States and the European Union remain significant global influencers, with Russia, China, and India emerging as major world-affairs players (Jowitt, 2023; Rolland, 2020).

Historical Context and Evolution of Afrofuturism 2.0

During the late colonial and decolonization phases, receptacle nation-states for the African peoples were constructed. These nation-states were organized around three central ideas. First and foremost, there was an appeal for humans around the globe to collectively understand and comprehend the intricate structure and organization of the vast continent, to harness and utilize its potential for the betterment of human welfare and the enhancement of life in all its diverse forms. This profound quest for enlightenment became the cornerstone on which the nation-states were built. Simultaneously, these African nation-states undertook the task of existing within a Britain-France-centric type of capitalist economy that was unabashedly resource-exploitive. However, it is essential to emphasize that the progressive leaders in these nations vehemently rejected any private foreign exploitation of their people and resources. This marked a pivotal shift in the economic development paradigm, as Africa attempted to resiliently struggle against any unjust exploitation, determined to establish a more equitable and self-reliant economic system that placed the welfare of its citizens at the epicenter of its endeavors.

Furthermore, the architects of these nation-states firmly believed in the paramountcy of sovereignty and the rule of law. They envisioned a society characterized by social justice, underpinned by a framework derived from the profound precedents and timeless principles established by thinkers such as Kwame Nkrumah. Drawing inspiration from these intellectual forerunners, the African continent aspired to construct a just and equitable society where the rights and dignity of every individual are considered sacrosanct, irrespective of their background or social standing. However, upon reflection, it has become evident that the colonial ideological foundation on which the African nation-states were built needed to be more robust. It ultimately led to the emerging nations' failure as practical tools for resolving the profound and multifaceted existential problems that plagued the continent.

Afrofuturism 2.0 takes further steps to recognize Africa's ongoing struggle by critically questioning and rejecting global structures that perpetuate the continent's exploitation. Additionally, Afrofuturism 2.0 supports a forward-looking approach based on the collective agency of the African people, which aims to create a prosperous and peaceful Africa. As part of the world and influenced by external issues and forces, Afrofuturism 2.0 is also deeply intertwined with the global order's complexities that shape our present reality. It acknowledges and engages with the multifaceted dynamics and challenges posed by the interconnectedness of nations, cultures, and politics across the globe. By exploring alternative narratives and possibilities, Afrofuturism 2.0 seeks to navigate and disrupt dominant power structures, working toward a future that is not only rooted in the empowerment of Africa but also in an equitable and just world for all (Müller-Mahn & Kioko, 2021).

Recognizing the limitations of these traditional nation-building ideals, Afrofuturism 2.0, building on previous African freedom initiatives, breaks free from their grasp, offering an alternative system that embraces the unique properties of Africa and its diaspora. Afrofuturism 2.0 propounds a radical departure from the dogmas of the past, placing prominent emphasis on the election and appointment of leaders with sound scientific and technical credentials. This transformative leap reflects the realization that leaders who are augmented with a sophisticated understanding of the complexities of the physical world will be better positioned to guide their nations toward a future of unprecedented challenges in an era of climate change and techno-autocratic capitalism.

Moreover, Afrofuturism 2.0 articulates a unique and effective ethic that provides an all-encompassing sociopolitical, economic, and environmental framework rooted in and developed under local conditions. This dynamic and context-sensitive framework aims to reconcile the progressive aspirations of the African people with the cultural and ecological tapestry of the continent itself, propelling Africa onto the global stage as a champion of sustainable development and equitable growth. In essence, Afrofuturism 2.0 stands as a profound paradigm shift, resonating with the pulsating heartbeat of Africa's vibrant and diverse communities. It dares to dream of a future where the intrinsic wisdom of the universe itself, amalgamated with scientific acumen, propels Africa toward unprecedented heights. It envisions a society where the tenets of justice, equality, and progress converge harmoniously, paving the way for a new era of African power on the world stage (Cooper, 2022; Miyoshi, 2023).

Climate Change and Afrofuturism 2.0

The consequences of the current climate-related events in Africa are increasingly getting more attention, particularly from an economic and cultural perspective. For example, in a 2021 article by Pohl et al., the authors try to gauge the economic impact of climate warming and human development in the Sahel region of Africa and point to the necessity of rethinking the shifting of resources in disciplinary settings away from the negative impact of climate change. Africa seems to hold the key to green energy systems for the world, particularly when it comes to the high demand for cobalt, which is a necessary ingredient in the production of lithium-ion batteries, which subsequently could be used in the production of electric cars. The European EU Green Deal also sees Africa as an essential partner in the global battery demand. The struggle to maintain this position, particularly in the light of its forced colonial economic past, can be observed in the fight to extract necessary materials like cobalt, for example, being a point in the political program of former US president Trump (Orlov et al., 2020; Dickerson et al., 2022).

Impacts of Climate Change on Afrofuturism

The potential indirect consequences of climate change pose significant risks to African people and their future opportunities, making these concerns essential considerations in decision-making. The African continent is the most exposed regarding what it has and produces due to the many people who have survived, and the small share of the wealth created. It is also particularly concerned about its ability to combat obstacles to and respond to threats to climate change. As we increasingly visualize atoms' subatomic particles and semi-superimpose the energy of waves and particles, by extending the Afrofuturism metatheory, human potentials could be enhanced through instruments such as bio-mecha—systems that combine biological and mechanical elements, designed to augment and expand human capabilities. By contrast, others can change human form with monumental presentations, underwater views, and appreciation of the elegantly beautiful and complex (Baarsch et al., 2020).

BRICS+ or Bandung 2.0

The intersection of climate change and migration poses significant challenges to global political and social constructs like Pan-Africanism, BRICS+, and Afrofuturism. These challenges just got steeper at the conclusion of the climate change meetings in the city of Baku, Azerbaijan. The limited commitment from the Western countries signified the lack of financial commitment and the growing absence of American influence on the issue of climate change with the coming of the second Trump administration. Addressing these challenges requires understanding their unique contexts and how climate-induced displacement impacts them. Pan-Africanism, the advocacy for political unity, cultural recognition, and economic cooperation among African countries and diasporas, faces new hurdles with climate migration. The United Nations estimates that climate change will displace millions of Africans by 2050 (Atwoli et al., 2022). This migration strains already fragile political borders and amplifies resource scarcity, challenging the solidarity that Pan-Africanism seeks. Immigrants often encounter hostility and xenophobia due to competition for employment and resources (Ottoh, 2021). Therefore, fostering cooperation and harmonizing policies within the African Union is crucial to address these stressors effectively (Nzaou & Ngome, 2020).

BRICS+—an association comprising Brazil, Russia, India, China, and South Africa, extended to other developing nations—faces its own climate migration issues. Member countries grapple with significant interregional migrations exacerbated by climate pressures. India's internal migration is an example, with rising sea levels threatening coastal areas (Senapati & Gupta, 2014). The economic and infrastructural demands of hosting displaced populations could strain BRICS+ alliances as each nation prioritizes domestic politics over collaborative responses. Coordinated climate policies and investment in resilient infrastructure and agriculture could mitigate these tensions (Leal-Arcas et al., 2022).

Afrofuturism envisions a future where African diasporas leverage technology to overcome historic injustices. However, climate migration poses existential questions for Afrofuturistic visions. Displacement due to climate may alter not just physical landscapes but cultural and traditional narratives as well (Anderson & Wadgymar, 2020). The threat to heritage and traditional knowledge underscores the need for digital preservation technologies and innovative storytelling to maintain identity despite displacement (Carter, 2022). Afrofuturism marries speculative thought with African diasporic / African frameworks, often exploring themes of speculative thought and presenting alternative futures. Integral to the genre is the reimagining of futures through an African lens, allowing for narratives that challenge hegemonic discourses and envision possibilities where marginalized communities are central to innovations and societal shifts (Nelson, 2002b).

Science fiction has long been a platform for exploring existential and societal dilemmas. Afrofuturism offers a unique perspective through which climate change can be examined. Works like Octavia Butler's *Parable of the Sower* (1993) integrate environmental collapse, illustrating climate change's potential societal impacts. These narratives are particularly poignant given Africa's historical exploitation of resources and the resultant environmental impacts, situating Afrofuturism as both speculative and prophetic. Climate change's disproportionate impact on marginalized communities underscores the importance of Afrofuturistic narratives. Historically, colonial practices and industrial exploitation have exacerbated environmental degradation. Afrofuturism posits futures where African-descended people utilize futuristic technology to combat ecological challenges, presenting climate resilience narratives that shift away from Western-centric paradigms (Eshun, 2003).

Important to Afrofuturism's engagement with climate change is the exploration of African spiritual and cultural traditions. Authors like Nalo Hopkinson (2012) integrate African cosmologies, presenting environmental symbiosis as a spiritual mandate rather than a mere utilitarian concern. These narratives posit an ecological ethics deeply intertwined with identity and cultural preservation. Moreover, Afrofuturism enables a reimagining of technological development that prioritizes sustainable and equitable practices. Works often depict advanced societies where technology harmonizes with nature, offering a vision of a future resistant to traditional colonial narratives that equate technological progress with exploitation (Womack, 2013). The relationship between Afrofuturism, speculative thought, and climate change highlights a critical interrogation of past and present injustices while dreaming radical futures where justice and environmental harmony prevail. It positions African narratives as crucial to the global discussions on climate change, asserting transformative possibilities beyond mere survival (Yaszek, 2006). Afrofuturism serves as a vital lens for exploring climate change, offering speculative visions grounded in justice and resilience. By centering African-descended narratives, it repositions African futurity and positions historically marginalized perspectives as essential to our understanding of climate futures. In conclusion, while Pan-Africanism, BRICS+, and Afrofuturism offer frameworks for a cooperative and technologically empowered future, climate migration challenges their foundational tenets. Collective action, strategic policy formulation, and technological innovation are essential to navigate the complexities imposed by climatic shifts.

The Bio-Mecha Revolution

Can technology exacerbate or solve issues related to gene and brain advancement? Afrofuturism 2.0 aims to minimize these problems by utilizing collective wisdom, culture, and resources to create a brighter future for humanity—that is, to initiate a bio-mecha revolution. This visionary movement focuses on the commoner, working to alleviate the oppressive homogeneity that characterized the Industrial Age. Its mission is to bridge the gap left by previous technological and industrial ideologies, offering innovative solutions to enhance social interaction and expand the horizons of space. Ta-Nehisi Coates, an influential figure, passionately encourages the upcoming generation to wholeheartedly embrace Afrofuturism, urging them not to settle for complacency. He emphasizes that Afrofuturism is not antitechnology or antiscience but a movement that seeks to unite communities and designers. By doing so, Afrofuturism aims to bring the inspiring inventions of Black inventors, once confined to the realms of science fiction, into the realm of reality. The ultimate objective of Afrofuturism 2.0 is to sow the seeds of knowledge within accessible, affordable, and sustainable technology. Simultaneously, it endeavors to stimulate fresh imagery and ideas through Afrocentric narratives. By fusing the power of technology with cultural richness, Afrofuturism 2.0 envisions a future where science and art harmoniously coexist, empowering diverse communities and inspiring collective progress (Asante, 2023; Laguarta Bueno, 2018).

The 20th century was known as the Information Age, while the 21st century is already called the Biological Age. Contemporary advancements in technology are allowing for the potential development of body parts, whole bodies, and parts of the brain. This could create a hybrid of man and machine, raising questions about the future and our identities. Rather than decoding the human genome, there is a focus on understanding and orchestrating intelligence instead of simply developing it. The key is the need for a new form of intelligence that understands complexity rather than simplification. The question remains: Will we be prepared to handle the ramifications of creating life (Rheinberger, 2023)?

Emerging Technologies and Implications

The Fourth Industrial Revolution is embedded in a mushrooming digital connection. Everyone is located either in the digital heart or the digital mirage. Cybersecurity, privacy, and big data are the immediate implications of this turbulence. 3-D printing is the precursor to a future likely dominated by bio-mecha processes that allow metals, ceramics, and plastics to be morphed by blending biology with mechanical and physical engineering. We refer to such processes as bio-mecha rather than just mecha process, and they include advances in memory devices using biological systems, transistors, synapses, touch and logic devices, biosensors, therapeutic membranes, and even the very complex semiconductor capacitors that need stringent structure for capacitor dielectric interfaces. The stock market has already begun to reward bio-mecha companies at valuations surpassing long-established contenders in the automotive and renewable energy spaces.

In Afrofuturism 2.0, excellent and leading scholars suggest that Afrofuturism may already be passé simply because it is, by its nature, an engagement with human imagination or the idea of a specific set of human imaginings about how specific aspects of the human collective future may develop considering a focus on the African diaspora. We propose that the romance or the vision is only one part of Afrofuturism. However, the reality of determining the future also comes into sharp focus, and it is in space technology and satellite technology that Africa is lagging without the specific content of the idea that will contradict what this book suggests. Afrofuturism 2.0 is about the complex realities and efforts to shape that future in ways and from a specifically African vantage point (Kroeker, 2022).

Challenges and Opportunities for Afrofuturism 2.0

In their seminal book *The Techno-Human Condition*, Braden Allenby and Daniel Sarewitz asked, "What if the Singularity arrives and the Africans have the only key?" This thought-provoking statement was meant to address the notion of the ongoing Fourth Industrial Revolution in which biotech advances, bio-environmental monitoring, such as the Intergovernmental Panel on Climate Change, EarthCube Science, the New Horizons program, or the African Center for Climate and Earth Observatory supported by the European Space Agency are causing great concern for the radical alterity of developing countries, in the context of biotechnological and bioclimatic leapfrogging, the capture of new forms of life on the planet and beyond. This work introduces another term into the current political lexicon—bio-mecha revolution—a rapidly developing phenomena within the so-called world order aimed at rapidly developing man–machine weaponry the likes of which the planet has not yet seen. It is obvious that if modern science fiction and cyberculture are based on significant countermythics of Afrofuturism, then we, in turn, in the era of bioclimatic leapfrogging, "bio-MECHA," and envy, should also overcome the old mythology of promised future victories (Dawley, 2024; Lenow, 2021).

Ethical Considerations and Social Justice

Furthermore, several inclusive choices fall under the broad governance category, such as significant issues in constitutional theory, profound discrimination, and exclusion. Ensuring top-quality medical care, governance, and ethical considerations is essential for establishing a society capable of coexisting in relative harmony and peace while working together to safeguard freedom and life satisfaction for all citizens. When developing a strategy for global governance, these factors must be carefully considered (Wright & Blackwill, 2020; Chancel, 2020). The world of modern medicine has justifiably been praised for scientific advances that have brought about remarkable cures that have extended and saved the lives of countless people. It continues to excel in creating an extensive array of gadgets and technologies that people can use to be more productive and have leisure time while living relatively longer, more healthful lives as time progresses. However, from a moral and ethical perspective, most healthcare professionals believe that modern medical professionals must go beyond mere scientific excellence and aspire to consider and value patients as unique individuals deserving of being treated humanely.

Conclusion

This book engages the concept of Afrofuturism 2.0 and suggests that it expand on its original foundation. As a result, the updated version of

Afrofuturism 2.0 should include a perspective on the future that not only is based on an African geography of reason and Afrocentric metaphysical concepts related to the universe but that also takes into account a broader environmental approach, perspectives, and stories on sustainable development, addressing climate change, the digital industrial revolution, and its potential advantages for an Indigenous fusion of technology and biology, and the subsequent repositioning of Africans in a world influenced by the digital age. At the heart of this argument is the belief that Africans and their communities have transitioned from external and internal battles for freedom from racial oppression, segregation, and armed conflicts against colonial and neocolonial regimes to the maintenance of freedom, sovereignty, and protection in favor of the governance of the majority, without disregarding minorities (Holbert et al., 2020; Brooks et al., 2023).

Afrofuturism 2.0 continues the trend of speculative thinking initiated by influential figures such as Sun Ra, George Clinton, Octavia Butler, Vusamazulu Credo Mutwa, and Lee Scratch Perry. These visionaries of the Black imagination offered glimpses of what the future might hold for humanity, especially people of African descent, envisioning a future in space. In this era of a new world order, characterized by a dominant ideology from the aftermath of the Cold War, declining higher education institutions, and a shifting global power structure, African people may find themselves politically influenced by a central African authority in a coalition with other major powers. The potential for chaos is not limited to climate change, the impacts of neoliberalism, or resurging racial tensions but also includes the uncertainties and potential consequences of the emerging bio-mecha revolution, which could alter the destiny of humanity (Asante, 2023; Adeniyi, 2023).

Reflections on the Future of Afrofuturism 2.0

The developed world's attempt not to see globalizing apartheid as sustainable begets global communities who live off the grid—who feed off the sun, purify water, and obtain the energy needed to sustain complex life from the cycle of life rather than from placing energy into deep states of concentration using distilled life. Afrofuturism prioritizes cultural formations that protest both the universalist narratives and discourses that sponsor techno-medical and techno-feudalist globalism and their production technologies, that is, they embody consumer behavior called "conspicuous consumption" by Veblen and "security" by authoritarian regimes because life still follows a simple second principle. Military development owed more to peacetime research and procurement than to wartime logic or technology. Councils for slave management and incubators for genetic engineering, built during the modern era, face periodic uprisings because construction is a hoax when it is based on tranquilizing unstable peoples instead of representing them equitably.

Afrofuturism represents a critical epistemology with Africana metamodernity while narrating cosmic complexity. It is the bridge between different imaginaries of humans and their futures, which colonial modernity sought to alienate: the mythology, eschatology, and cosmology represented by Africa and its diaspora. The Afrofuturistic movement is part of a deglobalization battle in which dominant actors attempt to fix whatever is possible and manipulate whatever is necessary to maintain their exclusive access to the parts of a planetary society that they need while treating everyone else as disposable. Coming at the intersection of climate change and both miniaturization and vertical dressing in biochemistry, our society's new forms of apartheid are the challenges and prospects of Afrofuturism 2.0.

ACKNOWLEDGMENTS

The completion of this book would not have been possible without the dedicated support and encouragement of several remarkable individuals. First and foremost, I extend my deepest gratitude to my friend, Andrew Rollins, former pastor, during graduate school at the University of Nebraska–Lincoln; our conversations have been a constant source of inspiration, intellectual insight, and motivation. Your unwavering belief in my vision and your encouragement during moments of uncertainty have been invaluable. Whether through late-night discussions or shared silences, your presence has been a guiding light in this journey. To my Saint Louis supporters that helped the movement get started with support and finances, Dr. Dwan Warmack, Shira Truitt, Mr. Ryan Branson El, Mr. Greg Carr, Ms. Hattie Weaver, Councilwoman Marlene Davis, and Dr. Betty Porter-Walls. To all the members of the Black Speculative Arts movement helping me build this movement for years, John Jennings, Dacia Polk, Stacey Robinson, Tim Fielder, Quentin Vercetty, Toneisha Taylor, Shannon Theus, Zaika dos Santos, Guilherme Xavier, Natasha A. Kelly, Nkolo Blondel, Frank Toh, Michael Bhatch, Gerald and Steven Vreden, Freddy Andrade, Steven Steele, Julian Chambliss, Lawanna Richmond. To my Temple colleagues, Molefi Asante, Kimani Nehusi, Nah Dove, Abu Abarry, Aaron Smith, thank you for the intellectual nourishment and constructive dialogues the last few years that helped shape this work. Your insightful feedback, critical reviews, and shared knowledge enriched the structure and depth of my research, and for this, I am deeply appreciative. I am thankful and grateful for the help I received from Christina Hudson, editing this document over the summer. I am especially grateful for the collaborative spirit and the stimulating discussions that inspired new ideas and directions for this book. I must also acknowledge the wider community of Afrofuturism scholars and creatives: Walter Greason, Erik Steinskog, Mark Dery, Nettrice Gaskins, Alondra Nelson, tobias van veen, Ytasha Womack, Tiffany Barber, Lonny Brooks, Sheree Renee Thomas, King Britt, and enthusiasts whose exceptional work laid the groundwork for many of the concepts explored within these pages. Your pioneering ideas provided a foundation and a compass that guided me toward unexplored territories. A special thanks goes to the series editors, Kinitra Brooks and Susana Morris, whose belief in this project and support throughout the process made this book a reality. Also, the editorial team's commitment, led by Ana Maria Jimenez-Moreno, to excellence, ensured that my vision was executed with precision and care. To my mom and dad, who encouraged my creative growth over the years, and my brother Terry, who stored my comic collection. Last, to my family, Denise, Zari, and Lauryn, whose love and support have been my bedrock, thank you for your patience and understanding throughout this process and all those long trips Daddy had to be away and miss events. Your support gave me the strength to continue, even when the road was long and uncertain. This book is a testament to the collective effort of all the individuals who have stood by me, contributed to, and believed in this work. With all my heart, thank you.

PORTIONS OF the introduction and the beginning of chapter 6 first appeared as "Afrofuturism: The Second Race for Theory" on the Council on Library and Information Resources' *Curated Futures* blog, "Afrofuturism 2.0: Dark Speculative Futurity and the Age of Acceleration" in *New African Thought* (2nd semester, 2024), and "Afrocentricity and Afrofuturism 2.0: Mapping African Futurity in a Changing World Order" in *The Routledge Handbook of Ethnicity and Race in Communication,* edited by Bernadette Marie Calafell and Shinsuke Eguchi (Routledge, 2025).

REFERENCES

Aaronson, S. A. (2024, April 22). *The age of AI nationalism and its effects.* Available at SSRN: https://ssrn.com/abstract=4803311 or https://doi.org/10.2139/ssrn.4803311

Acharya, A. (2008). *Bandung revisited: The legacy of the 1955 Asian-African Conference for International Order.* National University of Singapore.

Acharya, A. (2018). *The end of American world order.* Polity Press.

Adichie, C. N. (2008). *Half of a yellow sun.* Knopf Doubleday.

Adeniyi, I. (2023). *The politics of death in the selected Afrofuturist works of Nalo Hopkinson, Nnedi Okorafor, and Wanuri Kahiu.* University of Manitoba.

Adesanya, O. I. (2021). Ethnic-nationalism and politics of recognition in Africa: Towards a multicultural ideology. *BODIJA JOURNAL: A Philosophico-Theological Journal, 11,* 178–198. https://www.acjol.org/index.php/bodija/article/view/2136

Adler, E., & Drieschova, A. (2021). The epistemological challenge of truth subversion to the liberal international order. *International Organization, 75*(2), 359–386. https://doi.org/10.1017/S0020818320000533

African Union. (2015). *Agenda 2063: The Africa we want.* https://au.int/en/agenda2063/overview

Ahlbäck, A., & Braskén, K. (2023). *Anti-fascism and ethnic minorities: History and memory in Central and Eastern Europe.* Routledge.

Al Bidh, N. (2023). "Brave pessimism": The clash of Caesarism and democracy within Spengler's philosophy of history. *Philosophical Journal of Conflict & Violence, 7*(1).

Allenby, B. R. & Sarewitz, D. (2013). *The techno-human condition.* MIT Press.

Alkalimat, A. (2022). *The future of Black studies.* Pluto Press.

REFERENCES

Amoah, M. A. (2020). *FASHIONFUTURISM: The Afrofuturistic approach to cultural identity in contemporary Black fashion* [Master's thesis, Kent State University]. OhioLINK. http://rave.ohiolink.edu/etdc/view?acc_num=kent15960737328946

Anderson, E. (2023). *The first philosophers: The impact of indigenous thought upon Christianity and modernity.* US Catholic Historian.

Anderson, J. T., & Wadgymar, S. M. (2020). Climate change disrupts local adaptation and favours upslope migration. *Ecology Letters, 23*(1), 181–192.

Anderson, N. D. B. (2022). *Revolutionary Black faith: The contours of Black Christian socialist thought in the United States.* Union Theological Seminary.

Anderson, R. (2016). Afrofuturism 2.0 & the Black Speculative Arts movement: Notes on a manifesto. *Obsidian, 42*(1/2), 228–236.

Anderson, R. (2022a). Afrofuturism 2.0, Africana esotericism, and the geopolitics of Black Panther. *New Political Science, 44*(3), 444–449.

Anderson, R. (2022b). *Second race for theory.* Curated Futures [Blog]. https://futures.clir.org/afrofuturism-the-second-race-for-theory/

Anderson, R. (2022c). Afrofuturism and democracy: The age of disorder and the coming pluriverse. *Refraction Festival.* https://www.refractionfestival.com/editorial/afrofuturism-and-democracy-the-age-of-disorder

Anderson, R., & Carr, C. (2023). Afrocentricity and Afrofuturism 2.0: Mapping African futurity in a changing world order. In B. M. Calafell and S. Eguchi (Eds.), *The Routledge handbook of ethnicity and race in communication* (pp. 207–213). Routledge.

Anderson, R., & Curry, T. J. (2021). Black radical nationalist theory and Afrofuturism 2.0. In P. Butler (Ed.), *Critical Black futures: Speculative theories and explorations* (pp. 119–138). Palgrave Macmillan.

Anderson, R., & Fluker, C. (Eds.). (2019). *The Black Speculative Arts movement: Black futurity, art + design.* Lexington Books.

Anderson, R., & Jones, C. (Eds.) (2016). *Afrofuturism 2.0: The rise of Astro-Blackness.* Lexington Books.

Anderson, R., & Thomas, S. R. (2021). Curating the end of the world, Red Spring, and 2nd-wave Afrofuturism. *American Studies, 60*(3), 21–26.

Andersson, J. (2012). The great future debate and the struggle for the world. *The American Historical Review, 117*(5), 1411–1430.

Andersson, J. (2018). *The future of the world: Futurology, futurists, and the struggle for the post Cold War imagination.* Oxford University Press.

Andonopoulos, A. (2021). Posthuman others in twenty-first century women's science fiction [Doctoral dissertation, University of Newcastle].

Anyaduba, C. A. (2021). *The postcolonial African genocide novel.* Liverpool University.

Aragon, M. (2021). *A savage song: Racist violence and armed resistance in the early twentieth-century US-Mexico borderlands.* Manchester University Press.

Armillas-Tiseyra, M. (2023). Of freedom and the problem of the future in contemporary diasporic African speculative fiction. *Journal of the African Literature Association, 17*(1), 132–150.

Asante, B. (2022). *That bird is singing us an invitation to meet our future: Listening to the call of Sankofa to develop memory practice methodologies for performative practice* [Doctoral thesis, University of Westminster].

Asante, M. (1987). *The Afrocentric idea.* Temple University Press.

Asante, M. K. (1993). *Malcolm X as cultural hero: And other Afrocentric essays*. Africa World Press.

Asante, M. K. (2007). *An Afrocentric manifesto: Toward an African renaissance*. Polity Press.

Asante, M. K. (2017). The philosophy of Afrocentricity. In A. Afolayan & T. Falola (Eds.), *The Palgrave handbook of African philosophy* (pp. 231–244). Springer Nature.

Asante, M. K. (2023). *Afrocentricity in AfroFuturism: Toward Afrocentric futurism*. University Press of Mississippi.

Atkinson, W. W. (2023). *The secret doctrine of the Rosicrucians*. Double 9 Books.

Atwoli, L., Erhabor, G. E., Gbakima, A. A., Haileamlak, A., Ntumba, J. M. K., Kigera, J., . . . & Zielinski, C. (2022). COP27 climate change conference: Urgent action needed for Africa and the world. *The Lancet Oncology, 23*(12), 1486–1488.

Baarsch, F., Granadillos, J. R., Hare, W., Knaus, M., Krapp, M., Schaeffer, M., & Lotze-Campen, H. (2020). The impact of climate change on incomes and convergence in Africa. *World Development, 126*, Article 104699.

Babarinde, O., & Wright, S. (2017). Pan-Africanism, continental identity, and African foreign policy since 1945. *Conflict, Politics, and Human Rights in Africa* CPHR 4. Boston University.

Bacon, F. (1900). *The New Atlantis*. University Press.

Bacon, F. (2020). *Of the proficience and advancement of learning, divine and human*. Good Press.

Baghiani, A., & Kaouli, N. (2021). George W. Bush and Barack Obama's policies towards the "New Middle East": Promoting democracy or destroying social peace? *Algerian Review of Security and Development 10*(3), 1162–1174.

Balakrishnan, J. (2022). Building capabilities for the future of work in the gig economy. *NHRD Network Journal, 15*(1), 56–70. https://doi.org/10.1177/26314541211064726

Baldwin, A. (2022). *The other of climate change: Racial futurism, migration, humanism*. Rowman & Littlefield.

Balland, P. A., Broekel, T., Diodato, D., Giuliani, E., Hausmann, R., O'Clery, N., & Rigby, D. (2022). The new paradigm of economic complexity. *Research Policy, 51*(3), Article 104450. https://doi.org/10.1016/j.respol.2021.104450

Ballard, J. G. (2012). *Kingdom come: A novel*. W. W. Norton & Company.

Barberá, P. (2020). Social media, echo chambers, and political polarization. In N. Persily & J. A. Tucker (Eds.), *Social media and democracy: The state of the field, prospects for reform* (pp. 34–55). Cambridge University Press.

Bates, B. R., Lawrence, W. Y., & Cervenka, M. (2008). Redrawing Afrocentrism: Visual Nommo in George H. Ben Johnson's editorial cartoons. *The Howard Journal of Communications, 19*(4), 277–296.

Baur, D. G., & Dimpfl, T. (2021). The volatility of Bitcoin and its role as a medium of exchange and a store of value. *Empirical Economics, 61*, 2663–2683.

Baylis, J., Smith, S., & Owens, P. (Eds.). (2020). *The globalization of world politics: An introduction to international relations*. Oxford University Press.

Beatty, M. H. (2005). Martin Delany and Egyptology. *ANKH: Revue d'égyptologie et des Civilisations Africaines, 14–15*, 78–99.

Beauchesne, N. L. (2021). *Adepts of modernism: Magical magazine culture, 1887–1922* [Doctoral dissertation, University of Alberta].

Belkoli Houda, B. S. (2021). *The illusion of promoting democracy in Iraq during Obama's presidency* [Master's thesis, Guelma University]. http://dspace.univ-guelma.dz/jspui/handle/123456789/12698

Bell, D. (1973). *The coming of post-industrial society: A venture in social forecasting*. Basic Books.

Bell, D. (2022). *Dreamworlds of race: Empire and the utopian destiny of Anglo-America*. Princeton University Press.

Bell, D., Armitage, D., Blatt, J., Jagmohan, D., Hilfrich, F., & Philips, M. (2022). Duncan Bell, *Dreamworlds of race: Empire and the utopian destiny of Anglo-America*, Princeton University Press, 2020. *Contemporary Political Theory, 21*(2), 315–350.

Ben Salah, A., & Beggar, H. (2022). *Discourse in Francis Bacon's "The New Atlantis" (1626) and H. G. Wells's "The Island of Doctor Moreau" (1896)* [Master's dissertation, Mouloud Mammeri University of Tizi-Ouzou].

Berg, M. (2020). *The ticket to freedom: The NAACP and the struggle for Black political integration*. University Press of Florida.

Bernal, M. (1987/1991). *Black Athena: The Afroasiatic roots of classical civilization*. Free Association Books.

Bettiza, G., & Lewis, D. (2020). Authoritarian powers and norm contestation in the liberal international order: Theorizing the power politics of ideas and identity. *Journal of Global Security Studies, 5*(4), 559–577.

Bina, O., Inch, A., & Pereira, L. (2020). Beyond techno-utopia and its discontents: On the role of utopianism and speculative fiction in shaping alternatives to the smart city imaginary. *Futures, 115*, Article 102475.

Binetti, M. J. (2021). Philosophy and the speculative turn in the 21st century. *Philosophica: International Journal for the History of Philosophy, 29*(57), 53–67.

Birat, J. P. (2017). Musica universalis or the music of the spheres. *Matériaux & Techniques, 105*(5–6), Article 509.

Bird, P. (2021). An analysis of representations of African tribal society in "King Solomon's Mines" and "Heart of Darkness." *University of Nagasaki, Faculty of Global and Media Studies, 6*(6), 1–7. http://hdl.handle.net/10561/1787

Bistagnino, G. (2020). Liberalism, pluralism, and a third way. In V. Kaul & I. Salvatore (Eds.), *What is pluralism?* (pp. 62–78). Routledge India.

Bjørnskov, C., & Rode, M. (2020). Regime types and regime change: A new dataset on democracy, coups, and political institutions. *The Review of International Organizations, 15*, 531–551. https://doi.org/10.1007/s11558-019-09345-1

Blakey, J. (2021). The politics of scale through Rancière. *Progress in Human Geography, 45*(4), 623–640.

Blavatsky, H. P. (1891). *Isis unveiled: Mastery and key to the mysteries of ancient and modern science and theology*. University Library Basel.

Blavatsky, H. P. (1921). *The secret doctrine: The synthesis of science, religion, and philosophy*. Theosophical Publishing House.

Blum, C. S. (2023). *The other modernism: FT Marinetti's futurist fiction of power*. University of California Press.

Bogdan, H. (2024). Branding the Beast: Aleister Crowley as an advertiser of the occult. *Religion and the Arts, 28*(1–2), 13–65.

Bogues, A. (2015). *Black heretics, Black prophets: Radical political intellectuals*. Routledge.

Borst, E. M. (2009). *Cyborg art: An explorative and critical inquiry into corporeal human-technology convergence* [Doctoral dissertation, University of Waikato].

Börzel, T. A., & Zürn, M. (2021). Contestations of the liberal international order: From liberal multilateralism to postnational liberalism. *International Organization, 75*(2), 282–305. https://doi.org/10.1017/S0020818320000570

Boulding, E. (1996). Towards a culture of peace in the twenty-first century. *Social Alternatives, 15*(3), 38–40.

Braham, P. (2022). Afrofuturismo: Aesthetics and Interpretation. In Guillermina de Ferrari and Mariano Siskind (Eds.), *The Routledge Companion to Twentieth and Twenty-First Century Latin American Literary and Cultural Forms* (pp. 301–308). Routledge.

Bray, K., & Harrington, C. (2021, June). Speculative Blackness: Considering Afrofuturism in the creation of inclusive speculative design probes. In W. Ju, L. Oehlberg, S. Follmer, S. Fox, & S. Kuznetsov (Eds.), *Proceedings of the 2021 ACM Designing Interactive Systems Conference* (pp. 1793–1806). Association for Computing Machinery.

Brennan, J. R. (2021). The secret lives of Dennis Phombeah: Decolonization, the Cold War, and African political intelligence, 1953–1974. *The International History Review, 43*(1), 153–169.

Brzezinski, Z. (1970). *Between two ages: America's role in the technetronic era*. Viking Press.

Brock, A. (2020). Black technoculture and/as Afrofuturism. *Extrapolation, 61*(1/2), 7–28.

Brooks, K., Martin, K. L., & Simmons, L. (2021). Conjure feminism: Toward a genealogy. *Hypatia, 36*(3), 452–461.

Brooks, L. A., Best, A., & Fabello, J. (2023). Envisioning Africana futures in 2045: Dismantling white foresight to create community-centered Afrofuture pluriverses for all. *The Black Scholar, 53*(2), 71–82.

Browder, A. T. (1992). *Nile Valley contributions to civilization*. Institute of Karmic Guidance.

Brown, J. (2021). *Black utopias: Speculative life and the music of other worlds*. Duke University Press.

Brunton, J. (2018). Whose (meta)modernism? Metamodernism, race, and the politics of failure. *Journal of Modern Literature, 41*(3), 60–76. https://doi.org/10.2979/jmodelite.41.3.05

Bukowski, P., & Novokmet, F. (2021). Between communism and capitalism: Long-term inequality in Poland, 1892–2015. *Journal of Economic Growth, 26*(2), 187–239.

Butler, O. E. (1976). *Patternmaster*. Grand Central Publishing.

Butler, O. E. (1977). *Mind of my mind*. Grand Central Publishing.

Butler, O. E. (1979). *Kindred*. Doubleday.

Butler, O. E. (1993). *Parable of the sower*. Grand Central Publishing.

Butler, P. (Ed.). (2021). *Critical Black futures: Speculative theories and explorations*. Springer Nature.

Cachat-Rosset, G., & Klarsfeld, A. (2023). *Diversity, equity, and inclusion in artificial intelligence: An evaluation of guidelines*. Applied Artificial Intelligence.

Cadle, B. S. (2020). From Afrofuturism to "Afro-now-ism": Speculation on design as a transformative practice. *South African Journal of Art History, 35*(2), 67–85.

Camara, E. (2020). *The critical phenomenology of intergroup life: Race relations in the social world*. Lexington Books.

Canavan, G. (2016). *Octavia E. Butler*. University of Illinois Press.

Canavan, G. (2021). Science fiction and utopia in the Anthropocene. *American Literature, 93*(2), 255–282.

Cannavò, P. F. (2008). In the wake of Katrina: Climate change and the coming crisis of displacement. In S. Vanderheiden (Ed.), *Political theory and global climate change* (pp. 177–200). MIT Press.

Carter, B. W. (2022). *Afrofuturism and digital humanities: Show me and I will engage differently*. Routledge.

Çelik, Ş. (2020). The effects of climate change on human behaviors. In S. Fahad, M. Hasanuzzaman, H. Ullah, M. Saeed, I. A. Khan, & M. Adnan (Eds.), *Environment, climate, plant and vegetation growth* (pp. 577–589). Springer.

Césaire, A., & Pinkham, J. (2000). *Discourse on colonialism*. NYU Press. http://www.jstor.org/stable/j.ctt9qfkrm

Chalmers, D. J. (1996). *The conscious mind: In search of a fundamental theory*. Oxford University Press.

Chan, S. (2021). Challenging the liberal order: The US hegemon as a revisionist power. *International Affairs, 97*(5), 1335–1352.

Chancel, L. (2020). *Unsustainable inequalities: Social justice and the environment*. Harvard University Press.

Chapman, C. A., Abernathy, K., Chapman, L. J., Downs, C., Effiom, E. O., Gogarten, J. F., & Sarkar, D. (2022). The future of sub-Saharan Africa's biodiversity in the face of climate and societal change. *Frontiers in Ecology and Evolution, 10*, Article 790552.

Chapman, J. M. (2023). *Remaking the world: Decolonization and the Cold War*. University Press of Kentucky.

Chaves, A. O. L. (2018). From Kemet to the New World: History and reception of the first Egyptian collection in Latin America. *CIPEG Journal: Ancient Egyptian & Sudanese Collections and Museums, 2*, 13–26.

Chayt, E. B. (2014). *Disaster, dystopia, and exploration: Science-fiction cinema 1959–1971* [Doctoral dissertation, University of Texas at Austin].

Chiu, E. (2013). Hyperreality and consumer society: JG Ballard's *Kingdom Come*. *American & British Studies Annual, 6*, 165–173.

Christian, B. (1987). The race for theory. *Cultural Critique, 6*, 51–63.

Christopher, R. (2022). *Boogie down predictions: Hip-hop, time, and Afrofuturism*. MIT Press.

Chun, W. H. K. (2021). *Discriminating data: Correlation, neighborhoods, and the new politics of recognition*. MIT Press.

Clam, J. (2022). What is modern power? In C. Thornhill (Ed.), *Luhmann and law* (pp. 145–162). Routledge.

Coleman, D. B. (2023). Countering Afropessimist ontological nihilism: An Afrofuturist and Afro-diasporic cosmological rejoinder. *The Black Scholar, 53*(2), 48–57.

Coles, J. A. (2023). Storying against non-human/superhuman narratives: Black youth Afro-futurist counterstories in qualitative research. *International Journal of Qualitative Studies in Education, 36*(3), 446–464.

Colmon, C. D., Jr. (2020). *On becoming: Afrofuturism, worldbuilding, and embodied imagination* [Doctoral dissertation, University of Delaware].

Comaroff, J., & Comaroff, J. (2022). The wealth of ethno-nations: Notes on the identity economy. *Revue europeenne des migrations internationales, 3*(4), 31–55. https://doi.org/10.4000/remi.19004

Conermann, S. (2021). Mamluk Studies 2010–2020: An overview plus research gaps. In S. Conermann & T. Miura (Eds.), *Studies on the history and culture of the Mamluk Sultanate (1250–1517)* (pp. 7–56). https://doi.org/10.14220/9783737010313.7

Cooley, A., & Nexon, D. (2020). *Exit from hegemony: The unraveling of the American global order.* Oxford University Press.

Cooper, F. (2022). Decolonizations, colonizations, and more decolonizations: The end of empire in time and space. *Journal of World History, 33*(3), 491–526.

Coronelli, G. (2022). The futurist manifestos of early 1910: Dates and editions reconsidered. *International Yearbook of Futurism Studies, 12*, 3–49.

Courvisanos, J. (2005). Technological innovation: Galbraith, the post Keynesians, and a heterodox future. *Journal of Post Keynesian Economics, 28*(1), 83–102.

Cowls, J., Tsamados, A., Taddeo, M., & Floridi, L. (2023). The AI gambit: Leveraging artificial intelligence to combat climate change—opportunities, challenges, and recommendations. *AI & Society, 38*, 283–307.

Crowley, A. (2022). *The book of the law: Liber al vel legis.* Unicursal.

Csicsery-Ronay, I., Jr. (2003). Science fiction and empire. *Science Fiction Studies, 30*(2), 231–244.

Dai, J., Hiung, E. Y. T., Destek, M. A., & Ahmed, Z. (2024). Green policymaking in top emitters: Assessing the consequences of external conflicts, trade globalization, and mineral resources on sustainable development. *International Journal of Sustainable Development & World Ecology, 31*(6), 653–667.

Darity W. A., Jr., & Mullen, A. K. (2022). *From here to equality: Reparations for Black Americans in the twenty-first century.* University of North Carolina Press.

Davies, V. (2021). Pauline Hopkins' literary Egyptology. *Journal of Egyptian History, 14*(2), 127–144.

Dawley, W. (2024). Triangulating transhumanism: How risk, race, and religion in US culture produce futures (and Afro-futures). In M. E. Mogseth & F. H. Nilson (Eds.), *Limits of life: Reflections on life, death, and the body in the age of technoscience* (pp. 141–166). Berghahn.

Dean, A. (2017). Notes on Blacceleration. *e-flux journal, 87.* https://www.e-flux.com/journal/87/169402/notes-on-blacceleration/

De Cock, C. (2009). Jumpstarting the future with Fredric Jameson: Reflections on capitalism, science fiction and utopia. *Journal of Organizational Change Management, 22*(4), 437–449.

de Paor-Evans, A. (2018). The futurism of hip hop: Space, electro and science fiction in rap. *Open Cultural Studies, 2*(1), 122–135.

de Vries, L. (2022). *Reformation, revolution, renovation: The roots and reception of the Rosicrucian call for general reform.* Brill.

Deitelhoff, N., & Zimmermann, L. (2020). Things we lost in the fire: How different types of contestation affect the robustness of international norms. *International Studies Review, 22*(1), 51–76. https://doi.org/10.1093/isr/viy080

Delaney, T. (2020). *Darkened enlightenment: The deterioration of democracy, human rights, and rational thought in the twenty-first century.* Routledge.

Delany, M. R. (1880). *Principia of ethnology: The origin of races and color, with an archeological compendium of Ethiopian and Egyptian civilization, from years of careful examination and enquiry.* Harper & Brother.

Delices, P. (2021). At the center of world history, before Diop, there was Firmin: Great scholars on the Black African origin of the ancient Egyptians and their civilization. In C. L. Joseph & P. C. Mocombe (Eds.), *Reconstructing the social sciences and humanities* (pp. 147–170). Routledge.

Denisoff, D. (2021). *Decadent ecology in British literature and art, 1860–1910: Decay, desire, and the pagan revival.* Cambridge University Press.

Dery, M. (Ed.). (1994). *Flame wars: The discourse of cyberculture.* Duke University Press.

Descartes, R. (1644/2009). *Principles of philosophy.* Vrin.

Deterville, A. D. (2020). *Sankofa praxis—an Africentric meta-theory of sankofa and jegnaship—as a reclamation of Africentric episteme, psychology, spiritness, and personhood: A scholarly personal narrative of cultural retrieval, alignment, and actualization* [Doctoral dissertation, California Institute of Integral Studies].

Deveney, J. P. (1996). *Paschal Beverly Randolph: A nineteenth-century Black American spiritualist, Rosicrucian, and sex magician.* State University of New York Press.

Dias, L. (2022). Creating African unity through history: The question of the origin of the ancient Egyptians in Cheikh Anta Diop's Pan-Africanist historiography. *Revista Crítica Histórica, 13*(25), 1–32.

Dickerson, S., Cannon, M., & O'Neill, B. (2022). Climate change risks to human development in sub-Saharan Africa: A review of the literature. *Climate and Development, 14*(6), 571–589.

Diesen, G. (2022). *Russophobia: Propaganda in international politics.* Springer Nature.

Diesen, G. (2024). *The Ukraine War & the Eurasian world order.* Clarity Press.

Dikici, E. (2022). Nationalism is dead, long live nationalism! In pursuit of pluralistic nationalism: A critical overview. *Ethnicities, 22*(1), 146–173. https://doi.org/10.1177/14687968211063694

Dillender, K. (2020). Land and pessimistic futures in contemporary African American speculative fiction. *Extrapolation, 61*(1–2), 131–150.

Diop, C. A. (1967). *The African origin of civilization.* Présence Africaine.

Dolgoy, E. A., & Hale, K. H. (2020). Fiction and the science of self-reflection. In T. McCranor & S. Michels (Eds.), *Science fiction and political philosophy: From Bacon to "Black Mirror"* (pp. 15–36). Lexington Books.

Dorr, D. F. (1858). *A colored man round the world, by a quadroon.* Printed for the author.

Dove, L. M. (2023). Imagining a new world through Afrofuturism. In L. S. Abrams, S. E. Crewe, A. J. Detlaff, & J. H. Williams (Eds.), *Social work, white supremacy, and racial justice: Reckoning with our history, interrogating our present, reimagining our future* (pp. 424–439). Oxford University Press.

Dove, N. (1995). An African-centered critique of Marx's logic. *The Western Journal of Black Studies, 19*(4), 260–271.

Du Bois, W. E. B. (1903). *The souls of Black folk: Essays and sketches.* AC McClurg & Company.

Du Bois, W. E. B. (1910). *The souls of white folk.* The Independent.

Du Bois, W. E. B. (1920). *Darkwater.* Simon and Schuster.

Du Bois, W. E. B. (2011). *The Negro church*. Intro. by A. B. Pollard III. Wipf and Stock.

Du Bois, W. E. B. (2023). *The gift of Black folk: Historical account of the role of African Americans in the making of the USA*. DigiCat.

Du Bois, W. E. B., Brown, A., & Rusert, B. (2015). The Princess Steel. *PMLA, 130*(3), 819–829.

Duara, P. (2004). *Sovereignty and authenticity: Manchukuo and the East Asian modern*. Rowman & Littlefield.

Dubey, M. (2023). Afrofuturism and the speculative turn. In Y. Goyal (Ed.), *The Cambridge companion to contemporary African American literature* (pp. 81–95). Cambridge University Press.

Dunivin, Z. O., Yan, H. Y., Ince, J., & Rojas, F. (2022). Black Lives Matter protests shift public discourse. *Proceedings of the National Academy of Sciences, 119*(10), Article e2117320119.

Dunning, S. K. (2020). What is the future? Weirdness and black time in *Sorry to Bother You*. *Studies in the Fantastic, 9*(1), 44–62.

Duzgun, E. (2022). Radicalising global IR: Modernity, capitalism, and the question of Eurocentrism. *The Chinese Journal of International Politics, 15*(3), 313–333.

Dyer-Johnson, O. S. (2022). *Imagining a better world: Black futurity in contemporary Afrofuturism and speculative fiction* [PhD thesis, University of Nottingham].

Eddins, C. N. (2022). *Rituals, runaways, and the Haitian revolution*. Cambridge University Press.

Ehret, C., & Posnansky, M. (2023). *The archaeological and linguistic reconstruction of African history*. University of California Press.

Eisenhower, D. D. (1961). President Dwight D. Eisenhower's address. National Archives. https://www.archives.gov/milestone-documents/president-dwight-d-eisenhowers-farewell-address

Ekwensi, C. (1941). *An African night's entertainment*. Publisher unknown.

Elia, A. (2014). The languages of Afrofuturism. *Lingue e linguaggi, 12*, 83–96.

Eseonu, T., & Duggan, J. (2022). Negotiating cultural appropriation while re-imagining co-production via Afrofuturism. *Qualitative Research Journal, 22*(1), 96–107. https://doi.org/10.1108/QRJ-06-2021-0060

Eseonu, T., & Okoye, F. (2023). Making a case for Afrofuturism as a critical qualitative inquiry method for liberation. *Public Integrity*, https://doi.org/10.1080/10999922.2023.2251277

Eshun, E. (2022). Introduction: The art of the Black fantastic. In E. Eshun (Ed.), *In the Black fantastic* (pp. 8–28). MIT Press.

Eshun, K. (2003). Further considerations of Afrofuturism. *CR: The New Centennial Review, 3*(2), 287–302.

Everett, A. (2002). The revolution will be digitized: Afrocentricity and the digital public sphere. *Social Text, 20*(2), 125–146.

Fagan, P. (2024). Clicks and tricks: The dark art of online persuasion. *Current Opinion in Psychology*, Article 101844.

Fagunwa, D. O. (1938/2013). *Forest of a thousand daemons: A hunter's saga*. City Lights Publishers.

Failla, M. (2022). Assembling an Africana religious orientation: The Black witch, digital media, and imagining a Black world of being. *The Black Scholar, 52*(3), 30–40.

Fajardo, C. (2022). Jacques Rancière: Aesthetics, time, politics. *Journal of Aesthetics & Culture, 14*(1), Article 2049497.

Falcone, G. A. (2023). Futurism in the city of the future: Marinetti's avant-garde in New York 1909–1930. *Senior Projects Spring 2023*, Bard College, 352. https://digitalcommons.bard.edu/senproj_s2023/

Falola, T. (2020). Ritual archives. In N. Wariboko & T. Falola (Eds.), *The Palgrave handbook of African social ethics* (pp. 473–497). Palgrave Macmillan.

Falola, T., & Salau, M. B. (Eds.). (2021). *Africa in global history: A handbook*. De Gruyter.

Farbotko, C. (2005). Tuvalu and climate change: Constructions of environmental displacement in the *Sydney Morning Herald*. *Geografiska Annaler: Series B, Human Geography, 87*(4), 279–293.

Ferguson, N. (2008). *Empire: The rise and demise of the British world order and the lessons for global power*. Basic Books.

Ferguson, N. (2019). *The square and the tower: Networks and power, from the Freemasons to Facebook*. Penguin.

Ferris, E. (2020). Research on climate change and migration: Where are we and where are we going? *Migration Studies, 8*(4), 612–625.

Finley, L. (2015). Paschal Beverly Randolph in the African American community. In S. Finley, M. Guillory, & H. Page Jr. (Eds.), *Esotericism in African American religious experience* (pp. 37–51). Brill.

First, J. M., Danforth, L., Frisby, C. M., Warner, B. R., Ferguson, M. W. Jr., & Houston, J. B. (2020). Posttraumatic stress related to the killing of Michael Brown and resulting civil unrest in Ferguson, Missouri: Roles of protest engagement, media use, race, and resilience. *Journal of the Society for Social Work and Research, 11*(3), 369–391.

FitzGerald, M. (2020). *The Nazis and the supernatural: The occult secrets of Hitler's evil empire*. Arcturus Publishing.

Flint, C. (2022). *Introduction to geopolitics*. Routledge.

Fourcade, M., & Gordon, J. (2020). Learning like a state: Statecraft in the digital age. *Journal of Law and Political Economy, 1*(1), 78–108. https://doi.org/10.5070/LP61150258

Fox, T. (2023). *Black girl magic: History, identity, and spirituality in contemporary fantasy and science-fiction* [Master's thesis, University of Nevada, Las Vegas].

Francis, A. R. (2021). *Migrants can make international law*. Columbia Law School Scholarship Archive.

François, S., & Uskalis, E. (2023). *Nazi occultism: Between the SS and esotericism*. Routledge.

Fransen, S., & De Haas, H. (2022). Trends and patterns of global refugee migration. *Population and Development Review, 48*(1), 97–128.

Friedman, T. L. (2017). *Thank you for being late: An optimist's guide to thriving in the age of accelerations* (Version 2.0, with a new afterword). Picador USA.

Fukuyama, F. (2006). Identity, immigration, and liberal democracy. *Journal of Democracy, 17*(2), 5–20.

Fürstenberg, M. (2022). *Communities of hateful practice: The collective learning of accelerationist right-wing extremists, with a case study of the Halle synagogue attack* (Working Paper No. 2010). Max Planck Institute for Social Anthropology.

Galbraith, J. K. (1967). *The new industrial state*. Houghton Mifflin.

Galbraith, J. K., & Sharpe, M. E. (1977). The Veblen-Commons award. *Journal of Economic Issues, 11*(2), 185–200.

Galbraith, J. K., Weidenbaum, M. L., Hession, C. H., Deckard, B., Sherman, H., & Thompson, C. C. (1975). Economics and the public purpose. *Journal of Economic Issues, 9*(1), 87–100.

Gallagher, C. B. (2013). *Citizens of the empire: A molding of Victorian childhood identity* [Master's thesis, James Madison University].

Gallicchio, M. (2003). *The African American encounter with Japan and China: Black internationalism in Asia, 1895–1945*. Univ of North Carolina Press.

Gardell, M. (2023). Fascism and the violent replacement of the people. In S. Bracke & L. M. Hernández Aguilar (Eds.), *The politics of replacement* (pp. 245–261). Routledge.

Gaskins, N. R. (2019). Cosmogramic design: A cultural model of the aesthetic response. In M. F. Gage (Ed.), *Aesthetics equals politics: New discourses across art, architecture, and philosophy* (pp. 151–168). MIT Press.

Gates, H. L., Jr. (1988). *The signifying monkey: A theory of African American literary criticism*. Oxford University Press.

Gates, H. L., Jr. (2020). *Stony the road: Reconstruction, white supremacy, and the rise of Jim Crow*. Penguin.

Gaub, F. (2024). NATO and Libya: Operation Unified Protector, 2011. In J. A. Olsen (Ed.), *Routledge handbook of NATO* (ch. 15). Routledge.

Gaukroger, S. (2020). *Civilization and the culture of science: Science and the shaping of modernity, 1795–1935*. Oxford University Press.

Gazzini, T. (2022). *The changing rules on the use of force in international law*. Manchester University Press.

Geiselman, B. P. (2020). *Not slaves of another image: Black womanhood reimaged in the fiction of Frances E. W. Harper and Sutton E. Griggs*. Southern Illinois University at Carbondale.

Gellately, R. (2020). *Hitler's true believers: How ordinary people became Nazis*. Oxford University Press.

Geppert, A. C. T. (2012). Rethinking the space age: Astroculture and technoscience. *History and Technology, 28*(3), 219–223.

Geppert, A. C. T., & Siebeneichner, T. (2021). *Spacewar!* The dark side of astroculture. In A. C. T. Geppert, D. Brandau, & T. Siebeneichner (Eds.), *Militarizing outer space: Astroculture, dystopia, and the Cold War* (pp. 3–42). Palgrave Macmillan London.

Ghorban Sabbagh, M. R. (2020). Examining the relationship between "science" and "religion" in socio-cultural context of the Renaissance: A Kuhnian reading of Bacon's *New Atlantis*. *International Journal of Society, Culture & Language, 8*(1), 60–69.

Gibbs, D. N. (1995). Let us forget unpleasant memories: The US state department's analysis of the Congo crisis. *The Journal of Modern African Studies, 33*(1), 175–180.

Gill, J. I. (2022). Introduction: Toward Afrodiasporic and Afrofuturist philosophies of religion. In J. I. Gill (Ed.), *Toward Afrodiasporic and Afrofuturist philosophies of religion* (pp. 1–10). Wipf & Stock.

Gilroy, P. (1993). *The Black Atlantic: Modernity and double consciousness*. Harvard University Press.

Goode, J. P. (2021). Artificial intelligence and the future of nationalism. *Nations and Nationalism, 2*, 363–376.

Greenlee, S. (1969). *The spook who sat by the door*. Allison & Busby.

Griggs, S. E. (1899). *Imperium in Imperio: A study of the Negro race problem*. The Editor Publishing Co.

Gruesser, J. C. (2022). *A literary life of Sutton E. Griggs: The man on the firing line*. Oxford University Press.

Gunn, C. E. (2020). *Black cyborgs: Blackness narratives in technology, speculative fiction, and digital cultures* [Doctoral dissertation, University of Minnesota].

Gustafson, [tk]. (2001). [tk].

Haggard, H. R. (1885). *King Solomon's mines*. Cassell.

Haggard, H. R. (1926). *The ghost kings*. Cassell.

Hanchard, M. (1999). Afro-modernity: Temporality, politics, and the African diaspora. *Public Culture, 11*(1), 245–268.

Hancuff, R. (2018). Pan-African pessimism: *The Man Who Cried I Am* and the limits of Black nationalism. In S. Flynn & A. Mackay (Eds.), *Surveillance, race, culture* (pp. 247–265). Springer Nature.

Hanegraaff, W. J. (2020). Western esotericism and the Orient in the first Theosophical Society. In H. M. Krämer & J. Strube (Eds.), *Theosophy across boundaries: Transcultural and interdisciplinary perspectives on a modern esoteric movement* (pp. 29–64). SUNY Press.

Harel, T. O., Jameson, J. K., & Maoz, I. (2020). The normalization of hatred: Identity, affective polarization, and dehumanization on Facebook in the context of intractable political conflict. *Social Media + Society, 6*(2).

Harvey, M. (2020). Harnessed the Storm: Rereading Drexciya with The Black Atlantic. *Studies in Gender and Sexuality, 21*(2), 136–140.

Harrington, C. N., Klassen, S., & Rankin, Y. A. (2022). "All that you touch, you change": Expanding the canon of speculative design towards Black futuring. In S. Barbosa, C. Lampe, C. Appert, D. A. Shamma, S. Drucker, J. Williamson, & K. Yatani (Eds.), *Proceedings of the 2022 CHI Conference on Human Factors in Computing Systems* (pp. 1–10). Association for Computing Machinery.

Hartman, S. (1997). *Scenes of subjection: Terror, slavery, and self-making in nineteenth-century America*. Oxford University Press.

Harvey, J. (2021). Spaces of intervention: Politics, aesthetics, and archives in the films of John Akomfrah. In C. Nwonka & A. Saha (Eds.), *Black film British cinema 2* (pp. 126–142). Goldsmiths Press.

Haynes, J. (2020). Right-wing populism and religion in Europe and the USA. *Religions, 11*(10/490), 1–18.

Hedenborg White, M. (2020). From Chorazin to Carcosa: Fiction-based esotericism in the Black pilgrimage of Jack Parsons and Cameron. *LIR. journal, 12*(20), 52–73.

Hedenborg White, M. (2021). Rethinking Aleister Crowley and Thelema new perspectives. *Aries: Journal for the Study of Western Esotericism, 21*(1), 1–11.

Henshaw, A. L. (2020). Female combatants in postconflict processes: Understanding the roots of exclusion. *Journal of Global Security Studies, 5*(1), 63–79.

Herschthal, E. (2021). What kind of abolitionist was Benjamin Banneker? Reluctant activism and the intellectual lives of early Black Americans. *Slavery & Abolition*, 42(4), 669–690.

Higgins, D. M. (2021). *Reverse colonization: Science fiction, imperial fantasy, and alt-victimhood*. University of Iowa Press.

Hill, C. (2023). The roots and routes of Black emancipation in Sutton Griggs's *Imperium in Imperio*. *Texas Studies in Literature and Language*, 65(2), 209–228.

Holbert, N., Dando, M., & Correa, I. (2020). Afrofuturism as critical constructionist design: Building futures from the past and present. *Learning, Media and Technology*, 45(4), 328–344.

Holgado, M. E. (2020). Transforming the body, transculturing the city: Nalo Hopkinson's fantastic Afropolitans. In E. M. Durán-Almarza, A. J. Kabir, & C. R. González (Eds.), *Debating the Afropolitan* (pp. 68–82). Routledge.

hooks, b. (1994). *Outlaw culture: Resisting representations*. Routledge.

Hooper, M. C. (2024). "Racial greatness" reconsidered: Race theory, masking, and pragmatism in Sutton Griggs's *Imperium in Imperio*. *College Literature*, 51(1), 54–83.

Hopkins, P. E. (2022). *Of one blood: Or, the hidden self*. Broadview Press.

Hopkinson, N. (2012). *Report from Planet Midnight*. PM Press.

Hotta, E. (2007). *Pan-Asianism and Japan's War 1931–1945*. Palgrave Macmillan.

Houda, B. S. (2021). *The illusion of promoting democracy in Iraq during Obama's presidency* [Master's thesis: University of Guelma].

Howard, S. C. & Jackson, R. L., II (2013). *Black Comics: Politics of Race and Representation*. Bloomsbury Academic.

Hoyle, F. (1989). The steady-state theory revived. *Comments on Astrophysics*, 13(2), 81–86.

Hughey, M. W. (2021). Prometheus as racial allegory: The sociological poetics of W. E. B. Du Bois. *Journal of African American Studies*, 25(1), 102–123.

Hull, G. (2022). Epistemic ethnonationalism: Identity policing in neo-traditionalism and decoloniality theory. *Acta Academica: Critical Views on Society, Culture and Politics*, 54(3), 131–155.

Huntington, S. P. (1993). The clash of civilizations? *Foreign Affairs*, 72(3), 22–49.

Hurrell, A. (2006). Hegemony, liberalism, and global order: What space for would-be great powers? *International Affairs*, 82(1), 1–19.

Ibrahim, A. M. (2015). *Radical re-envisionings: Ancient Egypt, Afrofuturism, and FKA twigs* [Doctoral dissertation, University of Texas at Austin].

Ikenberry, G. J. (2020). *A world safe for democracy: Liberal internationalism and the crises of global order*. Yale University Press.

Ikenberry, G. J. (2020). *The crisis of liberal internationalism: Japan and the world order*. Brookings Institute Press.

Introvigne, M. (2021). An endless controversy: L. Ron Hubbard's "affirmations." *The Journal of CESNUR*, 5(6), 53–69.

Iuga, I. C., & Socol, A. (2024). Government artificial intelligence readiness and brain drain: Influencing factors and spatial effects in the European Union member states. *Journal of Business Economics and Management*, 25(2), 268–296.

Jackson, J. G. (1970). *Introduction to African civilizations*. Citadel Press.

Jackson, S. (2020). Religious education and the Anglo-world: The impact of empire, Britishness, and decolonisation in Australia, Canada, and New Zealand. *Brill Research Perspectives in Religion and Education, 2*(1), 1–98.

James, G. G. M. (1954). *Stolen legacy*. Philosophical Library.

Jameson, F. (2016). Postmodernism, or, The cultural logic of late capitalism. In F. Jameson, *Postmodernism, or, The cultural logic of late capitalism* (pp. 62–92). Routledge.

Jancovich, M. (2019). "Chained to the pendulum of our own mad clockwork": Science fiction, cyclicality and the new dark age during the Cold War. *European Journal of American Culture, 38*(3), 255–277.

Jansen, M. B. (1975). *Japan and China: From war to peace, 1894–1972*. Rand McNally.

Janz, B. B. (2017). The geography of African philosophy. In A. Afolayan & T. Falola (Eds.), *The Palgrave handbook of African philosophy* (pp. 155–166). Palgrave Macmillan. https://doi.org/10.1057/978-1-137-59291-0_11

Jemisin, N. K. (2015). *The fifth season*. Orbit.

Jemisin, N. K. (2016). *The obelisk gate*. Orbit.

Jemisin, N. K. (2017). *The stone sky*. Orbit.

Jenkins, C. M. (2021). Afro-Futurism/Afro-Pessimism. In J. Miller (Ed.), *The Cambridge companion to twenty-first century American fiction* (pp. 123–141). Cambridge University Press.

Jennings, J., & Fluker, C. R. (2020). Forms of future/past: Black Kirby Afrofuturism and the visual technologies of resistance. In R. Anderson & C. R. Fluker (Eds.), *The Black Speculative Arts movement: Black futurity, art+design*. Lexington Books.

Jerng, M. C. Y. (2011). A world of difference: Samuel R. Delany's *Dhalgren* and the protocols of racial reading. *American Literature, 83*(2), 251–278.

Jethro, D. (2020). *Heritage formation and the senses in post-apartheid South Africa: Aesthetics of power*. Routledge.

Johnson, A. (2019). Performing Black imagination: The critical embodiment of transfuturism. In R. Anderson & C. Fluker (Eds.), *The Black Speculative Arts movement: Black futurity, art+design* (pp. ix–xiii). Lexington Books.

Jones, N. H. (2021). Our democracy's founding ideals were false when they were written: Black Americans have fought to make them true. In S. Holt (Ed.), *The best American magazine writing 2020* (pp. 359–382). Columbia University Press.

Jones, S. V. M. (2022). *Afrofuturist feminism as theory and praxis: Rhetorical root working in the Black Speculative Arts movement* [Doctoral dissertation, Syracuse University].

Joseph, P. E. (2006). *Waiting 'til the midnight hour: A narrative history of Black power in America*. Macmillan.

Joslin, I. V. (2023). *Afrofuturisms: Ecology, humanity, and francophone cultural expressions*. Ohio University Press.

Jowitt, K. (2023). *New world disorder: The Leninist extinction*. University of California Press.

Joy, B. (2020, April 1). Why the future doesn't need us. *Wired*.

Kaczan, D. J., & Orgill-Meyer, J. (2020). The impact of climate change on migration: A synthesis of recent empirical insights. *Climatic Change, 158*, 281–300.

Kameda, T., Toyokawa, W., & Tindale, R. S. (2022). Information aggregation and collective intelligence beyond the wisdom of crowds. *Nature Reviews Psychology, 1*, 345–357.

Kaminski, J. D. (2022). On human expendability: AI takeover in Clarke's *Odyssey* and Stross's *Accelerando*. *Neohelicon, 49*(2), 495–511.

Kapcar, A. (2022). Spatial occultism: Placement and spaces of occult ritual practice within pop culture. In A. French & K. Waldner (Eds.), *Modernity and the construction of sacred space* (pp. 103–124). De Gruyter Oldenbourg.

Kaplan, R. D. (2013). *The revenge of geography: What the map tells us about coming conflicts and the battle against fate.* Random House Trade Paperbacks.

Keeling, K. (2019). *Queer times, Black futures.* New York University Press.

Keto, C. T. (1993). *The Africa centered perspective of history.* Research Associate School Times Publications.

Kgongoane, O. (2024). *We're digging the future: Afro-future mining in Africa* [Doctoral dissertation, University of Pretoria].

Khan, A., & Aazka, K. P. (2023). The Casino syndrome: Analysing the detrimental impact of AI-driven globalization on human & cultural consciousness and its effect on social disadvantages. *International Journal of English Literature and Social Sciences, 8*(6). https://doi.org/10.22161/ijels.86.31

Khan, S. A. (2021). *Star warriors of the modern Raj: Materiality, mythology and technology of Indian science fiction.* University of Wales Press.

Kilavuz, M. T., & Sumaktoyo, N. G. (2020). Hopes and disappointments: Regime change and support for democracy after the Arab uprisings. *Democratization, 27*(5), 854–873.

Kilgore, D. W. D. (2017). Arthur C. Clarke at 100. *Science, 358*(6369), 1393–1394.

Kimenyi, M. S., & Lewis, Z. (2011). The BRICS and the new scramble for Africa. In *Foresight Africa: The continent's greatest challenges and opportunities for 2011* (pp. 19–21). Africa Growth Institute at Brookings.

Kimmage, M. (2020). *The abandonment of the West: The history of an idea in American foreign policy.* Basic Books.

Kiran, S. (2021). A technological view of nineteenth century imperialism and globalization in science fiction and global history. In B. Cowlishaw (Ed.), *The rail, the body and the pen: Essays on travel, medicine and technology in 19th century British literature* (pp. 23–45). McFarland & Company.

Kissinger, H. A., Schmidt, E., & Huttenlocher, D. (2021). *The age of AI: And our human future.* Hachette UK.

Klein, M. C., & Pettis, M. (2020). *Trade wars are class wars: How rising inequality distorts the global economy and threatens international peace.* Yale University Press.

Kohso, S. (2020). *Radiation and revolution.* Duke University Press.

Krafft, P. M., Shmueli, E., Griffiths, T. L., & Tenenbaum, J. B. (2021). Bayesian collective learning emerges from heuristic social learning. *Cognition, 212*, Article 104469.

Krenn, M. L. (2022). The age of discrimination: Race and American foreign policy after World War I. *Genealogy, 6*(1), Article 16.

Kristóf, T., & Nováky, E. (2023). The story of futures studies: An interdisciplinary field rooted in social sciences. *Social Sciences, 12*(3), Article 192.

Kroeker, L. (2022). African Renaissance, Afrotopia, Afropolitanism, and Afrofuturism: Comparing conceptual properties of four African futures. *Africa Spectrum, 57*(2), 113–133.

Kuklinski, C. T., Mitchell, J., & Sands, T. (2020). Bipolar strategic stability in a multipolar world. *Journal of Politics & Law, 13*(1), 82–88.

Laguarta Bueno, C. (2018). Transhumanism in Dave Eggers' *The Circle*: Utopia vs. dystopia, dream vs. nightmare. *Revista de Estudios Norteamericanos, 22*, 165–188.

Lake, D. A., Martin, L. L., & Risse, T. (2021). Challenges to the liberal order: Reflections on international organization. *International Organization, 75*(2), 225–257.

Land, N. (2011). *Fanged noumena: Collected writings 1987–2007*. MIT Press.

Land, N. (2023). *The dark enlightenment*. Imperium Press.

Lane-Poole, S. (1990). *The story of the Moors in Spain*. Black Classic Press.

Langer, J. (2011). *Postcolonialism and science fiction*. Palgrave Macmillan.

Lauren, P. G. (1996). *Power and Prejudice: The Politics and Diplomacy of Racial Discrimination*. Westview Press.

Lavan, M. (2020). *Creating new suns: Early examples of Afrofuturist literature* [Doctoral dissertation, City University of New York].

Lavender, I. (2019). *Afrofuturism rising: The literacy prehistory of a movement*. The Ohio State University Press.

Lawson, L., Manick, C., & Jackson, G. (Eds.) (2021). *The Future of Black: Afrofuturism, Black Comics, and Superhero Poetry*. Blair.

Leal Filho, W., Wall, T., Mucova, S. A. R., Nagy, G. J., Balogun, A. L., Luetz, J. M., . . . & Gandhi, O. (2022). Deploying artificial intelligence for climate change adaptation. *Technological Forecasting and Social Change, 180*, Article 121662.

Leal-Arcas, R., Al Zarkani, M., Jbara, L., Margaritidou, M., & Mubwana, R. M. (2022). The BRIC and climate change mitigation. In *International trade and sustainability: Perspectives from developing and developed countries* (pp. 229–280). Springer International.

Lee, K. F. (2018). *AI superpowers: China, Silicon Valley, and the new world order*. Houghton Mifflin.

Leigh, J. (2020). *The emergence of global power politics: Imperialism, modernity, and American expansion 1870–1914* [Doctoral dissertation, London School of Economics and Political Science].

Lemprière, J., & Lord, E. (1825). *Lempriere's Universal Biography: Containing a Critical and Historical Account of the Lives, Characters, and Labours of Eminent Persons, in All Ages and Countries. Together with Selections of Foreign Biography from Watkin's Dictionary, Recently Published, and About Eight Hundred Original Articles of American Biography* (Vol. 1). R. Lockwood.

Lenow, J. E. (2021). Can we imagine a human future? Afrofuturism, transhumanism, and human life in Christ. *Political Theology, 22*(3), 1–18.

Leonard, N. (2020). The arts and new materialism: A call to stewardship through mercy, grace, and hope. *Humanities, 9*(3), Article 84. https://doi.org/10.3390/h9030084

Lerner, A. B. (2020). The uses and abuses of victimhood nationalism in international politics. *European Journal of International Relations, 26*(1), 62–87. https://doi.org/10.1177/1354066119850249

Levenda, P. (2008). *Stairway to heaven: Chinese alchemists, Jewish kabbalists, and the art of spiritual transformation*. A&C Black.

Levin, J. (2022). *The metaphysics of mind*. Cambridge University Press.

Levitin, D. (2022). *The kingdom of darkness: Bayle, Newton, and the emancipation of the European mind from philosophy*. Cambridge University Press.

Lispector, C. (1977). *The hour of the star*. New Directions.

Lofgren, M. (2016). *The deep state: The fall of the constitution and the rise of a shadow government.* Penguin Books.

Lok, M. (2023). *Europe against revolution: Conservatism, enlightenment, and the making of the past.* Oxford University Press.

Louv, J. (2018). *John Dee and the empire of angels: Enochian magick and the occult roots of the modern world.* Simon and Schuster.

Ma, G. (2023, December). Informetric analysis of researches on legal issues related to artificial intelligence. In 2023 *Asia Conference on Cognitive Engineering and Intelligent Interaction (CEII)* (pp. 130–134). IEEE.

Mack, C. A. (2011). Fifty years of Moore's law. *IEEE Transactions on Semiconductor Manufacturing, 24*(2), 202–207.

Mackay, R., & Avanessian, A. (Eds.). (2014). *#Accelerate: The accelerationist reader.* MIT Press.

Maddox, J. T., IV (2020). *Challenging the Black Atlantic: The new world novels of Zapata Olivella and Gonçalves.* Bucknell University Press.

Mamonova, N., & Franquesa, J. (2020). Populism, neoliberalism and agrarian movements in Europe: Understanding rural support for right-wing politics and looking for progressive solutions. *Sociologia Ruralis, 60*(4), 710–731. https://doi.org/10.1111/soru.12291

Manjapra, K. (2020). *Colonialism in global perspective.* Cambridge University Press.

Manning, P., & Trimmer, T. (2020). *Migration in world history.* Routledge.

Marable, M. (2011). *Malcolm X: A life of reinvention.* Penguin Books.

Marinetti, F. T. (2016). *The manifesto of futurism.* Passerino Editore.

Marino, D. (2024). The Tao of Julius Evola. *Vienna Journal of East Asian Studies.* Article online ahead of print, https://doi.org/10.30965/25217038-01501015

Matias, D. M. S. (2020). Climate humanitarian visa: International migration opportunities as post-disaster humanitarian intervention. *Climatic Change, 160,* 143–156.

Mbembe, A., & Balakrishnan, S. (2016). Pan-African legacies, Afropolitan futures. *Transition, 120,* 28–37.

McCauley, T. (2020). *A.I. nationalism: A new frontier in geopolitics.* Foreign Policy.

McGarity, K. A. (2009). *In memoriam Octavia Butler: For chorus, orchestra and speaker* [Doctoral dissertation, University of Texas at Austin].

McLarney, E. & Idris, S. (2023). Black Muslims and the angels of Afrofuturism. *The Black Scholar, 53*(2), 30–47.

McLeod, S. (2008). *Social identity theory in psychology.* Simply Psychology. https://www.simplypsychology.org/social-identity-theory.html#sthash.UsNnjwtA.dpbs

McMahon, M. (2021). *Questions of sovereignty and international institutional effectiveness on a global scale: The United Nations and the international courts.* Texas State University.

McQuaid, K. (2007). Sputnik reconsidered: Image and reality in the early space age. *Canadian Review of American Studies, 37*(3), 371–401.

Mihatsch, M., & Mulligan, M. (2022). Sovereignty in Africa and the specter of Wilson. In M-J. Lavellée (Ed.), *The end of Western hegemonies?* (pp. 35–62). Vernon Press.

Miller, P. D., a.k.a. DJ Spooky That Subliminal Kid. (2004). *Rhythm Science* [Mediaworks Pamphlets]. MT Press.

Mills, C. W. (1997). *The racial contract*. Cornell University Press.

Mills, C. W. (2022). Breaching cosmopolitan theory's global color line—Inés Valdez: *Transnational Cosmopolitanism*: Kant, Du Bois, and Justice as a Political Craft. (Cambridge: Cambridge University Press, 2019. Pp. 210.) [Book Review]. *The Review of Politics, 84*(1), 107–111.

Mirabella, V. (2023). Italian futurist books (1909–1944) at the British Library. *Electronic British Library Journal, 2022*, Article 10.

Mirsky, J. V. (2023). *What if there's no one pulling the strings? A cultural theoretical account of Trumpism and big tent conspiracy theories* [Bucknell Honors Thesis].

Mishra, S. (2023). The fluidity of world order and break from past: Opportunities and challenges. *Social Development Issues, 46*(1), Article 5.

Mitchell, J. (2023). Racial and social democracy in Sam Greenlee's *The Spook Who Sat by the Door*. *American Literary History, 35*(1), 187–200.

Mitchell, J. D. (2020). *The death and life of the American novel: Radicalism and the transformation of US literature in the 1960s* [Doctoral dissertation, Duke University].

Miyoshi, M. (2023). A borderless world? From colonialism to transnationalism and the decline of the nation-state. *Critical Inquiry, 19*(4), 726–751.

Modupe, D. (2003). The Afrocentric philosophical perspective: A narrative outline. In A. Mazama (Ed.), *The Afrocentric paradigm* (pp. 55–72). African World Press.

Moldbug, M. (2008). *The dark enlightenment*. Unqualified Reservations [Blog]. https://www.unqualified-reservations.org/

Monáe, J. (2018, April 7). *Janelle Monáe—Dirty Computer* [emotion picture] [Video]. YouTube. https://youtu.be/jdH2Sy-BlNE?si=c4PXAzHG1tjLxWk2

Monteiro-Ferreira, A. (2014). *The demise of the inhuman: Afrocentricity, modernism, and postmodernism*. SUNY Press.

Moody-Turner, S. (2020). Double consciousness: African American writers at the turn of the twentieth century. *A Companion to American Literature, 2*, 455–469.

Morgan, T. V. (2020). Pushing the frontiers of Nigeria's cultural communication through digital media practice. *Virtual Creativity, 10*(2), 175–190.

Morlino, L. (2020). *Equality, freedom, and democracy: Europe after the great recession*. Oxford Academic, https://doi.org/10.1093/oso/9780198813873.001.0001

Morris, A., Schwartz, M., & Itzigsohn, J. (2021). Racism, colonialism, and modernity: The sociology of W. E. B. Du Bois. In S. Abrutyn & O. Lizardo, *Handbook of classical sociological theory* (pp. 121–143). Springer Nature.

Morris, S. M. (2019). "Everything is real. It's just not as you see it: Imagination, utopia, and Afrofuturist feminism in Octavia E. Butler's 'The book of Martha.'" In R. Anderson & C. Fluker (Eds.), *The Black Speculative Arts movement: Black futurity, art+design*. Lexington Books.

Morrow, A. (2022). Conceptualising secret societies and conspiracy theories in Imperial Japan. In F. Piraino, M. Pasi, & E. Asprem (Eds.), *Religious dimensions of conspiracy theories: Comparing and connecting old and new trends* (chap. 5). Taylor & Francis.

Mpande, S. M. N. (2021). *The diaspora's role in Africa: Transculturalism, challenges, and development*. Routledge.

Mulkey, R. L. (2024). *Black birth, culture, and community: A Hoodoo perspective explored through Black birthing narratives* [Master's thesis, Bastyr University].

Müller-Mahn, D., & Kioko, E. (2021). Rethinking African futures after COVID-19. *Africa Spectrum, 56*(2), 216–227.

Mullins, M. R. (2021). *Yasukuni fundamentalism: Japanese religions and the politics of restoration*. University of Hawai'i Press.

Murinde, V., Rizopoulos, E., & Zachariadis, M. (2022). The impact of the FinTech revolution on the future of banking: Opportunities and risks. *International Review of Financial Analysis, 81*, Article 102103.

Murray, D. (2017). *The strange death of Europe: Immigration, identity, Islam*. Bloomsbury Continuum.

Nathaniel, S. O., & Akung, E. J. (2022). Afrofuturism and Africanfuturism: Black speculative writings in search of meaning criteria. *Research Journal in Advanced Humanities, 3*(3), 1–14.

Nehusi, K. S. (2023). Kemet and the philosophy of Afrofuturism. *The Black Scholar, 53*(2), 4–16.

Nelson, A. (2002). *Afrofuturism: A special issue of Social Text*. Duke University Press.

Nelson, A. (2019). Afrofuturism and the archive: Black radical imagination and digital humanities. *Journal of African American Studies, 23*(4), 357–372.

Neptune, C. (2023). *Ah new riddim: A marked (Black) axiological shift across space and time* [Doctoral dissertation, Massachusetts Institute of Technology].

Newman, B. (1992). *Brave New World Revisited* revisited: Huxley's evolving view of behaviorism. *The Behavior Analyst, 15*, 61–69.

Nilsson, P. E. (2022). Manifestos of white nationalist ethno-soldiers. *Critical Research on Religion, 10*(2), 221–235. https://doi.org/10.1177/20503032211044426

Noys, B. (2023). *Apocalypse and crisis: Literary, cultural and political essays, 2009–2021*. Brill.

Nunn, A. J. (2023). *Racial imaginaries: Limit and resistance in contemporary Black women's speculative fiction* [Doctoral dissertation, University of Maryland, College Park].

Nzaou, A., & Ngome, F. E. (2020). African Union. *Yearbook of International Environmental Law, 31*(1), 313–319.

Oboe, A. (2019). Africa's planetary futures. *From the European South, 4*, 1–104.

Ojha, H., & Schofield, N. (2022). *Climate change and water security in the Indo-Pacific region: Risks, responses, and a framework for action*. Australian Water Partnership.

Okakura, K. (1903). *The Ideals of the East*. John Murray.

Okidegbe, N. (2022). Of Afrofuturism, of algorithms. *Critical Analysis of Law, 9*, 35–48.

Okorafor, N. N. (2019, October 19). African Futurism defined. *Nnedi's Whala Zone Blog*. http://nnedi.blogspot.com/2019/10/africanfuturism-defined.html

Okoro, D. (2021). *Futurism and the African imagination: Literature and other arts*. Routledge.

Olsen, K. M. (1987). *Jean Toomer's "Cane": A work in the American grotesque genre* [Master's thesis, Eastern Illinois University].

Ong, J. M. (2019). Imperial ecologies and extinction in HG Wells's island stories. In L. W. Mazzeno & R. D. Morrison (Eds.), *Victorian environmental nightmares* (pp. 185–206). Springer Nature.

Orlov, A., Sillmann, J., Aunan, K., Kjellstrom, T., & Aaheim, A. (2020). Economic costs of heat-induced reductions in worker productivity due to global warming. *Global Environmental Change, 63*, Article 102087.

Osei, E. A. (2023). Wakanda Africa, do you see? Reading *Black Panther* as a decolonial film through the lens of the Sankofa theory. *Critical Studies in Media Communication, 37*(4), 378–390.

Osei-Tutu, A. A. Z. (2023). African-centered hybridity: A reconceptualization of Africanness in this colonially guised globalized era. *Alliance for African Partnership Perspectives, 2,* 61–73.

Ottoh, F. O. (2021). International migration and xenophobia. *Journal of African Union Studies, 10*(1), 9–27.

Owens, I. D. (2013). *At the crossroads: African American and Caribbean writers in the interwar period.* Columbia University.

Page, C., & Woodland, E. (2023). *Healing justice lineages: Dreaming at the crossroads of liberation, collective care, and safety.* North Atlantic Books.

Pak, C. (2010, June). Ecocriticism and terraforming: Building critical spaces. *FORUM: University of Edinburgh Postgraduate Journal of Culture & the Arts, 10,* 1–14.

Parhizkar, M. I. (2015). *The planet is the way it is because of the scheme of words: Sun Ra and the Performance of Reckoning* [Master's thesis, City University of New York].

Parrinder, P. (2021). Science fiction and the scientific world-view. In P. Parrinder (Ed.), *Science fiction: A critical guide* (pp. 67–88). Routledge.

Parsi, V. E. (2021). *The wrecking of the liberal world order.* Palgrave Macmillan.

Patterson, O. (1982). *Slavery and social death: A comparative study.* Harvard University Press.

Peattie, P. (2022). Afrofuturism revelation and revolution: Voices of the digital generation. *Journal of Communication Inquiry, 46*(2), 161–184.

Pedretti, F. (2021). Race and Zen: Julius Evola, fascism, and DT Suzuki. *Arc: The Journal of the School of Religious Studies, 49,* 48–82.

Peters, M. A. (2023). The emerging multipolar world order: A preliminary analysis. *Educational Philosophy and Theory, 55*(14), 1653–1663.

Pfeiffer, C. (2022). *Future scenarios on multilateralism: Global governance models for efficient (economic) policy coordination.* Global Solutions: World Policy Forum.

Phillips, R. (2014). *Recurrence plot (and other time travel tales).* Afrofuturist Affair / House of Future Sciences.

Phillips, R. (2023). Black quantum futurism. *Journal of Architectural Education, 77*(1), 9–19.

Pirker, E. U. & Rahn, J. (Eds.) (2024). *Afrofuturism's Transcultural Trajectories: Resistant Imaginaries Between Margins and Mainstreams.* Routledge.

Pohl, B., Dos Santos, S., Bai, G. M., Compaoré, Y., Dianou, K., Diallo-Dudek, J., & Janicot, S. (2021). Indoor temperature variability in the Sahel: A pilot study in Ouagadougou, Burkina Faso. *Theoretical and Applied Climatology, 146,* 1403–1420.

Porter, P. (2020). *The false promise of liberal order: Nostalgia, delusion and the rise of Trump.* Polity Press.

Rabaka, R. (2010). *Against epistemic apartheid: W. E. B. Du Bois and the disciplinary decadence of sociology.* Lexington Books.

Rancière, J. (1992). Politics, identification, and subjectivization. *October, 61,* 58–64.

Rancière, J. (2021). *The emancipated spectator.* Verso Books.

Rancière, J. (2022). *The time of the landscape: On the origins of the aesthetic revolution.* John Wiley & Sons.

Rapanyane, M. B. (2021). The new world [dis] order in the complexity of multi-polarity: United States of America's hegemonic decline and the configuration of new power patterns. *Journal of Public Affairs, 21*(1), Article e2114.

Rapp-Hooper, M. (2020). From primacy to openness: US strategic objectives in Asia. In L. Bitounis & J. Price (Eds.), *The struggle for power: US-China relations in the 21st century* (pp. 105–111). Aspen Institute.

Remmling, G. W. (2022). Francis Bacon and the French Enlightenment philosophers. In G. W. Remming (Ed.), *Towards the sociology of knowledge* (pp. 47–59). Routledge.

Rheinberger, H. J. (2023). Beyond nature and culture: Modes of reasoning in the age of molecular biology and medicine. In M. Lock, A. Young, & A. Cambrosio (Eds.), *Living and working with the new medical technologies: Intersections of inquiry* (pp. 19–30). Cambridge University Press.

Riesenberg, E. L. (2014). *Taboos and primitivism: James Frazer, HG Wells, and the intersection of anthropology and science fiction* [Honors thesis, College of William and Mary].

Robinson, C. J. (2020). *Black Marxism: The making of the Black radical tradition* (rev. and updated 3rd ed.). UNC Press Books.

Roediger, D. R. (2022). *The wages of whiteness: Race and the making of the American working class*. Verso.

Rogers, M. M. (2021). Exploring the domestic abuse narratives of trans and nonbinary people and the role of cisgenderism in identity abuse, misgendering, and pathologizing. *Violence Against Women, 27*(12–13), 2187–2207.

Rolland, N. (2020). *China's vision for a new world order* [NBR Special Report 83]. National Bureau of Asian Research.

Rollefson, J. G. (2008). The "robot Voodoo power" thesis: Afrofuturism and anti-anti-essentialism from Sun Ra to Kool Keith. *Black Music Research Journal, 28*(1), 83–109.

Rose, T. (1994). *Black noise: Rap music and Black culture in contemporary America*. Wesleyan University Press.

Rose, T. (2008). *The hip hop wars: What we talk about when we talk about hip hop*. Basic Civitas.

Rosenboim, O. (2015). Geopolitics and empire: Visions of regional world order in the 1940s. *Modern Intellectual History, 12*(2), 353–381.

Rowell, C. H., & Butler, O. E. (1997). An interview with Octavia E. Butler. *Callaloo, 20*(1), 47–66.

Rustin, B. (1965). *From protest to politics: The future of the civil rights movement*. League for Industrial Democracy.

Rustin, B. (1966). *"Black Power" and coalition politics*. American Jewish Committee.

Rutledge, G. E. (2000). Science fiction and the Black Power/Arts movements: The transpositional cosmology of Samuel R. Delany Jr. *Extrapolation, 41*(2), 127–142.

Saaler, S., & Koschmann, J. V. (2007). *Pan-Asianism in modern Japanese history*. Routledge.

Safranchuk, I. A., & Lukyanov, F. A. (2021, June 3). The modern world order: Structural realities and great power rivalries. *Russian International Affairs Council*. https://russiancouncil.ru/en/analytics-and-comments/analytics/modern-world-order-structural-realities-and-great-power-rivalries/

Sakib, S. M. N. (2022). Assessing the impact of Arctic melting in the predominantly multilateral world system. *Asian Pacific Journal of Environment and Cancer, 5*(1).

Samatar, S. (2017). Toward a planetary history of Afrofuturism. *Research in African Literatures, 48*(4), 175–191.

Sandrin, P. (2021). *The rise of right-wing populism in Europe: A psychoanalytical contribution.* In B. De Souza Guilherme, C. Ghymers, S. Griffith-Jones, & A. Ribeiro Hoffmann (Eds.), *Financial crisis management and democracy* (pp. 227–239). Springer.

Saramago, A. (2022). Post-Eurocentric grand narratives in critical international theory. *European Journal of International Relations, 28*(1), 6–29.

Saz-Carranza, A., Rueda-Sabater, E., Vandendriessche, M., Moreno, C., & Jordana, J. (2024). The future(s) of global governance: A scenarios exercise. *Global Policy, 15*(1), 149–165.

Schmidt, N. (2022). *Present futures: Speculative infrastructure at the turn of the twentieth century* [Doctoral dissertation, Indiana University].

Schmitt, C. (2005). *Political theology: Four chapters on the concept of sovereignty.* University of Chicago Press.

Scholz, O. (2023). The global Zeitenwende: How to avoid a new cold war in a multipolar era. *Foreign Affairs*, January/February. https://www.foreignaffairs.com/germany/olaf-scholz-global-zeitenwende-how-avoid-new-cold-wars

Schwartz, H. M. (2022). Global secular stagnation and the rise of intellectual property monopoly. *Review of International Political Economy, 29*(5), 1448–1476.

Scott, D. K. (2021). Afrofuturism and Black futurism: Some ontological and semantic considerations. In P. Butler (Ed.), *Critical Black futures: Speculative theories and explorations* (pp. 139–163). Palgrave Macmillan.

Senapati, S., & Gupta, V. (2014). Climate change and coastal ecosystem in India: Issues in perspectives. *International Journal of Environmental Sciences, 5*(3), 530–543.

Serjeantson, R. (2024). Francis Bacon, colonisation, and the limits of Atlanticism. *History of European Ideas, 50*(7), 1155–1168.

Shalf, J. (2020). The future of computing beyond Moore's law. *Philosophical Transactions of the Royal Society A, 378*(2166), Article 20190061.

Shepperson, G. (1962). Pan-Africanism and "Pan-Africanism": Some historical notes. *Phylon (1960–), 23*(4), 346–358.

Siepe, D. (2022). Wewelsburg Castle in thrillers and comics. In K. John-Stucke & D. Siepe (Eds.), *Myths of Wewelsburg Castle* (pp. 113–142). Brill Schöningh.

Sites, W. (2021). *Sun Ra's Chicago: Afrofuturism and the city.* University of Chicago Press.

Skya, W. A. (2023). The other Japan: Back to Japan's religious roots for a new Japanese nationalism? *Journal of Right-Wing Studies, 1*(1), https://doi.org/10.5070/RW3.1500

Smedley, A., & Smedley, B. D. (2005). Race as biology is fiction, racism as a social problem is real: Anthropological and historical perspectives on the social construction of race. *American Psychologist, 60*(1), 16–26.

Sneed, R. (2021). *The dreamer and the dream: Afrofuturism and Black religious thought.* The Ohio State University Press.

Spickard, P., Beltrán, F., & Hooton, L. (2022). *Almost all aliens: Immigration, race, and colonialism in American history and identity.* Routledge.

Staudenmaier, P. (2020). Racial ideology between Fascist Italy and Nazi Germany: Julius Evola and the Aryan myth, 1933–43. *Journal of Contemporary History, 55*(3), 473–491.

Steinskog, E. (2017). *Afrofuturism and Black sound studies: Culture, technology, and things to come.* Springer.

Stern, A. M. (2022). From "race suicide" to "white extinction": White nationalism, nativism, and eugenics over the past century. *Journal of American History, 109*(2), 348–361.

Stiglitz, J. E. (2008). *Globalization and its discontents.* Norton.

Stoddard, L. (1920). *The rising tide of color against white world-supremacy.* Scribner.

Stross, C. (2005). *Accelerando.* Penguin Publishing Group.

Sunga, L. S. (2014). Does climate change worsen resource scarcity and cause violent ethnic conflict? *International Journal on Minority and Group Rights, 21*(1), 1–24.

Sunstrum, P. P. (2013). Afro-mythology and African futurism: The politics of imagining and methodologies for contemporary creative research practices. *Paradoxa, 25,* 113–130.

Szwed, J. F. (1997). *Space is the place: The lives and times of Sun Ra.* Da Capo Press.

Tamplin, W. (2020). The Anglo-Saxon New Negro: Sutton E. Griggs's Anglo-Saxonism and the quest for cultural paternity in *Imperium in Imperio* (1899). *Utopian Studies: The Journal of the Society for Utopian Studies, 31*(1), 97–117.

Tate, G. (2017, September 1). Kalahari hopscotch: A freewheeling manifesto on tricksters, healers, and hoodoo. *The Believer,* https://www.thebeliever.net/kalahari-hopscotch/

Taylor, J. L. (2021). The politics of the Black Power movement. *Annual Review of Political Science, 24*(1), 443–470.

Taylor, M. (2022). Teaching to transgress: Cheikh Anta Diop and the African intellectual reformation. *The Imhotep Research Journal,* 28–37.

Teitelbaum, B. R. (2021). Traditionalism in the American Right. In T. Bar-On & B. Molas (Eds.), *The Right and Radical Right in the Americas: Ideological currents from interwar Canada to contemporary Chile* (pp. 215–238). Lexington Books.

Teixeira, C. P., Spears, R., & Yzerbyt, V. Y. (2020). Is Martin Luther King or Malcolm X the more acceptable face of protest? High-status groups' reactions to low-status groups' collective action. *Journal of Personality and Social Psychology, 118*(5), 919–944.

Thaxter, H. (2020). "I want to live forever and breed people!": The legacy of a fantasy. In G. J. Hampton & K. R. Parker (Eds.), *The Bloomsbury handbook to Octavia E. Butler* (pp. 15–34). Bloomsbury Academic.

Thomas, S. R. (2019). Twenty-five years in a 500-year-long song. In R. Anderson & C. Fluker (Eds.), *The Black Speculative Arts movement: Black futurity, art+design* (pp. ix–xiii). Lexington Books.

Thondhlana, J., Roda Madziva, R., & Garwe, E. C. (2021). What can the African diaspora contribute to innovation and knowledge creation? The case study of Zimbabwean innovators. *Journal of the British Academy, 9*(s1), 101–125.

Thornton, B. J. (2023). *Afro-Atlantic Catholics: America's first Black Christians* by Jeroen Dewulf [Book Review]. *The Americas, 80*(3), 506–507.

Toliver, S. R. (2021). Beyond the problem: Afrofuturism as an alternative to realistic fiction about Black girls. In D. Price-Dennis & G. E. Muhammad (Eds.), *Black girls' literacies: Transforming lives and literacy practices* (pp. 153–169). Routledge.

Toliver, S. R. (2023). It will take nations of billions to obstruct our dreams: Extending BlackCrit through Afrofuturism. *Journal for Multicultural Education, 18*(3), 230–244.

Trafton, S. (2004). *Egypt land: Race and nineteenth-century American Egyptomania*. Duke University Press.

Truby, J. (2020). Governing artificial intelligence will benefit the UN's Sustainable Development Goals. *Sustainable Development, 28*(4), 946–959. https://doi.org/10.1002/sd.2048

Truscello, M. (2020). *Infrastructural brutalism: Art and the necropolitics of infrastructure*. MIT Press.

Tucker, J. (2004). *A different engine: Samuel R. Delany's science fiction*. Wesleyan University Press.

Tufekci, Z., & Wilson, C. (2012). Social media and the decision to participate in political protest: Observations from Tahrir Square. *Journal of Communication, 62*(2), 363–379.

Turpin, C. A. (2021). Strategic disruptions: Black feminism, intersectionality, and Afrofuturism. *CEA Mid-Atlantic Review, 29*, 21–34.

Tuters, M. (2020). Esoteric fascism online: 4chan and the Kali Yuga. In L. D. Valencia-García (Ed.), *Far-Right revisionism and the end of history* (pp. 286–303). Routledge.

Tutuola, A. (1952). *The palm-wine drinkard; And my life in the bush of ghosts*. Grove Press.

Tynes, B. M., Coopilton, M., Schuschke, J., & Stewart, A. (2023). Toward developmental science that meets the challenges of 2044: Afrofuturist development theory, design, and praxis. In D. P. Witherspoon & G. L. Stein (Eds.), *Diversity and developmental science: Bridging the gaps between research, practice, and policy* (pp. 245–270). Springer International.

Underwood, B. E. (2022). The poetics of hope: Utopian desires, Afrofuturism, and Black girl magic at the inauguration. *CLA Journal, 65*(1), 88–105.

Van Dijck, J. (2013). *The culture of connectivity: A critical history of social media*. Oxford University Press.

Van Sertima, I. (Ed.) (1993). *Golden age of the Moor*. Transaction.

van Veen, T. (2014). *Other planes of there: The mythsciences, chronopolitics and conceptechnics of Afrofuturism* [Doctoral thesis, McGill University].

Varela, C. (2017). Africa finds its voice in the halls of Manchester. *History in the Making, 10*(1), Article 6.

Vass, V. (2017). *Aspects of narration and voice in Zora Neale Hurston's "Their Eyes Were Watching God"* [Master's thesis, University of the Western Cape].

Vince, G. (2022). *Nomad century: How climate migration will reshape our world*. Macmillan.

Vinson, H. A. (2011). *"The Time Machine" and "Heart of Darkness": HG Wells, Joseph Conrad, and the fin de siècle* [Master's thesis, University of South Florida].

Vint, S. (2021). *Science fiction*. MIT Press.

Vinuesa, R., Azizpour, H., Leite, I., Balaam, M., Dignum, V., Domisch, S., & Fuso Nerini, F. (2020). The role of artificial intelligence in achieving the Sustainable Development Goals. *Nature Communications, 11*(1), 1–10.

Vitalis, R. (2018). *White world order, Black power politics: The birth of American international relations*. Cornell University Press.

Waghid, Z., & Ontong, K. (2022). Exploring the phenomenon of Afrofuturism in film in decolonizing the university curriculum: A case study of a South African university. *Citizenship Teaching & Learning, 17*(1), 27–48.

Waite, A. E. (2020). *The brotherhood of the Rosy Cross: A history of the Rosicrucians*. Read Books Ltd.

Walker, E. N. (2014). *Beyond Banneker: Black mathematicians and the paths to excellence.* SUNY Press.

Wallerstein, I. M. (1991). *Geopolitics and geoculture: Essays on the changing world-system.* Cambridge University Press.

Walton, H., Jr. (2020). *American politics and the African American quest for universal freedom.* Routledge.

Warren, C. A., & Coles, J. A. (2020). Trading spaces: Antiblackness and reflections on Black education futures. *Equity & Excellence in Education, 53*(3), 382–398.

Welton, B. M. (2021). The Anglo-Saxons—Stoddard and Lovecraft: Ideas of Anglo-Saxon supremacy and the New England counter-revolution. *Madison Historical Review, 18*(1), Article 3.

Wertheim, S. (2020). The price of primacy. *Foreign Affairs,* March/April. https://www.foreignaffairs.com/articles/afghanistan/2020-02-10/price-primacy

West, M. W. (2021). *Sex magicians: The lives and spiritual practices of Paschal Beverly Randolph, Aleister Crowley, Jack Parsons, Marjorie Cameron, Anton Lavey, and others.* Simon and Schuster.

Wester, P., Mishra, A., Mukherji, A., & Shrestha, A. B. (Eds.). (2019). *The Hindu Kush Himalaya assessment: Mountains, climate change, sustainability and people.* Springer Nature.

Wilderson, F. B., III (2008). *Incognegro: A memoir of exile and apartheid.* Duke University Press.

Wilderson, F. B., III (2020). *Afropessimism.* Liveright Publishing.

Wilhite, I. A. (1999). *Rhetorical theory: Discourse practices of utopian communities* [Doctoral dissertation, Louisiana State University and Agricultural & Mechanical College].

Wilkinson, T. (2020). *A world beneath the sands: The golden age of Egyptology.* Norton.

Willard, T. (2022). *Thomas Vaughan and the Rosicrucian Revival in Britain: 1648–1666.* Brill.

William, A., & Srnicek, N. (2013). #Accelerate: Manifesto for an accelerationist politics. In J. Johnson (Ed.), *Dark Trajectories: Politics of the Outside* (pp. 135–155). [Name] Publications.

Wilson, G. M. (2019). *Radical nationalist in Japan: Kita Ikki, 1883–1937.* Harvard University Press.

Wilson, W. (1851). *A little earnest book upon a great old subject.* Darton and Co.

Winchester, W. W., III (2019). Engaging the Black ethos: Afrofuturism as a design lens for inclusive technological innovation. *Journal of Futures Studies, 24*(2), 55–62.

Womack, Y. (2013). *Afrofuturism: The world of Black sci-fi and fantasy culture.* Chicago Review Press.

Wood, B. (2020). *Invented history, fabricated power: The narrative shaping of civilization and culture.* Anthem Press.

Woodson, J. (2015). The Harlem Renaissance as esotericism: Black Oragean modernism. In S. C. Finley, M. S. Guillory, & H. R. Page Jr. (Eds.), *Esotericism in African American religious experience* (pp. 102–122). Brill.

Wright, M. A. (2021). Sex and the future of history: Black politics at the limit in Sutton E. Griggs' *Imperium in Imperio*. *The Black Scholar, 51*(4), 32–46.

Wright, T., & Blackwill, R. D. (2020). *Why COVID-19 presents a world reordering moment.* Brookings Institution.

Yaffe, M. D. (2020). How Francis Bacon's new organon co-opts biblical theology for his *New Atlantis*. In S. Frankel & M. Yaffe (Eds.), *Civil religion in modern political philosophy* (pp. 34–52). Pennsylvania State University Press.

Yancy, G. (2004). Geneva Smitherman: The social ontology of African American language, the power of Nommo, and the dynamics of resistance and identity through language. *The Journal of Speculative Philosophy, 18*(4), 273–299.

Yao, X. (2021). *Disaffected: The cultural politics of unfeeling in nineteenth-century America*. Duke University Press.

Yaszek, L. (2006). Afrofuturism, science fiction, and the history of the future. *Socialism and Democracy, 20*(3), 41–60.

Yette, S. F. (1971). *The choice: The issue of Black survival in America*. G. P. Putnam & Sons.

Young, K., & Reid, V. (2023). *Afrofuturism: A history of Black futures*. Smithsonian Institution.

Young, L. (1998). *Japan's total empire: Manchuria and the culture of wartime imperialism* (Vol. 8). Univ of California Press.

Young, L. (2020). Imperial culture: The primitive, the savage and white civilization. In L. Back & J. Solomos (Eds.), *Theories of race and racism* (pp. 336–355). Routledge.

Yousef, T. (2017). Modernism, postmodernism, and metamodernism: A critique. *International Journal of Language and Literature, 5*(1), 33–43.

Yuan, J. (2022). What is scientific culture? *Cultures of Science, 5*(3), 124–127.

Zamalin, A. (2019). *Black utopia: The history of an idea from Black nationalism to Afrofuturism*. Columbia University Press.

Zamalin, A. (2022). Afrofuturism as reconstitution. *Afrofuturism and the Law, 9*(1), 9–15.

Zavala, S. (2022). A general view of the colonial history of the New World. In A. T. Bushnell (Ed.), *Establishing exceptionalism* (pp. 1–17). Routledge.

Zeitlin, S. G. (2021). "The heat of a feaver": Francis Bacon on civil war, sedition, and rebellion. *History of European Ideas, 47*(5), 643–663.

INDEX

accelerationism, 58; and Dark Enlightenment, 102–6, 113. *See also* Blacceleration; Dark Enlightenment; Land, Nick

African futurism, 13, 89–91, 114, 116, 147

Africanfuturism, 90

Africology, 9, 12, 43

Afro-Caribbean futurism, 137

Afrocentricity, 14–16

Afrofuturism: aesthetic politics of, 123–25, 141–44 (*see also* Rancière, Jacques); as aesthetic-philosophical discourse, 141–43; in African diaspora, 113–14, 146–47, 168–69; and Afrocentricity, 14–16; with Afrofuturism 2.0, 15, 113, 141–43; and Afropessimism, 14; in Alondra Nelson, 139; and Black Speculative Arts Movement, 125–26, 129–31, 141–43; as coherent cultural phenomenon, 101; coining of, 8–9, 15; and contemporary technology, 146–47; and Dark Enlightenment, 112–16; definition and history, 1–3, 168–69; in dialogue with Jacques Rancière, 141–43; as epiphenomenal time, 132–34, 136; impacts of climate change on, 166–67; importance of African mythology to, 89–91; as innovative way to reject racism, 143–44; as lens for climate change, 168–69; and metamodernism, 5–7; in multipolar world, 155–61; from mythology, 90; and Pan-Africanism, 17–20; proto-, 97; and social change in 21st century, 147–48; as speculative counter-rhetoric, 35–36; and Web 3.0, 135. *See also* Afrofuturism 2.0; astro-Blackness; Black Arts Movement; Black Speculative Arts Movement

Afrofuturism 2.0, 22–23; and accelerationism, 116–17; and climate change, 166–67; and new world order, 145–47; definition of, 15, 169–72; edited volume, 130; historical context and evolution of, 164–66; initiating a biomecha revolution, 169–70; political efficacy of, 113; reflections on future of, 172–73

Afropessimism, 10, 13–14, 114–16

AI, 13, 20, 22–23, 105, 161; nationalism, 23, 145, 150–51, 155–57

203

Akomfrah, John, 83, 139
antiracism: in potential societies, 39; in speculative thought, 74
Artificial Intelligence. *See* AI
astro-Blackness, 116; and *Afrofuturism 2.0*, 11, 15, 130; conferences, 129; as global political identity, 157; signaling subversiveness or power, 126
astro-theology, 38, 43. *See also* Banneker, Benjamin
astroculture, 21; definition of, 78–79; and science fiction, 81–84. *See also* Galbraith, John Kenneth

Bacon, Francis, 26–30, 33; *The New Atlantis*, 3, 20, 26–27, 30, 33
Bandung Conference, 87–89
Banneker, Benjamin, 21; Astro-Liberation Theology, 38–39; and Black speculative thought, 41, 43
Baraka, Amiri, 140. *See also* Black Arts Movement
Blacceleration, 114–16. *See also* accelerationism
Black Arts Movement (BAM), 94, 101, 140
Black Lives Matter (BLM), 110, 128–29
Black nationalism, 10; and Martin Delany, 40
Black Power: and Black Arts Movement, 140; and modern Black studies, 12; in Octavia Butler, 99–100; post–Black Power era, 8; as resisting mainstream American art, 138; in Samuel R. Delany, 98–99; science fiction, 94–96; spirit of, in Pan-Africanism and Bandung Conference, 87–89. *See also* Malcolm X
Black Quantum Futurism (BQF), 129, 136–37
Black Speculative Arts Movement (BSAM), 121; Afrofuturist aesthetic politics of, 22, 122–24; background on emergence of, 126–29; birth of, 129–31; as kind of Black visual alchemy, 140; Nommo and, 125–26; and Rancière's distribution of the sensible, 141–44
Butler, Octavia: and Black Speculative Arts Movement, 129; as key figure in Afrofuturism, 21, 95, 114, 137, 147; *Kindred*, 99–100; *Mind of My Mind*, 100; *Parable of the Sower*, 115, 168; *Patternmaster*, 100; significance and works, 99–101

CCRU (Cybernetic Culture Research Unit), 104. *See also* Eshun, Kodwo; Land, Nick
climate change, 8, 16; acceleration of, 17–19; and African diaspora, 155–58, 162, 168–69; and Afrofuturism 2.0, 23, 145, 165–68, 172–73; and AI nationalism, 155–57; as existential threat, 23, 146; global response to, 154–55; Intergovernmental Panel on, 171; and mass migration, 152–54, 158, 167. *See also* Friedman, Thomas
Coates, Ta-Nehisi, 169
Cold War, 8, 12, 16; Africa and, 87, 91–92; and Afrofuturism, 97, 113, 145; and Black Power, 94–95; as cultural war, 9; and futurology, 81, 83–84, 90–92; overview of, 86–87; multipolarity, 149; new world order, 172; and occult, 61; post–Cold War era, 2, 9, 121, 146, 154
colonialism: and climate change, 158; and epiphenomenal time, 133; influence of, on science fiction, 89, 94, 124–25; justifications for, 49, 116; and social death, 13; struggles against, 7, 13, 62, 89, 93, 128. *See also* imperialism
conjure feminism, 21, 37–38. *See also* Vodun
critical race theory, 135. *See also* race; racism
Crowley, Aleister, 39; and F. T. Marinetti, 58–59; influence of, on astroculture, 77–78; life and works, 57–58. *See also* esotericism; Thelema

Dark Enlightenment, 21–22, 117; and Afrofuturism, 112–14; concept of, 102–3; critique of, 104; and ethnonationalism and xenophobia, 111; rise of, 105. *See also* Land, Nick; Yarvin, Curtis
Delany, Martin, 21; and Egyptology, 40–41
Delany, Samuel R., 21; *Dhalgren*, 98; as key figure in Afrofuturism, 9, 95,

137, 147; significance and works, 98–99
Dery, Mark, 8, 13; as coining "Afrofuturism," 9, 15
Du Bois, W. E. B.: and Afrocentrism, 16, 37; and Black speculative philosophy and fiction, 67, 72, 74; and color-line, 64; *The Comet*, 70–71; double consciousness, social contract, and the veil, 65; *Encyclopedia Africana*, 8, 12; Harlem Renaissance, 21; psychological wages of whiteness, 5. *See also* Griggs, Sutton E.; Harlem Renaissance; racial contract

Egyptology: and Enlightenment, 26, 30–31; history of, 31–32; influence of, on European thought and culture, 32–33; and Martin Delany, 40–41
Eshun, Kodwo, 8; and chronopolitics and epiphenomenal time, 90, 133; and climate resilience narratives, 168; and counter-futures of Afrofuturism, 23, 96, 114; on hijacking accelerationism, 116. *See also* Ra, Sun
esotericism, 59; Africana, 11, 70; and Harlem Renaissance, 68–70; influence of, on futurist avant-garde, 56–59; in Jean Toomer, 68–70; in Martin Delany, 41; in Paschal Beverly Randolph, 39–42; and Third Reich, 59–61; in Zora Neal Hurston, 69–70. *See also* Crowley, Aleister; occult; Ra, Sun; Thelema
Everett, Anna, 9, 14, 16

Friedman, Thomas, 16–17
futurism (Italian), 58
futurology, 79–81; in Africa, 91–93; and Cold War, 83–86; in science fiction, 81–83

Galbraith, John Kenneth: and futurology, 81–85; impact and legacy, 83; in postwar science fiction, 80–81; and theory of astroculture, 78–79; and theory of technostate, 76–77, 79–80. *See also* futurology
Gaskins, Nettrice, 134–35
Griggs, Sutton E.: *Imperium in Imperio*, 66; significance and works, 66–67; speculative philosophy, 72, 74

Haitian Revolution, 35; Vodun in, 36–38, 41–43
Harlem Renaissance, 8, 21; esotericism and occult in, 67–70, 74; as threat to white race, 44
Hoodoo, 37–38. *See also* Vodun
Hopkins, Pauline, 40, 67, 74; *Of One Blood*, 39, 71–72
Hopkinson, Nalo, 125, 137–38, 168; *Brown Girl in the Ring*, 137
Hubbard, L. Ron, 77–78
Hurston, Zora Neale, 21, 67–70, 72, 74

imperialism, 6; and colonialism, 49–52; and color-line, 64; influence of, on science fiction, 50–51, 53–54, 89; justifications for, 44, 48–49, 156; struggles against, 6–7, 35, 43, 62–63, 93

Jennings, John, 124, 130, 138–39; Black Kirby, 140

Kaplan, Robert, 16–17

Land, Nick, 21, 102, 117; and belief in destructive and transcendent humanity, 112–13; and Dark Reformation, 104; and embrace of capital as "alien life-form," 115. *See also* Dark Enlightenment; Yarvin, Curtis

Malcolm X, 9; life and assassination of, 93–94. *See also* Black Power
Marinetti, Filippo Tommaso, 56–58; and esotericism, 58–59. *See also* futurism (Italian)
Moldbug, Mencius. *See* Yarvin, Curtis

Nelson, Alondra, 8, 15, 23, 139, 168

occult: and Afrofuturism, 9; and (Western) futurism, 58–59; and Harlem Renaissance, 68–70; and Imperial Japan, 61–64; influence of, on Jack Parsons, 77–78; and Paschal Beverly Randolph, 39–40; Rosicrucianism, 28–30; and science fiction, 52–53. *See also* Crowley, Aleister; esotericism; Ra, Sun; Rosicrucianism
Occulture. *See* occult

Okorafor, Nnedi. *See* Africanfuturism

Pan-Africanism, 127; and Afrofuturism, 16–20; and Bandung Conference, 87–89; and climate change, 167–69
Parsons, Jack, 77–78
Phillips, Rasheedah, 34, 116, 129, 135–37. *See also* Black Quantum Futurism

Ra, Sun, 10, 14, 172; and Black Arts Movement, 101; extraterrestrial mythos of, 21; life history, film, and music, 96–98; as key figure in Afrofuturism, 95, 114, 172. *See also* Szwed, John
race: African, 162; and Afrofuturism, 9–10, 15, 45, 125, 139–41; alien, 47, 52–53, 84, 96; Angel, 96; Aryan, 59, 61; -based policies, 151; and Black Power, 94–95, 98–99; and Black Speculative Arts Movement, 22; and civilization, 44–47; concept of, 24, 34, 45, 72; development (international relations), 64–65; and epiphenomenal time, 133–34; and esotericism, 70; and intersectionality, 38; preoccupation of whites with, 44–46; and politics, 66, 72–74, 127, 140; relations, 122. *See also* Du Bois, W. E. B.; racism; social Darwinism; Stoddard, Lothrop
race for theory, 11–15, 65
racial capitalism, 3, 13, 115
racial contract: C. W. Mills's definition of, 4–5; and W. E. B. Du Bois, 64–65
racism: Afrofuturism as counterdiscourse to, 6, 11, 35–36, 42–43; background of, 33–34; in Christianity and American polity, 73; and Deep State, 111; Enlightenment, 3, 21, 41–42; Enlightenment resistance to, 39; in H. G. Wells, 53–54; in Lothrop Stoddard, 45–46; negative qualities of, 143; in Paschal Beverly Randolph, 40; and police violence, 128–29; and race, 13; as refuted by Martin Delany, 41–42; resistance to, 101 (*see also* antiracism; Black Power); scientific, 21, 25, 74; and social contract, 65; and social Darwinism, 49; systemic, 93, 136; as transcended by Sun Ra's cosmic identity, 97

Rancière, Jacques, 122–24, 141–42
Randolph, Paschal Beverly, 21, 43, 55; overview and works, 39–40
Reed, Ishmael, 139
Robinson, Stacey, 130; Black Kirby, 140
Rosicrucianism: and Enlightenment, 26–27, 33–34; in Paschal Beverly Randolph's *Ravalette*, 40; overview and beliefs, 28–30. *See also* esotericism; occult

Sankofa: historical consciousness of, 132; as living metaphor, 131
Schmitt, Carl, 102
science fiction: 19th-century, 36, 44, 52–54; 20th-century, 52–53, 67, 79–85; African, 89–90, 92, 131; Afro-Caribbean, 137–38; and Afrofuturism, 9, 14–15, 21–22, 147; and AI, 150; astropolitics in, 83–85; Black Power, 93–96, 98–101, 129–30, 139; and climate change, 158, 168; and cognitive estrangement, 124; and esotericism, 45–46, 55, 77–78; futurology in, 81–83, 86; imaginative possibilities of, 51, 56; and imperialism, 48, 50–52, 55; *Last Angel of History*, 83, 139; postcolonial, 87–89, 137–38; *Space Is the Place*, 97; technostate themes in, 80–81, 83–85 (*see also* Galbraith, John Kenneth); Western, 34–36, 79–80, 137, 171. *See also* Butler, Octavia; Delany, Samuel R.; Hopkinson, Nalo; speculative fiction; Wells, H. G.
Snircek, Nick, 114, 116. *See also* accelerationism
social Darwinism, 49
social death, 13. *See also* Afropessimism; Wilderson, Frank
speculative fiction: African, 91; antiracist usage of, 39; and Black Speculative Arts Movement, 22; and cyberspace, 135; in old and new media, 140; sociopolitical and temporal agency of, 73, 94, 98–99, 136; as tool for radical organizing, 41–43
Stoddard, Lothrop, 44; concepts of race, 46; *Rising Tide of Color*, 21, 45–46
Szwed, John, 21; *Space Is the Place*, 97. *See also* Ra, Sun

Tate, Greg, 9, 139
technostate. *See* Galbraith, John Kenneth
Thelema, 57, 77–89. *See also* Crowley, Aleister

Vodun, 21; and astro-theology, 39; in Haitian Revolution, 36, 41–43; overview and origins, 37. *See also* Hoodoo

Wells, H. G., 48, 52, 56, 84; overview and works, 53–54
Wilderson, Frank, 13–14. *See also* Afropessimism
Womack, Ytasha, 90, 129, 168

Yarvin, Curtis, 103–4. *See also* Dark Enlightenment

NEW SUNS: RACE, GENDER, AND SEXUALITY IN THE SPECULATIVE
Susana M. Morris and Kinitra D. Brooks, Series Editors

Scholarly examinations of speculative fiction have been a burgeoning academic field for more than twenty-five years, but there has been a distinct lack of attention to how attending to nonhegemonic positionalities transforms our understanding of the speculative. New Suns: Race, Gender, and Sexuality in the Speculative addresses this oversight and promotes scholarship at the intersections of race, gender, sexuality, and the speculative, engaging interdisciplinary fields of research across literary, film, and cultural studies that examine multiple pasts, presents, and futures. Of particular interest are studies that offer new avenues into thinking about popular genre fictions and fan communities, including but not limited to the study of Afrofuturism, comics, ethnogothicism, ethnosurrealism, fantasy, film, futurity studies, gaming, horror, literature, science fiction, and visual studies. New Suns particularly encourages submissions that are written in a clear, accessible style that will be read both by scholars in the field as well as by nonspecialists.

Afrofuturism and World Order
REYNALDO ANDERSON

Dispelling Fantasies: Authors of Color Reimagine a Genre
JOY SANCHEZ-TAYLOR

Reading in the Postgenomic Age: Race, Discipline, and Bionarrativity in Contemporary North American Literature
LESLEY LARKIN

Black Speculative Feminisms: Memory and Liberated Futures in Black Women's Fiction
CASSANDRA L. JONES

Anti-Blackness and Human Monstrosity in Black American Horror Fiction
JERRY RAFIKI JENKINS

Gendered Defenders: Marvel's Heroines in Transmedia Spaces
EDITED BY BRYAN J. CARR AND META G. CARSTARPHEN

The Dreamer and the Dream: Afrofuturism and Black Religious Thought
ROGER A. SNEED

Diverse Futures: Science Fiction and Authors of Color
JOY SANCHEZ-TAYLOR

Impossible Stories: On the Space and Time of Black Destructive Creation
JOHN MURILLO III

Literary Afrofuturism in the Twenty-First Century
EDITED BY ISIAH LAVENDER III AND LISA YASZEK

Jordan Peele's "Get Out": Political Horror
EDITED BY DAWN KEETLEY

Unstable Masks: Whiteness and American Superhero Comics
 EDITED BY SEAN GUYNES AND MARTIN LUND

Afrofuturism Rising: The Literary Prehistory of a Movement
 ISIAH LAVENDER III

The Paradox of Blackness in African American Vampire Fiction
 JERRY RAFIKI JENKINS

www.ingramcontent.com/pod-product-compliance
Lightning Source LLC
Chambersburg PA
CBHW030137240426
43672CB00005B/167